THE TEUTONIC WAY

Book One: Teutonic Magic

BY KVELDÚLF GUNDARSSON

ISBN: 978-1-959350-09-5
Set in: Georgia 11/14 pt, Merriweather 14/13/12

©The Three Little Sisters LLC
USA/Canada

NOTES

THIS BOOK WAS WRITTEN IN THE LATE 90'S, REFERENCES, MATERIALS, ILLUSTRATIONS AND OTHER MENTIONS OF SOURCES HAVE CHANGED MEANING OVER TIME. WHERE POSSIBLE, THE MOST PROBLEMATIC SOURCES HAVE BEEN REMOVED AS WE BELIEVE THAT STEPHAN WOULD HAVE DONE SO, IF HE WAS ALIVE. AS A STAUNCH SUPPORTER OF HUMAN RIGHTS, STEPHAN WOULD NOT ENDORSE WRITERS WHO PROMOTE, DISSEMINATE OR FOSTER WHITE SUPREMACY OR PROMOTE OR SPREAD HATE ABOUT TRANS/LGTBQ+ OR OTHER MINORITIES.

FORWARD BY LARISA HUNTER

There are very few books in life that one can say shaped their path, but the Teutonic series by Kveldúlf was, for me that book. When I first came to heathenry, the push to read the Edda above all else seemed to be the only way one could enter the community, after reading them, I didn't really find that this alone helped me form a way to actually practice my faith. I, like many, found the 'recommended reading lists' that frequented the Internet, and that is where I found the Kveldúlf work. I found his writing relatable, informative and broad. I devoured the books, and then sought out more.

I found his fiction, his articles, his poetry, and more. I admired this man who had formed a spark in me that led me to write my own work, and forge my path to find my gods. When I formed the publishing house, I had no idea that I would have the great privilege and honor of working with Kveldúlf, but I am very glad that the road led me to his doorstep. I have admired Kveldúlf for a long time, and take it as a great honor and privilege to preserve and reprint his works. He has been supportive of me and supported me through illness and loss. His wife Melodi, has been instrumental in helping us keep this project going and has also provided us many crucial missing pieces.

The two are a writing powerhouse that we are so proud to represent. It is my hope that those coming to heathenry, take up the path that lays before them and walk it with pride. I hope that this book, helps you to forge that path. There are so many people that helped us in acquiring this book, but two in particular have been pivotal in arranging the contract and also in tracking down original copies. With that, I would like to thank Michael Ransom Wilson and Internet Archive for all that they have done to get this fantastic series back in print. To Kveldúlf, I have no words to express my gratitude to you, your trust and respect has been something I deeply treasure, and I want to express the deepest of thanks for instilling in me the power to believe in myself again, and to call you my friend.

TEUTONIC MAGIC

The Magical & Spiritual Practices
of the Germanic Peoples

The Wisdom of Odhinn

Here are written, for those who have the strength to grasp them, the hidden secrets with which our ancestors ruled wind and wave, fire and earth and the minds of men. For nine nights the great god Odhinn hung on the World-Tree, pierced by his own spear, the winds between the worlds blowing cold about him. At last he saw, in a blinding moment of might, the runes written at the great tree's roots. He took them up: great in power, great in wisdom, growing ever in might and lore from the secret his sacrifice won him. He taught the mysteries of the runes to his children among the human race, and these songs of might were sung and carved on wood and stone from Ger- many to England, to Denmark, Norway, Sweden, and Iceland, wherever the Teutonic peoples walked in their bright paths of battle and hidden wisdom.

Though stilled by the Christian church for a time, the secrets of magic lived on, passing in whispers through the ties of love and blood. Only in this last century, by the work of a few hid- den heroes, has this wisdom been recovered. Now, in this book, it is set out as fully as possible for those who dare. Learn how to use the ancient runic magic of Odhinn: how to read the future written in the runes, how to write and chant the songs of power so that you yourself may shape the windings of your life. Learn the secrets of magical poetry, of ritual, of the Teutonic herbs and trees of enchantment, of the Nine Worlds and the ways between them, and of faring forth in the spirit to learn things hidden and work your will. Learn of the gods and wights known by our ancestors, whose might will aid you in your magic and your life: Odhinn, Thorr, Freyja, Freyr, Tyr; the elves and dwarves; the spirits of your family and those who follow you. Take back the might of your ancestors, that you may grow in strength and wisdom and aid in the knowledge and healing of the earth.

Acknowledgments

Teutonic Magic is dedicated to the members of my first rune class, Erik (Eirikr) Malmstrom, Larry Pettit (Asgar), and Judith Pruett, who listened to this book in its first lifetime as a collection of scribbled notes and found it worthy of continued existence. Thanks are also owed to Patricia Paterson, Gloria Calasso1 and Hendrix Tolliver III of the Athanor Bookstore, who twisted my arm until I started doing the teaching work which led to this book; and to my endlessly supportive parents, who paid all the library fines incurred in two years of research.

HERITAGE OF MAGIC: OUR TEUTONIC PAST

The word "Teutonic," which once referred to the members of a specific Germanic tribe, has now come to encompass a heritage as large and varied as Northern Europe. One thinks of the Germans as Teutonic; but so, too, are the descendants of the Vikings, the Anglo-Saxons, and even the Normans. If any of your ancestors came from Northern Europe, you yourself are probably heir to the old thoughts and ways of the Teutonic people, long forgotten though these may have been in the rushing modern world. If not, you are still part of the culture they helped to shape, a speaker of a language that grew out of the world-view of the Anglo-Saxons for the sake of telling what they held true and understood. The ways and works of our Teutonic heritage lie just below the surface of the world we know, like gold forgotten beneath the grass covering a mound. It is up to those whose blood and souls ring with the old songs, who feel the secret might of the runes and hear the whispering of our ancient gods, to bring this treasure forth into the light of day again. The working of the magic and worshiping the gods of our ancestors are two of the most important first steps in re-quickening our hidden roots: only by matching wisdom and works can aught of worth be achieved. But to work the magic rightly, you must first know more of the minds from which it came and the world giving birth to its might. This book Contains both a practical guide to the working of Teutonic magic and some clarification of ways of thought which the modern world has largely forgotten, but which the mage who wills to reclaim the ancient might of our Teutonic ancestors must learn again.

THOUGHT AND CULTURE RECLAIMED:
AN INTRODUCTION

In the life of the person who follows the old ways of the Teutonic people, there should be nothing unholy, no time at which you shut yourself off from an awareness of the workings of your soul simply because the thing you are doing is not openly magical or religious in its goal. Rather, you should be aware of the presence of the gods in everything. When you weed your garden or plant a window box, think of the body of Nerthus, Mother Earth, in which you dig; when you eat a hamburger, give thanks to Freyr and Freyja for their bounty which fattened the cattle and ripened the grain for the bun! The more fully you can know how the gifts the gods have aided you in every aspect of your life, the closer you will be to them as you use these gifts. The same holds true for meditating on the runes: as you think on the workings of their various powers in every aspect of your life, you will become more and more adept-not only at reading the staves, but at using them in ways which work more directly upon the part of the world you can see. Closely related to the duality of holy/unholy is the question of good and evil. The West has inherited a great deal of its own viewpoint on this matter from the Middle East, in which it is a frequent practice to separate being into absolute Good and absolute Evil.

The problem with this, of course, is that when absolute concepts are applied to the relative world, they are generally applied according to local prejudices. The effect of this can be seen in, among other things, the incredible psychological devastation wreaked on the Western world by the declaration: "Sexuality is evil; absence of sexuality is good." The first, and most important, re-turning of thought back to the ancient ways comes in dealing with the duality of sacred and profane as seen by the modern world. The terms themselves come from Latin roots; rooted in Anglo-Saxon, the words become "holy" and "unholy," having very different meanings and connotations. Holy comes from a root meaning "healthy, whole," showing that in the Germanic mind something holy is not cut off from the physical world, but rather is strong in both the earth and the worlds of the soul which are woven into it. Something unholy is not simply mundane or "non-spiritual" in the way that a profane thing is; it is something sick or flawed. To hallow a place or item is not to set it apart from the world- it is not taboo or untouchable in the sense of the Judea-Christian (Norse spelling of Christian) "sacred"-rather, it is filled with such a power of holiness as to ward it from any unholy-warped or woe-working-wights. Rather than this extreme and absolutist view of good and evil, the Teutonic peoples viewed right as being that justice and correctness which maintains a living society, while wrong was injustice, incorrectness, or anything breaking the bonds of fairness and law on which society is founded. This Teutonic belief in right as justice and fairness is one of the foremost Germanic contributions to civilization as a whole, especially when you see it as the main barrier against Western civilization's advance into totalitarianism: the deep-rooted belief that "no one is above the law," that neither private people nor the government has the right to step outside the bounds of the legal system for any purpose and even a king or a president can be brought before the courts if due cause exists.

Related to the question of right and wrong is the dichotomy of weal-working and woe-working. In cases of magical action, where lawful justice is more difficult to determine, these are the aspects which must be considered. Simply stated, weal is that which works towards your welfare and the welfare of others; woe is that which harms yourself and/or others. From this standpoint, there is no excuse for crusading under the banner of "my enemy is evil and Iam good"; instead, you must honestly be able to say, in a case where you are forced to take action against another, "he/she is causing harm to others and must be stopped; I am willingly causing woe in hopes that a worse woe may be averted, and I know that I maybe working my own doom as well." With further study, you will notice that there is nothing intrinsically evil in the Germanic legends; only creatures which cause harm and must therefore be slain or banished. However, the giant kindreds are capable of working weal as well as woe; the gods work woe as well as weal; and in the sagas and legends we see that the most innocent of acts performed without forethought may lead to either result. The nature of runic magic's effectiveness is such that it should always be handled with the greatest of care lest you should unwittingly write the doom of yourself or of others, or write woe where you had meant weal; this will be dealt with more fully later. It should also be remembered that the common weal is more important than your personal good.

SECTION I: THE TEUTONIC WORLD

1: THE NINE WORLDS OF YGGDRASIL

The Nine Worlds of the Teutonic cosmos are arranged in two major patterns: the horizontal and the vertical (see figs. I and 2). The two are not complementary: the vertical model represents a refinement of the horizontal, which shows the traditional levels of being-the Overworld, the Earth, and the Underworld passed through in the spiritual journey. The most significant aspect of the horizontal world-pattern is its emphasis on boundaries: the ocean which separates the world of humans from the worlds surrounding it the second fence protecting Midgardhr (lit. "Middle enclosure") from the foes without and the inner circle of Asgardhr ("enclosure of the gods"). The basic idea is shown in the practice of putting up a fence around the farmstead Gardhr) which divides the innangardhs (the social space within) from the uncontrolled, unknown, and hence dangerous utangardhs (the wild space without). [1] The term Utgardhr refers to the entire area outside the ocean surrounding Midgardhr, in which a number of uncanny and often woe-working beings dwell. The ocean itself represents the spiritual plane which is the boundary between worlds. It is, however, notable that in the legends one can fly, ride, or walk to these worlds. Your precise vision of this plane will vary according to your personal awareness, but the root idea of the journey will not. The horizontal world-view shows the location and arrangement of the "elemental worlds," which are considered to be on the same level as Midgardhr in the sense that beings from any one of these worlds can cross into another without a great deal of spiritual preparation. Alfheimr and Svartalfheim do not appear on this map at all because they share the central space with Midgardhr, Asgardhr and Hel; they are considered respectively to occupy the upper and lower realms of Midgardhr itself. To view the vertical alignment correctly, the elemental world Niflheimr, Jotunheimr, Muspellheimr, and Vanaheimr should still be pictured as horizontally arranged, with the Asgardhr/Hel axis passing through the center of Midgardhr at right angles to the flat plane. The pattern contained in the tree Yggdrasill, which defines the organic structure maintaining the shape of the cosmos and holding the worlds in the proper relationship to each other, manifesting the shape of being concealed in the well at its foot. The worlds are connected by the multiple "roots" and "branches" of this tree; these are the roads which may be traveled between them and the channels through which the forces of each world pass to interact with the others.

ASGARDHR

The highest of the Nine Worlds is called Asgardhr, "enclosure of the gods." In the Prose Edda, Snorri Sturluson describes this inner gardh (enclosure) as being built in the center of Midgardhr, the hallowed space within the enclosure of human society. Asgardhr's place above the horizontal plane shows its separation from the elemental worlds; it requires either the aid of the Valkyrie in crossing the bridge Bifrost or exceptional strength of purpose and will to reach Asgardhr by any other means. Bifrost is composed of air, water, and fire, burning with a purifying flame. It is warded by the god Heimdallr, the personification of the hallowed air/water/fire triad and father of the kin-bindings between gods and humans. The crossing of this bridge is only for the initiated; its fire guards Asgardhr against the thurses, and neither the warriors who come to Valhalla nor Thorr, least spiritually refined of the Aesir, can cross it, but must instead force their way through the rivers surrounding Asgardhr. Thund roars and fish live in the flood of Thiothvitnir. That river's current seems too strong for the throng of the slaughtered to wade... Kormt and Ormt, and the two Kerlaugs, these Thor shall wade each day when he fares to doom at the ash Yggdrasil. The bridge of the Gods is all ablaze with fire and the holy waters seethe. [2] The river Thund ("the noisy") represents the passage through water of death. Only the strongest of soul can force their way upward to Valhalla; the rest sink to the still realms of Hel while strength and determination are enough for the warrior, it is the goal of the vitki to gain the Valkyrie's aid and be able to cross over Bifrost. Within Asgardhr are the halls belonging to the various gods, described in detail in Grimnismal. A knowledge of these dwellings is good both for the clues they provide to the nature of the gods and for invocational precision. These halls are Thrudheimr, the dwelling of Thorr, Ydal (Yew-dale) plains for Ullr, Valaskjalf for Odhinn, Sokkvabekk for Saga (possibly a hypostasis of Frigg) and Odhinn, Gladhome where Valhalla is built, Thrymheimr for Skadhi, Breidhablik for Baldr, Himinbjorg for Heimdallr, Folkvangr where Freyja keeps her half of the battle-slain, Glitnir for Forsett, Noatun for Niord, and Vithi, where Vidar dwells. It has also been suggested that each of the twelve halls represents a different sign of the Zodiac/month of the year, beginning with Thrudheim as Capricorn, since the Teutonic year starts on Mother-night (Dec. 20-21). Colors associated with Asgardhr are gold, silver and white.

ALFHEIMR

Alfheimr is the dwelling of the Light Alfar. It is close to Asgardhr, being listed among the halls of the gods (though not numbered among the twelve). A frequent refrain in Eddic poetry is "How fare the Aesir? How fare the alfs?" [3] Alfheimr is ruled by Freyr and characterized by the higher aspects of light and air. Alfheimr is the realm through which the flows of energy from Asgardhr are often transmitted to Midgardhr. In this world, the highest energies of the realm of humans mingle with the lower energies of the realm of the gods. It is the highest realm which can be reached from Midgardhr without the necessity of making a crossing. The colors associated with Alfheimr are yellow, light blue, light green, and white.

SVARTALFHEIM

As Alfheimr, the dwelling of the Light Alfar, overlaps the highest reaches of Midgardhr, so Svartalfheim, the dwelling of the Black Alfar, interpenetrates the subterranean regions of the earth. In this realm are found the mysteries of earthly manifestation, represented by the matchless smith craft of the dwarves. Svartalfheim contains the lowest frequencies of Midgardhr and the highest of Hel, standing in much the same relationship to Hel that Alfheimr does to Asgardhr. This realm can be reached with ease from Midgardhr, often inadvertently, as described in a number of tales. The colors of Svartalfheim are dark brown, gray, and red-gold.

HEL

The lowest of the Nine Worlds is Hel, ruled by the goddess Hel, mistress of the chthonic [subterranean] mysteries. As Asgardhr is at the crown of Yggdrasill, Hel is at its base. Like Asgardhr, Hel cannot be reached directly from Midgardhr one must "ride over a bridge," or travel between worlds with the aid of one's fylgja. The bridge to Hel crosses the river Gjoll and is guarded by the giant maiden Módgrudr. As Bifrost is fiery and narrow, the bridge to Hel is icy and wide. Hel is also called Nifelhel, meaning "Misty Hel" or "Dark Hel," which refers to the goddess' primary aspect of concealment. Hel borders very closely on the world Niflheimr; it is located "down and to the north," and it is the implied location of the venom-filled halls on Na Strand and home of the dragon Niddhogg, embodiment of the concealed powers of destruction/transformation within Hvergelmir, the original source of which was Niflheimr! Hel is the hidden root to which all things sink, as all the waters wend their way to Hvergelmir, and from which all things rise again. Although the realm of Hel is described as horrible in part the lifeless, lightless, joyless dwelling of the dead-it is written elsewhere that Hel is brightly bedecked to welcome Balder after his death.

This dual nature can be seen in the figure of the goddess Hel herself; she is half a beautiful woman and half a corpse, her concealment both that of the womb and that of the tomb. Hel receives those souls who cannot struggle through to Valhalla, but in time, as her name "Mother Holle" suggests, she bears them forth again. The colors of Hel are black, dark green, and dark brown.

JOTUNHEIMR

The most characteristic world of the utangardhs is Jotunheimr. This land is the dwelling of the thursar, rises, and etins (various types of giant; see Chapter 19, Out-dwellers), the children of Ymir. It is frosty and rocky, lashed by violent winds and storms. Jotunheimr is located in the east, the direction (roughly) from which the Teutonic peoples have migrated; the Anglo-Saxon Rune Poem describes the ancestor-hero Ing faring forth from the east. Jotunheimr is the land of primeval ancestry; Edrid Thorsson mentions that "to go into the east" is a term used to describe the act of faring into the realm of preconscious forces.[4] It is inhabited by beings of great wisdom such as the etin Vafthrudhnir, from whom even Odhinn can learn, by the giants and by the semi-sapient hrimthursar or ice-giants who continually seek to break and destroy the walls of the ordered world. It is these beings specifically against whom Midgardhr has been walled off and against whom Thor wards us; they characterize one aspect of the foes dwelling outside the gardh. Jotunheimr is the turbulent world of elemental air which, through its endless seething and struggling, both breaks down and fertilizes. Its nature is seen in the shattering, icy might of the wind from the east. The colors of Jotunheimr are red and gray.

VANAHEIMR

Jotunheimr is balanced by Vanaheimr, which is characterized by peace and plenty. The Vanir are gods of fertility, riches, and joy. Vanaheimr represents the world of water, its nature being shown by the life-bringing and gentle winds from the west. As well as ruling over fertility, the Vanir are also described as "the wise Vanir"[5] and are noted for their powers of foresight. Seidh-magic is the power used and taught by the Vanic Freyja. It is characterized by the journeying of the spirit and the power of prophecy. While the Vanir are not without their warlike aspects, they are not generally considered gods of war but of peace, prosperity, and harvest. The Vanir are also gods of death, and Vanaheimr, the watery world of the west may be associated with the "final far-faring," the ship-voyage of death. The colors of Vanaheimr are dark green, dark blue, brown, and red-gold.

NIFLHEIMR; MUSPELLHEIMR

Niflheimr and Muspellheimr, the worlds of primal ice and primal fire, are set respectively in the northern and southern parts of the utangardhs, through which their mights are filtered and mixed to bring about the forces working through Midgardhr. Both worlds and their inhabitants, being the pure forces of fire and ice, would be endlessly destructive if released onto the worlds of the innangardhs. As the High One (an Odhinnic hypostasis) says in Gylfagynning, "there is nothing in the world that can be relied upon when the sons of Muspell are on the warpath." [6] Muspellheimr is ruled by Surtr, who will meet Freyr in battle at Ragnarok. The color of Niflheimr is black; the color of Muspellheimr is red.

MIDGARDHR

The central world of all is this earth, Midgardhr, also known as Middle-Earth. This world brings together and melds the might of all the other worlds and is connected to them by the roots, branches, and trunk of the tree Yggdrasill. This world represents the element earth, which in Teutonic thought, as in establishment Western magic, encompasses all of the other elements. Unlike the earth of establishment magic, however, the earth of the Teutonic tradition also incorporates the workings of spirit as received directly from Asgardhr by way of Bifrost and indirectly through Alfheimr. It is essential that the vitki be able to maintain her/his footing in Midgardhr and preserve the middle world's balance of power within him/herself; otherwise he/she runs the risk of being over- come by the energies of a world with which she/he has worked too closely Folklore is filled with the stories of those who have become "captive" in other worlds; i.e., so closely attuned to the energies of those worlds that they went mad or became otherwise unable to function in this world.

2: URHDR'S WELL: THE WORKINGS OF WYRD

Perhaps the most notable difference between modern thought-patterns and those of the ancient Germanic people, which relates to the most essential theory of runic working, is the concept of time and being in relationship to time. Modern Western culture has absorbed the threefold Greco-Roman concept of time as "past" (that which has gone before), "present" (that which is), and "future" (that which will be). It is easy to associate these concepts with the three Norns Urdhr, Verdhandi, and Skuld. It is also incorrect. The Germanic time-sense is not threefold, but twofold: time is divided into "that- which-is," a concept encompassing everything that has ever happened-not as a linear progression, but as a unity of interwoven layers and "that-which-is-becoming," the active changing of the present as it grows from the patterns set in that-which-is. That- which-is is the Germanic "world," a word literally cognate to the Norse veröld [Old Norse veröld], "age of a man."

One will notice that even in modern English, there is no true future tense; the future can only be formed through the use of modal auxiliaries. For the Teutonic mind, all that has been is still immediate and alive; the present only exists as it has been shaped by the great mass of what is, and the future only as the patterns of that which is becoming now should shape in turn. Without this understanding of time in the Teutonic world, your power of reading and writing the runes will be at best limited, at worst in error and unpredictable in result. The Teutonic conception of time and being is fully expressed in one of the most ancient images of the Germanic peoples the ever-green tree with the well at its foot. This is best known as the Norse Yggdrasill, described thus in the Poetic Edda: I know an ash that stands, called Yggdrasil a tall tree, wet with white dews dripping down into the dales. Ever green it stands over Urth's well.

From there come three maidens, deep in lore, from the water that stands under the tree. One is called Urth, the other Verthandi, the third Skuld. Scores they carved, laws they laid, lives they chose. They worked Ørlög for the sons of men. [1] The tree upholds the Nine Worlds; it is the ever-growing manifestation of that-which-is and that-which-is-becoming, rooted in and shaped by the well which defines and contains time as the tree defines and contains space. The tree represents the body of Ymir, the set form and space; the well and the nourishing, shaping waters flowing up from through the tree and back are the powers embodied, at the beginning of all things, in the cow Audhumbla. The maidens referred to are the three Norns; their names mean "that-which-has-become" (Urdhr), "that-which-is-becoming" (Verdhandi) and "that-which should become" (Skuld). Urdhr is the greatest of the three, the other two being extensions of her power. Her name is cognate to the Anglo-Saxon Wyrd or modern English weird, the root of which means "to turn" and from which several Germanic verbs meaning "to become" are derived. The word "Wyrd" has been translated as "fate," but the essential concept behind it is entirely different from the Greco-Roman idea of fate.

In the Prose Edda, Yggdrasill is described as having three roots with a well under each:

> *"The third stands over Niflheimr, and under that root is Hvergelmir, and Nidhoggr gnaws the tree from below. But under that root which turns towards the Rime-Giants is Mimir's Well, wherein wisdom and understanding are stored; and he is called Mimir, who keeps the well... The third root of the Ash stands in heaven, and under that root is the well which is very holy, that is called the Well of Urdhr."* [2]

In The Well And The Tree, Bauschatz suggests that this is an overspecialization, that in fact each of the three wells represents a certain level of the single Well of Urdhr or Wyrd. The name Hvergelmir means "seething kettle"; it is obviously the containment of the primal rivers (laguz) flowing from Niflheimr at the beginning, whose names appropriately denote their seething, active nature. This is the source of the power pushing the waters upward through the Well-the special "active" quality indicated by the term brunnr which is usually applied to this well, the "brunnr" or burne being a well which is built around an active, flowing spring rather than the standing water of an ordinary well.[3]

The term implies both force and containment, which makes possible the accumulation of the events of becoming and hence the maintaining of the ever-growing world of being. The creation of the world out of chaos indicates the restraint of the well around the seething waters and the binding of Audhumbla's proto-force to make her power an integral part of the preservation and ordered growth of the world. Hvergelmir is associated with the gnawing of the dragon Nidhoggr, who on one level represents the venom of corrosion present along with the yeast of life, in the primal waters, and on another embodies the concealment integral to the understanding of the well of Wyrd (see Wyrm). The second level of the Well of Wyrd is the well of Mimir, whose name means "memory."

Mimir is described as "wisest of the etin-kind," having gained his wisdom by drinking every day from this well, which is to say, by the continual internalization of the entire temporal unity of the ever-growing world. It is significant that Mimir is an etin and that the description of Mimir's well places it in Jotunheimr, the dwelling of preconscious forces, when you consider the nature of this level of the well: the primeval forces welling from Hvergelmir are here filtered through the awareness of every- thing that has happened since the first union of fire and ice. It is in this level of the well that the intertwined layers of that-which-is may be found and understood; students of general occultism will see a resemblance to the Akashic Record here. Everything that has happened-all the events and patterns making up the entirety of the world ("veröld") exists within Mimir's well.

This is the aspect of the Well to which one comes in order to reawaken the ancestral memories, as described in the Rite of Mimir (See Section V: Appendices). The Well of Urdhr, the "top" level, or that which most directly affects manifestation, is the aspect by which that-which-is continues to form that-which-is-becoming. The Norns are described as sprinkling water and clay from the Well over the tree Yggdrasill for the purpose of healing and nourishing it. This may be seen as analogous to the lög [leggja], the laying of laws which literally means "laying layers," the layers which form the structure of the world. The Norns also ørlög seggja, "speak the primal layer," which is to say that they have the power of determining which layers of action within that- which-is shall be the mightiest in shaping becoming.[4]

The process of becoming is a process of accretion; the patterns of the layers below determine the pattern in which the layers now being laid shall fall and the patterns that should result. The shaping waters, their path determined by the patterns already formed and the choice of the Norns, flow up through the roots of Yggdrasill, which are deeply sunken in that-which-is, to shape the growth of its branches-becoming within the manifest realms of the tree, and then drip back from its leaves into the Well (the cycle described by the rune uruz), adding another layer to the world and providing the continuation of the patterns which shape the next cycle. The understanding of Teutonic thought is that the continuum of being is essentially organic and interactive, with each part growing naturally from the other.

Bauschatz suggests that only those actions which are directly derived from the major paths of the water from the Well are significant in shaping the turnings of Wyrd [5], but it would seem more fitting to suggest that, since the Well of Wyrd encompasses all of being, that the distinction lies in the level of the Well upon which various types of action operate. In this context one may see that the major actions determined by the Well of Urdhr flow back to Urdhr, their out-coming in becoming determining the shape of major events that should follow. Those lesser events, which are shaped by the greater turnings of Wyrd but which do not affect it except insofar as they bear out the patterns determined by the actions derived from the workings of Urdhr, flow back into the Well of Mimir, where they are incorporated into the general world. Finally, the force from all the events which do not flow directly into Urdhr sinks to Hvergelmir (from which it will push upward again in due course); "from there all waters have their way." [6] The individual weird is that pattern which the actions of your ancestors and previous lifetimes have shaped for your own life. It is not in any way predestination; your own actions can be consciously changed for the sake of shaping your own weird. This process of actively shaping the patterns of Wyrd is done by, among other things, cutting and coloring the runes, which has the effect of writing them straight into the Well of Urdhr, from which they will flow to directly influence the manifest worlds of Yggdrasill.

Because of the all-holding nature of Mimir, what has been written can never be unwritten. Wyrd is inescapable; but it can be written around. You may see this in the story of Starkadhr, in which Odhinn and Thorr take turns writing and rewriting the weird of Starkadhr, one writing for weal and the other for woe. Odhinn says that Starkadhr will always be victorious in baffle, Thorr replies that he will always be wounded grievously; Odhinn gives Starkadhr the gift of poetry. Thorr decrees that he will never remember his own staves; Thorr dooms Starkadhr to be the last of his line, Odhinn gifts him with a life three times as long as an ordinary man's, Thorr adds that Starkadhr must do one dastardly deed (of betrayal) in each lifetime1 and so forth. This same idea shows up in the Germanic children's story of Sleeping Beauty, in which one of the fairies (a survival of the lesser Norns who attend each person at childbirth) cannot take off the other's curse of death for the young princess but can only modify it to a hundred years of sleep. This is precisely the power of the runes: to write Wyrd, and write around it at need (nauthiz), For this reason, it is good to cast the runes several times in a working so as to avoid unknowingly writing your own doom. You should read the runes before acting to see what is likely to happen if you do nothing, again if you do the work as planned, and a third time after the work has been done to see what is now written.

3: THE TEUTONIC MAGICIAN: BODY, SOUL, AND MIND

In Teutonic thought, your being is divided into several different parts which work differently, but must all function harmoniously if you are to do well on any level. As Teutonic magical workings call for the working of these several sides of the mage's being, it is necessary to know the form and function of each. Preferred terminology varies greatly with practitioners; Old Norse, archaic English, and modern English will be used as seems fitting. An index of terms is provided in the Glossary.

LICH (body): The Teutonic magician is expected to be strong of body as well as mind and soul. The body is the earthly vehicle for your magical force, and it must be capable of carrying, sustaining, and feeding that power as mightily as possible. Physical control is important; you will do well to take up the study of martial arts along with magic, if possible. Fasting is useful only as an aid to meditation and vision; active magic requires your fullest energies. Hence it is good to eat two to four hours before a ritual, so that you may be receiving the strength of your food, but not suffer any loss of sensitivity (food does tend to close down or dull psychic activity). It is also healthy to eat something with a lot of protein when you have completed your working. Vegetarianism is wholly outside of any Northern tradition; while a meatless diet that contains a full ration of protein and other nutrients will not be harmful to Teutonic workings, it will certainly not aid your spiritual growth in any special way as it would in most Eastern traditions.

Alcohol should be drunk in religious and inspirational rituals, but not before or during works of active magic where the vitki's control needs to be at its fullest. With the possible exception of the highly poisonous fly agaric [a muscimol mushroom], there is no clear tradition of using mind-altering substances in Teutonic mysticism. There are hints in the Eddic writings concerning the use of various parts of the yew tree (taxus baccata), but all parts of this tree are exceedingly poisonous. I personally know of one modern rune-worker who almost killed himself by inhaling smoke from burning yew berries. DO NOT experiment with these plants. Hair and beard, as the signs and embodiments of your life-force, play a great role in Teutonic thought and mysticism. These should be grown as long as your circumstances permit and carefully tended. Before rituals, you should brush till the hair literally crackles and sparks with electricity, concentrating on the might of the hamingja-force (life energy/mana) you are bringing forth to readiness, Hair, blood, and bodily warmth are all the earthly embodiments and the vehicles of the hamingja-force. SOUL: The term soul is used in this book to include all the non-physical aspects of the magician: hamingja, hide, fetch, valkyrja, and mind are all parts of the soul.

SPIRIT: The term spirit is used descriptively here to distinguish that which functions on the earthly realm from that which functions in the hidden realms: "vision of the spirit" as the capability to see the non-physical, for instance.

HAMINGJA: The hamingja will be somewhat discussed under Ritual. It is your personal reserve of power, roughly analogous to the general concept of mana. In later sources, the hamingja is sometimes confused with the fylgja (fetch). It is certainly the source of the fylgja's power, so the strength of that spirit is always relative to the strength of your hamingja, though the exact degree of relation may vary with a number of factors. The hamingja power can certainly be separated from the fetch, or that part of the soul can be given extra might. The hamingja is characterized as fiery energy.

HAMR (hide, shape): The hamr is the subtle body underlying your earthly body, which normally has the same shape as the physical form, though it can be changed. It maybe compared to the astral body of traditional Western workings. It is the shape in which the soul-complex fares forth from the lich.

FYLGJA (fetch): The fylgja is the animal-form showing the soul's inner nature and the person's condition. It can be seen by those gifted with spirit-sight; to the nonmagical, it only appears just before one's death. It is usually a guardian, whose might works-both in magical and in physical struggles, the outcome of which often depends on the strength of the fylgja-form and the hamingja which empowers it. The fetch is often confused with the disir (see Wights, Chapter: 18) or the valkyrja, and the fact that some fylgjur appear as women rather than animals adds to this confusion. For the same reason, the hamingja is also confused with these, especially with the kinfylgja who holds the reservoir of a family's ancestral hamingja and wisdom (see Othala, Chapter:7). The disir, however, are independent wights, while the Valkyrie, unlike the fylgja, cannot be commanded or seen by spirit-sight at any given time. The knowledge told you by the fetch should not, unless it is a message from another being, be taken as any sort of higher wisdom; its judgment is that of an animal, which may sense antipathy or danger and can perceive information that is not normally available to the vitki. It should be treated only as a guide in a limited sense, like a seeing-eye-dog rather than a teacher.

VALKYRJA: The Valkyrie is the highest aspect and the guardian and guide of the soul. She is the source of spiritual wisdom and the intermediary between Asgardhr and the individual. She acts at all times like an independent being, and it requires a great deal of spiritual effort to reach a state of conscious communication with her. Her nature is highly complex. She is described fully in Chapter 8.

MIND: The term mind is used in this book to describe the awareness and cognitive ability which encompasses both hugr, "thought," and minni, "memory" (embodied by Odhinn's ravens Hnginn and Muninn). The hugr is consciousness and analytical reason; the minni, the storehouse of all forms of memory, including that of the semi-independent parts of the soul, ancestral memory, and the Jungian collective unconscious. This memory is eidetic and endless, and one of the greatest goals of the Teutonic magician is to bring forth the wisdom that lies hidden in its darkness - to learn from "Mimir's Head." Until the hugr has been trained to receive knowledge through the sight and hearing of the spirit, messages from the hidden wights about one will reach it only through the minni, often surfacing as "feelings" or seemingly irrational choices. Although one's thought and memory seldom communicate fully, they are never separated from each other.

SECTION II: MAGICAL THOUGHT AND WORKING

4: EARTHLY HISTORY OF THE RUNES

The runic alphabet, or futhark, seems to have come forth into earthly being sometime between the third and first centuries B.C.E. (Before Common Era). Before that, the Germanic people had no writing as such, although they did have the holy and magical signs such as the quartered sun-wheel, swastika, ship, and so forth, which they carved in rock in their burial mounds and other ritual places, and which they may have carved into wood for purposes of divination. The Elder Futhark as we know it seems to have grown largely from the North Italic script of the last few centuries B.C.E., although Latin and Greek influences can be seen in it as well, as can some of the native Germanic holy symbols. It is thought that the knowledge of the runes must have spread northward and eastward from the alpine area; though no runic artifacts have survived along the path of the migration, the North Italic origin is virtually certain. Runic symbols may have first been used on perishable materials for casting lots, a practice with which the Germanic peoples were already familiar.

The art of carving them into stone and metal would then have come later, although a helmet (the Negau helm) exists which bears a North Italic inscription in a Germanic language, reading HARIGASTI TEIWAI, a usage which is typical of runic working. The inscription may mean either "to the god harigast" or "Harigast and Teiwaz" (Odhinn and Tyr).[1] The oldest known runic inscription is that of the Meldorf Brooch, which was found in western Jutland and is dated at roughly 50 C.E. The Elder Futhark developed into a number of slightly differing runic alphabets as a consequence of sound-shifts in changing languages. In Scandinavia, some of the symbols were dropped and others were used for more than one sound, while many of the runes were simplified or altered. This eventually led to two slightly different sixteen-rune futharks, the Danish and the Swedish-Norwegian. The Danish form, dating from the ninth century to the eleventh, is considered to be roughly the standard, and is generally referred to as the Younger Futhark.

The Anglo-Saxon Futhark added nine runes to the Elder Futhark and' changed some of the stave-shapes and sound values slightly. The reason for expanding the futhark instead of condensing it may lie in the fact that the Anglo-Saxon Futhark was becoming more and more used for writing and mundane purposes, while the Younger Futhark remained largely a magical script for a long time, making readability a secondary concern. As this purpose diminished in Scandinavia, a system of dots to distinguish phonetic value evolved. The runes seem to have reached Scandinavia and the eastern part of Europe sometime around the third century C.E. [2] It is thought that they were spread by wandering tribes, in particular the Heruli, who were known for their runic wisdom and whose name, Erilar, seems to have become a title for someone especially skilled in rune-craft. The Scandinavian inscriptions which show the full Elder Futhark date from the fifth and sixth centuries. These inscriptions have been found on both bracteates (medallions) and stones.

The futhark order is consistent except for the last two runes, dagaz and othala, which are frequently inverted both in the oldest and more recent futharks, and a single inscription which reverses the thirteenth and fourteenth runes, perthro and eihwaz. The division of the aettir ("eights" or "families") is also consistent. The 24-rune futhark is divided into three aettir of eight runes each, and the attributions of runes to their aettir was preserved even when the futhark no longer contained three sets of eight runes. With the slow growth of Christianity in the north, the use of runes in magic was forced to diminish, although the evidence of memorial stones that were carved in nominally Christian times shows that some of the old lore remained above ground centuries after it had supposedly been suppressed. In the more isolated parts of Iceland and Scandinavia, the practice of the native magic survived among the folk for a long time.

Some hints of runic knowledge also survived in rural areas in Germany, but such lore as might have been hidden in the traditions of the German folk was largely destroyed by the immense upheavals suffered by that country as a result of World Wars I and II. [3] The magical revival of the runic system was begun by Guido von List at the beginning,of the twentieth century. Von List guided by the Havamal and a mystical experience he underwent during eleven months of blindness (following a cataract operation), worked the Younger Futhark into an eighteen-rune system which is known as the Armanen Futhark. The magical groups working with this system were generally suppressed during the Nazi regime; the Armanen Orden was not revived until 1969. Although a fair body of writing on runic magic existed in German, there were no reliable books on runic workings published in English until A Handbook of Rune Magic came out in 1984[1]. As well as reviving the oldest and most magically powerful runic system, the Elder Futhark, within the traditional context of Germanic magic and world-view, he made the most useful elements of the German system available to the English-speaking public. Thorsson is the founder of the Rune-Gild, an organization formed for the systematic teaching and study of rune craft.

5: MAGICAL HISTORY OF THE RUNES

While the time of human discovery of the runes can be charted and analyzed, it is only a small part of runic lore. Far more important is their origin outside of human time and workings, which holds the mystery of their power-their discovery by Odhinn, the gift of the runes to humankind, and the use made of them by those who were heir to the full body of runic lore, a body which the modern vitki seeks to both reconstruct and expand. The runes existed in a potential state within the ice of Niflheimr, the fire of Muspellheimr, and the void of Gingunnagap before the world was created. The interaction of ice and fire created the proto-being Ymir, whom Thorsson identifies with hagalaz, the rune which is the "seed crystal" of the order of the Teutonic cosmos,[1] and the cow Audhumbla, the shaping force working to bring forth the full runic order and manifestation. This process was completed when Odhinn/Vili/Ve' slew Ymir and shaped the cosmos from his body, bringing the runic forces into full being by setting them forth into form.

[1] This publication is no longer considered valid due to views of the author not being in alignment with modern heathenry

The runes can be found in all things, especially things of power, as listed in the Sigrdrifumal: On the shield that stands before the shining god . . On the paw of the bear and on Bragi's tongue, on the wolf's claw and on the eagle's beak, on the bloody wings and on the bridge's end, on the loosening palms and on the healing step... [2] Some of these items literally have runes written on them; others seem to be mighty carriers of the power which is that of the runes. Although the workings of the runes in coming forth into being had guided the shaping of the cosmos, they could not be known by conscious beings until the final union of thought with form, which was realized by Odhinn's sacrifice of himself on Yggdrasill. By hanging himself on the World-Tree, which held the entire shape of being, he performed a rite of shamanic initiation that enabled him to fare downward into Hel, the silent keeper of the roots of the World-Tree and, in a single instant of inspiration, realize the entirety of the runes. His sacrifice of self to self-of the god to the greater needs of the god-gave him the might which he needed to carry forth this faring, remaining aware through his death and descent.

I know that I hung on the wind-tossed tree, all of nine nights, wounded by spear, and given to Odhinn, myself to myself, on that tree of which no man knows from what roots it doth rise. They dealt me no bread, nor drinking horn. I looked down, I drew up the runes Screaming I took them up, and fell back from there." [3] This cry was the first galdra single proto-word of power that encompassed the entire essence of the runes, filling Odhinn's whole being with their might. Having learned the runes, Odhinn gave them to other beings through a draught of holy mead, which was probably Odhroerir, the mead of poetry.[4] The potential to learn and use their power was given to humankind at their creation by Hoenir, one side of Odhinn's being (see Odhinn, Chapter: 16) as the gift of odhr, godly inspiration.

This potential was brought forth fully by Heimdallr, who, after fathering the three classes of human society, taught runic wisdom to the first noble and his youngest son, Kon. Runic wisdom is also taught directly by a hero's valkyrja, by Odhinn in some of his many disguises, and, it is hinted, by Mimir. Magical lore was usually, though not always, passed down through direct family lines or the family ties of fostering. There were no particular restrictions on gender in learning, teaching, or practicing runic magic; the common modern belief that wisdom must pass from man to woman and woman to man has no place in Teutonic tradition, with the theorized exception of certain teachings involving sexual exchange together with and as a part of magical lore. [5]

Most of what is known today about the historical use of runes in magic is either reconstructed from the inscriptions on surviving items or from references in the sagas, which hold a number of useful descriptions of the method of practicing runic magic. The entire futhark was written on some items, particularly bracteates, which might have been worn as talismans by practicing rune-masters or used as symbols of the Odhinnist cult, since a number of them also bear images which are characteristic of Odhinn-worship.[6] Most of the inscriptions state their purpose or a part of their purpose, although encoding is common even within these writings.

You must remember that, especially in the earlier runic period, that which was written was meant magically and could be read only by initiates; even seemingly ordinary memorial inscriptions were not to be read by the general public and often contained a number of layers of meaning hidden beneath the known words. Other inscriptions are wholly secret and cannot be understood except by considering the magical purpose of the individual runes. Runic magic in the sagas is done by carving and coloring the runes, together with magical chanting, as written forth in the Grettis saga: A woman cuts runes on the root of an uprooted tree, reddening them with her blood, sings over them, and walks backwards and widdershins [counterclockwise] about the tree while casting her spell. She then sends it into the ocean, saying over it that it shall go to Drangey and do Grettir harm.

The tree floats up on the shore of the island; when Grettir tries to cut it for firewood, his ax bounces off and gives him a wound which becomes mortally infected, and his foes are finally able to kill him.[7] This is characteristic of the working of Teutonic magic: rather than the fireballs of Tolkien's Gandalf, it is the subtle turning of Wyrd. Of course, as your experience and power grow, you will be able to cause results more swiftly, depending on the complexity of your working. Egill Skallagrimsson, the greatest rune-master of the Viking Age (d. 990), was able to cause a horn of poisoned ale to burst with a carving composed of a single rune repeated several times (see laguz, Chapter: 7), and by scraping off and re-carving runes written by an unskilled boy, was able at once to heal a girl who had been suffering under the miscast spell for some time. The swift effect in both these cases was due to the simplicity and immediacy of the situation, and also to the fact that Egill was working a counter-magic which broke the effect of bale at once.

However, when he carved a nidhing-pole to drive Eirik Bloodaxe and Queen Gunnhild out of the land, a much more complex formula and ceremony were needed, and the spell took some time to work, as it involved a great turning of Wyrd for a whole country. The most direct and effective workings are those which affect mind and soul, such as the laying of battle-fetter (frozen panic in a crisis) or the seeming change of a person into an animal that occurs when the animal-fylgja is forced (or allowed) to take over that person's body and mind completely (as described in the Hrolfs Saga Kraka when the witch Hvit turns the king's son Bjorn into a ravening bear by striking him with a wolf skin glove). In most cases, these workings belong more properly to the class of seidh-magic, which deals directly with affecting soul and consciousness rather than the turning of external events and circumstances. However, it is possible to use runic magic for these purposes. Odhinn caused a frenzy in Vali's mother Rind by touching her with a rune-written piece of bark, and a rune-written horn of mead was given to Guthrun so that she could recover from her sorrow over Sigurdhr.[8]

6: RUNIC THEORY: LEARNING THE RUNES

The goal in runic workings is to control the power of the runes so as to create the effect you want. For this purpose, it is first necessary to have a deep knowledge of the runes themselves and secondly necessary to understand the ways in which they may be used and the reasons why they work as they do. Something of this has already been spoken of under the Well of Wyrd; this chapter: will deal with the more active aspects of runic theory. The runes may be thought of as forces which come forth into being and shape it: collectively, they embody the entire that-which-is/is becoming/should become. There are many different ways of coming to know and use their might, but all of these come down to the drawing of these forces into yourself and guiding them forth to work your will. Some forms of runic magic require no tools other than the trained mind and will.

The most durable and complex, however, call for an earthly vessel into which the runes may be carved so that their might continues to flow from it until the streams of power are actively broken by the destruction of the "body." The advantage of these practices is sometimes offset by the fact that it is more difficult to carve and color runes unnoticed than it is to shape and send their force out to your target; but something which is properly charged with runic force and bound can hold the charge as long as is needed for most purposes, though it cannot renew its flow as a carved taufr (talisman) does. While the nature of Teutonic terminology may make it seem rather paradoxical to talk about setting the runes into the Well of Wyrd in one chapter and about using their forces directly to achieve an end in the next, there is actually no paradox implied.

When you make a medicine to heal someone, for instance, you may have laid a layer in the process of writing them a weird of health, but until you have caused it to be used for that purpose, you will not have completed the writing of that weird. To be effective, the magic of the runes must be applied and directed according to their own rules and the basic laws that rule all forms of esoteric power. To write weird is to act; but to write it wittingly, you must understand your actions and their effects. In learning the runes you will find that there are two ways by which you must approach them; the way of the mind and the way of the soul. The way of the mind is that of research, logic, numerical calculation, and experimental evaluation; the way of the soul is that of meditation, feeling, and practice. Neither way alone can teach you the workings of the runes.

The first by itself leads to barrenness, the second to delusion. In this book I have striven to present a well- rounded basis for the vitki to build her/ his own working and understanding on, but as this is largely a work of the mind, it is needful for each person to balance what he/she learns here with personal thought and practice. With the methods of meditation, as with one's practical workings, it is necessary to keep a galdrabok (magical diary) in which one records new lore and rites, all that one experiences in meditation and practice, as well as everything that happens in daily life which seems to touch on one's path as a vitki.

MEDITATION

The first step in understanding the runes in one's soul, after one has set them firmly in one's mind, is meditation. It is best to begin by meditating on each rune on your own. This can be done in many ways, each of which has a somewhat different effect. It is good to begin by staring at the shape of the rune and intoning either its name or the galdr-sound (mantra) associated with it. Thorsson suggests that each rune be painted in red on an index card [1] and this is likely the easiest way to set them into one's awareness. This should be done for five minutes or so, at a rate of one rune a day. It is best to do it in the morning when getting up, trying to visualize the rune at intervals during the day; or else just before going to bed, writing down one's dreams in the morning. Of course, meditation can be performed at any time.

Another practice which some people find works well is the use of stadhagaldr or runen yoga (standing with one's body in the shape of a rune for the purpose of drawing in its force). This practice was developed by the Armanen-rune workers in Germany. Its antiquity is not too well known, although artifacts showing the human body twisted into shapes like those of the runes, and the modem Icelandic practice of teaching children the alphabet by having them stand in letter-shapes, may support it. This method is beyond the scope of this book; a full description of how to use it and its effects, together with the positions, may be found in A Handbook of Runic Magic[2].

Meditation may also be done by simply sitting and concentrating one's entire self on a single rune to see what one can feel or find within it. The key to successful meditation of any sort is the ability to concentrate on one's object in all ways. To do this, it is necessary first to clear the mind and body of what is unwanted, and then to fill them with what is wanted. True concentration-letting nothing within or without pull one from one's goal-is one of the hardest things to learn and one of the most necessary in any kind of magic. When your concentration breaks, do not be angry or upset; this will only make your distraction much worse. Settle down and try again. In practice, the aim of full concentration can best be reached by good meditative breath control, such as is used in yoga and some martial arts.

Inhale deeply, not with the chest and shoulders, but from the gut. Your stomach should swell outward, your shoulders staying utterly still. Pull the breath in slowly, filling your lungs from the bottom; hold the air in for a couple of seconds, then let your breath out just as slowly as you let it in, and hold it out for a couple of seconds before breathing in again. It will help to begin with a slow, regular mental count which is the same for the inward and outward breath, and for the short holding of fullness and emptiness. The exact number is not important, although it should be the same for each cycle; a number may be chosen according to personal convenience and understanding of Teutonic number lore.

[2] This book is no longer viewed as a legitimate source within modern heathenry.

GUIDED MEDITATIONS

The purpose of the guided meditations supplied in this book is to provide a footing for an emotional and psychic understanding of the runes, in addition to the mental understanding gained by study and rational contemplation. These meditations may, and indeed should be used in conjunction with individual meditation as scribed above, so that you can balance a personal understanding of. Each rune with an understanding of the runic force and cultural background evoked by the guided meditation. These meditations offer a series of images and mental processes designed to aid your spiritual attunement to the force of each rune and to use the understanding of each rune's essential nature to tie together some of the various levels on which and ways in which it operates. Using them should serve to bring your personal awareness (consciously and subconsciously) closer to the mindset of the Teutonic world in which the force of the runes was expressed and defined, thus making it easier, both psychologically and psychically, to tap, channel, and control the might of the runes.

The meditations may be thought of as a psychic tuning fork, which you use initially to achieve the desired vibrational quality and level (the vibration of the rune) for the purpose of being able to recognize, touch, and use that particular stream of power at will. The guided meditations offered here may be changed to fit your individual needs; they are certainly not meant to limit anyone in any way. If you do not choose to use them as guided meditations, you may find it worthwhile to simply think on the images within the context of the rune with which they are associated. I created these meditations for the benefit of my first rune class in order to synthesize the historical and magical data I was giving them into a form capable of speaking to heart, mind, and soul at once. I had previously observed the effectiveness of path workings in my own assimilation of Qabalistic symbolism and lore, and felt that some of the techniques used in that school would also work in runic studies.

These guided meditations are based on images and understandings reached by myself in my own contemplation of the runes, combined with my research into the thought-patterns and imagery (both visual and poetic) of the Teutonic folk. If you choose to use these writings as guided meditations, you may either tape yourself reading them aloud or have them read by a friend or one person in a small group. To perform them, you should sit or lie with your eyes shut in a comfortable position which is not likely either to become cramped or to encourage you to fail asleep. Wear clothes which do not bind, particularly about the chest and abdomen. Allow a little time in which you can breathe in a deep, regular rhythm, letting all your tension and distracting thoughts flow out, before you begin the meditation itself. At the end of the meditation, it is very important to picture yourself in your own body again with your feet firmly grounded on the earth, as written forth in the text. This is called grounding, and it is done to prevent the psychic and mental disorientation which occurs when your awareness, having functioned outside of your earthly body, is not fully brought back into it; or when you have brought a great deal of magical energy into yourself which, unless it is directed to some purpose at once or settled by the act of grounding which brings one back to full earthly functioning, can disorder the mind - sometimes severely.

GALDR–SONGS

In the Norse texts, runic magic is often described as galdr-magic, as opposed to the more shamanic forms of spae- and seidhmagic. The word galdr comes from a root meaning "to sing or chant," which shows the needfulness of vibrating the rune-sounds and magical songs on all levels in order to bring their power into full being. As a meditative means, the chanting of the galdr-sounds will cause your very body, as well as the world around you, to vibrate with the might of the rune upon which you are calling. You should begin training yourself by practicing meditative breathing for some time until it feels quite natural. When you are able to control your breath and establish a strong regular rhythm, you should start singing the galdr-sound (given individually with each rune) on the outward breath and sub-vocalizing it on the inward breath, being sure to continue to breathe from the diaphragm. The sound should, at least at first, be sung on a single tone. This should be as low and loud as is comfortable for your voice, in order to create the maximum resonance within your body.

You should be able to feel the resonance within and around you growing in power as you sing the galdr-sounds on the outward breath of each cycle, while the sub-vocalized songs of the inward breath intensify the runic might in your spirit so that you can bring it forth more mightily on the exhalation. After a while, you may find alterations of tone to be more powerful; once you have mastered the basic skill of galdr-singing, this is a worthwhile path of experiment. If the full rune name is used, each of the sounds should be prolonged as long as possible, so that one complete exhalation is required to sing the name once. This should hold true in magical rites when one is using runic sounds or names as well as in meditation. The use of galdr-sounds in meditation is also a good way to learn to vibrate one's galdrar ("magical songs"-vocal part of the enchantment) in active magic so that the words resonate through your body and all the levels of being, bringing the silent and hidden force of the runes on which you call and of the words which shape and guide their might forth into earthly being. The resonance of the song is one of the major gateways through which power is brought between the worlds!

BRINGING THE RUNES FORTH

When you have worked your way through the futhark in one, or all if possible, of these manners, you will be ready to begin using the runes outside of yourself. Meditation and seeking, of course, never end as long as you live, but after you have brought these basics within yourself, your individual path is up to you. The best way to start bringing the runes forth is by sitting in a dark room with your eyes open. Choose a rune with which you have done well in meditation and begin to breathe, singing the name of that rune until you can feel its might within. Slowly stretch out your strong hand, index finger out, and trace the stave-shape in the air. The shining power, in red or a fitting color, should flow through your hand and eyes in a brilliant beam so that you can in some manner see the rune you have written there.

Should this not be easy for you, close your eyes and visualize its bright lines before you, looking through the eyes of your soul. When you can see it in this manner, open your eyes again. This may take some practice, but in time you should be able to see at least the shining ghost of the lines of power you have written. Once you have finished your practice, you should either draw the rune's energies into yourself or dissipate it back into the universe. It is bad practice to leave about any sort of magical energy which is not clearly bound to a specific goat and done over a period of time it can be dangerous. This should be practiced until you are able to do the Circle Rite easily and comfortably. When you are comfortable with the basic internalization and theoretical function to the point that you can use this simple ritual to ward yourself you will be ready to begin performing active runic magic.

RUNIC WORKINGS

"Know'st how to write, know'st how to read, know'st how to stain, how to understand, know'st how to ask know'st how to offer, know'st how to supplicate know'st how to sacrifice?" (Havamal, 144)

The most traditional means of puffing runic magic into effect is the carving and coloring of a runic inscription. This may be done on any suitable material-wood, bone, stone, and metal were the most common materials of the early days, but this should not cause a vitki to feel limited. Although synthetic materials lack hamingja-force of their own, by the same token, they are suitable for taking any sort of charge which you want to impress upon them. Anything which can be carved, engraved, and/or painted can be made into a runic talisman. It was usual for Germanic people to have the items which were most important to them, such as their weapons, written with fitting runes of success; this practice can easily be adjusted to fit modern needs. If wood is used for the talisman, or taufr, the following should be done. Go out into the woods with a bottle of ale or mead and a small loaf of bread. Quietly whisper your purpose and the runes of the rite to the earth, asking Mother Nerthus to show you a suitable tree.

Wait silently until you feel an urge to walk in one direction or another, then follow the feeling until you come to a tree that you sense is the one chosen. Perform the first part of the Rite of Tree-Gift (p.284) and leave without looking back or speaking to anyone until you are home. Return in the same silence to your tree at sunset or just after, or sunrise or just before, and perform the second part of the rite. With your ritual knife or, if needful, a hallowed ax, strike off the twig or branch you have chosen; it should be one bending to a quarter of the earth or an aett of the heavens, north and east being preferred. Cover the wood with a black cloth and carry it home, again without speaking in any way. In a ritual of healing or other rite concerned with a person's growth and well-being, it is actually better to cut the runes into the living tree, on a bough bending towards the east. When carving the runes, you should sing the name or galdr-sound of each as long as you work on it, prolonging the initial sound as long as possible.

This should be done in a slow rhythm of deep, regulated breathing from the center of your body, as should all galdr-singing. As you inhale, you should feel the streams of power flowing into your body, filling you with brilliant, tingling might; as you carve and sing, you should be able to see the power flowing forth into the grooves you cut, shining brightly in the runes, and feel it thrumming through the sax-knife in your hand. The coloring of the runes is the most important part of the process, as it is through coloring that they are brought to life. They are almost always colored red. The blood of the vitki is the most traditional pigment for the runes, as it fills them with her/his life and hamingja-force.

Red ocher is also a traditional pigment for the runes; its Anglo-Saxon name, teafor, is cognate to the Old Norse word for talisman, taufr, and the German word for magic, Zauber. The root of all of these words means "to make red," showing the essential tie between the act of reddening the runes and the working of magic. Red ocher is sometimes difficult to find in America, though usually art stores will carry either the dry pigment or an ocher-based paint. Red madder is another good traditional coloring that is much easier to come by in the pure form (though somewhat expensive).

If red ocher or madder is substituted for blood, you should grind the raw pigment with linseed oil, singing the names of the runes and charging the pigment with them through the pestle as you would charge recels (incense) during its grinding; this may also be well-empowered with a single drop of blood. The blood or ocher should be laid into the runes with the point of the sax or, if you prefer, with a special tool. While doing this, you should sing the lines of galdr for each rune by which you are guiding the sphere of its workings, feeling the runic might flow ever more powerfully through your body to glow in the newly livened runes. It is best in every way to have the entire ritual thoroughly memorized so that you may concentrate fully on the might which you summon and guide into the runes written on the taufr.

Further steps are more or less optional depending on your needs and level of experience with rune-magic: someone who has worked with runic energies and ritual for many years will naturally have less need of outward forms than someone who has just been doing it for a while. The practice of full ritual is of great benefit to the beginning and intermediate students, both because the changes it makes within the worker. As with all skills, constant practice and testing your limits are the keys to growth and success. An example of a full scale ritual for creating a runic taufr may be found in Chapter 21 under Rite of Carving.

7: RUNES OF THE ELDER FUTHARK

ᚠ **FEHU**

Galdr-sound: ffffffff
(A hissing f; like the crackle of flames)
Letter: F

Money is a comfort to everyone though every man ought to deal it out freely
if he wants to gain approval from the lord.
— Anglo-Saxon Rune Poem

(Gold) causes strife among kinsmen the wolf grows up in the woods.
— Old Norse Rune Rhyme

(Money) is the strife among kinsmen and the fire of the flood-tide and the
path of the serpent.
— Old Icelandic Rune Poem

One is called help and will help you in all sickness / sorrow and affliction.
— Havamal

The rune name fehu literally means "cattle," which were the measure of wealth in the earliest period of Germanic history. As the society developed, the power embodied by the cattle themselves was transferred to the gold with which one could buy them. Both served in turn as the physical representation of the mobile energy which manifests as money in human dealings. The rune fehu is translated as "wealth" or "gold" in the rune poems, but its etymological origin continues to suggest the strength of fertility and life-force which are essential aspects of this stave. War between the Aesir and the Vanir.[3] This war could only be ended by the giving of hostages the use of the power of gebo to harness fehu (as hinted at in the Anglo-Saxon Rune Poem) by channeling its energies into the binding of exchange.

The tales centering around Andvari's hoard- the Sigurdhr poems, Volsunga Saga, Niebelungenlied, etc., Which tell of a repeated cycle of kin-murder-how the terrible woe which fehu can work if its energies are not carefully controlled and directed in their flowing. The energy of fehu must be kept in motion or it becomes tainted. This is the meaning behind the stories of dragons gold being poisoned. The connection between wealth, fertility, and general life-energy is visible in the nature of the goddess Freyja and the god Freyr, whose powers govern prosperity and well-being in all their forms. Both Freyja and Freyr are deities of the fertile earth and of riches-one of Freyr's titles is Frodhi, the Fruitful, and Freyja weeps tears of gold. The life-force of these two deities is expressed as joy, sexual energy, and courage in battle. Both Freyr and Freyja are mighty warriors as well as rulers of prosperity and peace; their nature is energetic in all aspects of being.

This is the stave of elemental fire as the primal energy working through the worlds, the source of fertility, prosperity, and strength. The word "fire" is often used in kennings for gold, such as "fire of the dragon's bed"[1] and "fire of the creek,"[2] and gold is often described as "glow-red," indicating its essentially fiery nature. The woe-working aspect of fehu is its capability of causing discord, even within the kin-grouping, among those who should be most closely bound. As the rune of elemental fire, fehu is always a potential source of disruption as well as strength. The working of fehu in this aspect can be seen in the description of how Freyja came to the Aesir as the witch Gullveig, "power of gold" or "intoxication of gold," with power over fire and the energies of seidhr magic, and how the discord caused by her presence became the war between the Aesir and the Vanir.[3]

This war could only be ended by the giving of hostages the use of the power of gebo to harness fehu (as hinted at in the Anglo-Saxon Rune Poem) by channeling its energies into the binding of exchange. The tales centering around Andvari's hoard- the Sigurdhr poems, Volsunga Saga, Niebelungenlied, etc., Which tell of a repeated cycle of kin-murder-how the terrible woe which fehu can work if its energies are not carefully controlled and directed in their flowing. The energy of fehu must be kept in motion or it becomes tainted. This is the meaning behind the stories of dragons gold being poisoned. The fires of fehu in the personal sphere are expressed as the "libido"; that energy which, sexual in origin, is sublimated and channeled to provide the force behind most human actions. In magic, fehu governs the transfer of energies. You can use it either for projection or for the sake of drawing energy into yourself to temporarily increase your own power for a working.

Repeated use of the rune for this purpose will gradually increase the quantities of energy that you can handle at any given time and will aid the growth of your personal reserves of power. In general the use of fehu with another rune will cause a fiery increase in the second rune's power if fehu is used in a supplementary manner. If, for instance, you were to use fehu with jera for the purpose of enhancing your development of runic skills, it would speed and strengthen your natural spiritual growth to the fullest extent possible while bringing a rapid increase in your general power, although the control exerted by jera would prevent that power from outstripping your wisdom or your ability to shape and guide it.

In working woe, however, you might combine fehu with thurisaz to induce a violent and destructive rage, although this combination could be used to aid you in fighting, perhaps as part of a formula for bringing on the berserker rage; or you could generate an illness characterized by extreme fever and pain. In this case, the fiery and discordant energies of fehu would strengthen and inflame the breaking power and brute force of thurisaz. You must remember that the effects of these combinations, as well as being determined by the spoken galdrar which call upon certain aspects of the runes, are as dependent on the understanding and skills of the rune worker as on the runes themselves. A skilled worker could combine the forces of fehu and isa, fire and ice, for a mighty making, but in the hands of a novice this pairing could work great woe indeed. As well as drawing external energies into yourself, fehu can also be used for awakening your personal power and sending it outward.

The rune poems' references to "the path of the serpent" (Icelandic Rune Poem) and "the wolf grows up in the woods" (Old Norwegian Rune Rhyme) refer to the nature of fehu as magical energy itself which is a hidden force in the ordinary person and needs a special effort to bring it into play. The line about the wolf also may refer to Sigurdhr of the Volsungs, whose father Sigmundr was known for changing shape by means of a wolf's hide. According to one tradition, Sigurdhr was raised in the forest, ignorant of his lineage. Only when the time comes for him to slay Regin's brother, the dragon Fafnir who holds Andvari's gold, does he receive the reforged sword of his father which represents the strength that had been hidden within him.

In Richard Wagner's version of the story, the sword's name is Nothung, a suggestion of the need-rune nauthiz which holds the means by which the hidden fire may be brought forth. Ritually, fehu shows the hamingja or life-force. It is also seen in the unshaped flame of the fire-pot or recels-burner. Fehu can be used for increasing fertility, sexual desire, and riches. The stone carnelian, whose name derives from the Latin word for "flesh," is appropriate to fehu. Its red-gold color represents the fiery gold of the rune's energies; it is said to energize its holder and bring "good 1uck"- the positive working of energy in your personal sphere.

Carnelian is also said to be an aid to fertility, and it is used traditionally as a protection against envy and strife, the woe-working aspects of fehu. Green tourmaline works well together with fehu, its swift- moving energies directing the life-force of fehu into the personal sphere. The green color is fitting when you think of the closeness of fehu to Freyr and Freyja. Green tourmaline is also associated with physical fertility, being used in modern times as an aid for female hormone problems. Amber is also connected with fehu, being a Freyja associated twin to gold. It is said that Freyja's tears turn to gold on the land and to amber on the sea. Amber's energetic properties are visible on every plane, including the physical, where its energies are expressed as an electrical charge.

Fehu: Meditation

You stand in the middle of a furrowed field. The sun is setting in a blaze of red-gold fire on your right. The air is warm with spring. A soft, mild breeze blows your hair back, stirring your green tunic and cloak. As the sky gets darker, you can see little pinpricks of flame dancing over the soil. You know that this is May Eve, and the fire is burning over the flecks of gold in the earth. Far ahead of you, in the shadow of a hill, you see a ghostly blaze burning strongly, marking the place where a treasure lies buried. You walk across the field towards it, stepping lightly over the damp furrows. As you walk, you see the faint fiery shapes of women flying across the sky. These are followers of Freyja at their seidh-magic; they have left their woman-hides at home and are visible only as flashes of magical energy as they fly to their works. They pass closer and closer to you. You feel your hair prickling up with surges of power. Looking down, you see that you are also glowing with a faint flame under your skin. You reach the little rise in the ground where the fire burns most strongly.

It tingles as you plunge your hands into the earth, filling you with the strength to dig more deeply. The soil comes away in great rich chunks until you reach a huge stone. You breathe deeply and the fire within you flares up as you lift the stone and easily toss it away. Beneath is a deep hollow filled with glowing red gold, and a gray serpent is coiled around it in slumber. You reach down carefully, but as soon as your bright aura touches the snake it raises its head and hisses at you. It brightens until you can hardly look at it glowing red as molten gold. You stretch out your arms, standing in the position of fehu, chanting: "Fehu-might flow / From gold's grim worm-warder.

"Your watchful strength stolen / Sleep now in silence!" As you chant, a stream of energy flows from the serpent into your upraised left arm until you are entirely filled with its fiery strength, and it drops its head in sleep, gray and drained. You reach into the hollow and take out the gold. Walking away, you scatter the pieces along the furrows like seed, a candle-flame burning over each coin. The blazing power that had filled you drains away slowly as you do this, until the entire hoard has been sown. Although you still feel full of life and strength, the urgent flaming might has flowed out of you.

Looking back over your path, you see that the field has grown up where you walked and is now tall and green. An intense green fire seethes through the earth, pushing up new leaves even as you watch. The bonfires are springing up around the edges of the field. You can hear the sound of distant singing, and in the shadows cast by the flames, you can see young people coming together and moving off among the new green stalks of wheat. You raise your head and hands in thanks to Freyr and Freyja for what you have been given as you return to your own body, feet firmly planted on the earth, knowing that you can always draw upon this might through the rune fehu.

ᚢ URUZ

Galdr-sound: uuuuuuu (oo as in "moon." Prolonged, steady, forceful, like the lowing of a bull)
Letter: U

(Aurochs) is fearless and greatly horned a very fierce beast, it fights with its horns, a famous roamer of the moor it is a courageous animal.
— Anglo-Saxon Rune Poem

(Slag) is from bad iron oft runs the reindeer on the hard snow.
— Old Norwegian Rune Rhyme

(Drizzle) is the weeping of clouds and the diminisher of the ring of ice and the herdsman's hate. — Old Icelandic Rune Poem

I know another that is needed by the sons of men, who want to be leeches.
— Havamal 147

The rune-name uruz means "aurochs," the mighty, wild bovine of ancient times, which was an object of veneration among the Germanic peoples. As fehu, the domestic beeve [a beef creature], is the rune of energies suited to conscious control and shaping, so uruz, the wild animal, is the rune of the powerful unconscious-shaping energies of the universe which can only be guided by the wise one. The rune poems link this stave to the process of purification and shaping embodied by the cow Audhumbla and the alchemical process of evaporation and condensation. Both "slag" and "drizzle" speak of the endless process of patterning, cleansing, and reshaping which is the work of uruz. In the larger context of world and being, the runes shape shows the path of the water rising from the Well of Urdhr shaping the growth of the World-Tree, and flowing back down from its leaves into the well, continually renewing the life of the tree and healing the wounds made by all the wights that gnaw on it.

Uruz is the rune of Wyrd as an active force (the upward stroke) and also the rune used to direct the magical shaping will into the Well of Urdhr (the downward stroke). As well as embodying the process of shaping and setting forth into being throughout the Nine Worlds, uruz also represents the unconscious life-force shown by the strength and "fierceness" of the aurochs. As Audhumbla was the first source of nourishment for all wights, so the rune uruz makes the primal, "ur" energies available for use. The twinned might of uruz as shaping power and nourishing might is written forth as the two beasts on the roof of Valhalla. Heithrun, the goat is called, who stands in Warfather's hall and eats of Laerath's limbs, She fills the vat full of bright mead.

That drink cannot be drained. Fikthyrnir, the hart is called who stands in Warfather's hall and eats of Laerath's limbs. Drops fall from its horn to Hvergelmir. From there all waters have their way. 1 The stave-shape of uruz also shows the horns of the aurochs. They point downward rather than upward, showing the animal ready to charge. The best-known quality of the historical aurochs was its untameable ferocity, which to the ancient Germanic people was a sign of its overflowing spiritual vitality. Its horns were embodiments of this potency, and also represented the capability to pierce into other worlds. The Germanic peoples sometimes wore horned helms in ritual for this reason: the warrior/vitki has access to all realms and is master of all.

By defeating the aurochs and drinking from his horn, the warrior assumed the animal's strength, power, and pride of place. Uruz is the rune by which the vitki rules the "lands" around him/herself, just as the aurochs ruled the moors. The rune uruz is best known as a rune of healing, since it draws life-force from all the realms and brings it into being according to the initial pattern which is held in the genetic structure of the body (see hagalaz). It both shapes and maintains the health and strength which are necessary to sustain the intense efforts of magic and to withstand the strain which prolonged use of energies puts on the user. Uruz is used to aid in the growth of "wisdom" within you; that is to say, the deep-rooted, semiconscious awareness of the patterns of being and the way in which the waters of Urdhr are flowing. It can be used to bring your awareness to the workings of nature and the ebb and flow of natural energies. Uruz can be used in the personal sphere to bring you courage and physical strength and to enhance your independence and leadership abilities.

In workings of woe, uruz can be used either to control another directly or to put that person at the mercy of internal or external forces which he/she cannot control. More frequently, it is used to strengthen yourself and bring you wisdom needed to gain victory in a struggle. In using uruz to enhance your own power, you must remember that it is a primal and wild force which requires strength to work with. As the Germanic warrior had to overcome the physical aurochs to prove his fitness, so the vitki must be able to do this on the mental and spiritual plane. Used with other runes, uruz works to bring them into being on all levels of reality and to send them into the Well of Urdhr, as described above. It is the power by which you can shape the patterns of your weird and by which those patterns are brought forth; it is the working of Wyrd's water, as laguz is the water itself and perthro is the Well.

As a rune of warding, uruz can be used against forces of breaking both to maintain the patterns that already exist within your own sphere and to either turn those energies back to their source or to use them for your own weal. Ritually, uruz represents the act of drinking or pouring a hallowed draught from the horn or cup. In its aspect as the horns piercing the walls between the worlds, uruz can be called upon to bring about visions or to make speaking between realms easier. The stone associated with uruz is tiger's eye, which is traditionally said to bring courage, confidence, and strength, and which calls forth life force and brings it into your own being. The eye-like gleam of light in this stone hints at the horns of uruz piercing the realms of being so that a ray of brightness shines through. Your mouth is dry and parched with thirst in spite of the cold. You scoop up a freezing handful of water and taste it, but it is so frothy and bitter that you spit it out at once. As you watch, a cloud begins to rise from the churning torrent shedding bitter black venom which mingles with the sparks arching across the void to form a roaring giant-shape towering far above your head. Clear water begins to drizzle down from the purified cloud. You toss your head back to drink of it and it is sweet, cool and good.

Uruz: Meditation

You stand at the edge of a huge, dirty glacier, the icy wind that blows down from it chilling you to the bone. You can see that the muddied ice has formed in rippled layers. A murky, seething torrent flows down the glacier's side, freezing as it flows. At your back is a distant warmth. Looking behind you, you see a great fire far away in the darkness, shedding light over the nothingness and throwing off torrents of flames and glowing sparks. The cloud slowly draws together, solidifying into the form of a great wild cow. She licks eagerly at the soiled rim of ice, her tongue wearing it away. A river of sweet milk flows from her udders; as you drink, you feel her untamed might strengthening you. The shaggy, dark giant who stands above you reaches up to his full height, stretching over the great cow, his head so high that you cannot make out any of his features. With one last mighty roar he spreads his arms and they turn into huge branches. The cow blurs into a mist, surrounding you with cloudy grayness. When the mist clears, you see that you are standing on a lush green field at the foot of a tree whose trunk reaches up into the clouds, growing out of the great well before you.

Sparkling water pours over the sides of the well, splashing over the tree and healing the ragged gashes in its bark. A shower of dew drips down from the needles above you, some of it falling back into the well and some of it soaking into the white clay around it. Moving forward, you put your hand to the side of the tree, where it emerges from the well and feel the mighty waters pulsing up through it with a rhythm like a vast heartbeat. Tilting your head back and looking up the trunk of the tree, you see a golden shimmering near the crown. As the clouds drift away from it, you can see the hall clearly despite the distance.

It is Valhalla, the Hall of the Slain; its roof is made of golden shields and its pillars are spears. A she-goat and a great-antlered stag stand on the roof of the hall, chewing at the twigs of the World-Tree. Drops of shining dew fall from the horns of the stag into the well far below; golden mead flows from the udders of the goat into a great cauldron at the door of the hall. A few drops drip over its side and you open your mouth to catch them. The mead is sweet and powerful, filling you with a great rushing might. Behind you - You hear the thundering of hooves and you turn to look at the beast which is trampling across your moor. It is an aurochs in his prime, a huge bull covered with shaggy black hair, six feet tall at the shoulder with long curling horns.

With a joyful shout you rush at him. He dips his horns down, ready to gore and toss. Easily you leap up over his head, holding the rough horns to balance yourself as you ride his back. You are almost overwhelmed by the might of the beast beneath you; but slowly you gain control, melding into him until you yourself have become the mighty aurochs, the fierce warrior-beast who rules this land. When you have run long enough, you stop and stand up, the aurochs-power still flowing through you as you regain your human form.

On your head is a horned helmet, the sign of your mastery. Like the aurochs, you toss your head, and light flows through the air where your horns pierce it. You know that you have the power to pierce the veils between the realms at will and to master the other worlds as you have mastered this one, but the time has not yet come for you to fare further. You reach out and the shaping power within you knits shut the rip in the air before you. This done, you return to your own body, feet firmly planted on the earth, knowing the ur-might which you can always reach and draw forth through the rune uruz.

ᚦ **THURISAZ**

Galdr-sound: thu-thu-thu
(a deep, violent, explosive grunt, pronounced and cut off very
sharply, repeated rather than pro longed)
Letter: voiceless th as in "thorn"

(Thorn) is very sharp; for every thane who grasps it; it is harmful, and
exceedingly cruel I to every man who lies upon them.
— Anglo-Saxon Rune Poem

(Thurs) causes the sickness of women; few are cheerful from misfortune.
— Old Norwegian Rune Rhyme

(Thurse) is the torment of women, and the dweller in the rocks and the
husband of Vardh-runa. — Old Icelandic Rune Poem

I know a third for the event that I should be in dire need of fettering a
foeman.
I can dull the blades of my attackers so that they can strike by neither
weapons nor wile.
— Havamal 148

The rune-name thurisaz means "giant"; etymologically it means "strong one"
and, as such, is appropriate both to the race of thurses and to their chief foe, Thorr,
whose name also begins with this stave. The nature of thurisaz is phallic and
aggressive, as is the shape of the rune itself. The rune-poem references make clear
the forceful aspects of phallo-centric sexuality shown by thurisaz. Thurisaz is the
rune of forth rushing power as brute force; it is the strength which makes the
thurse-kind so frightful to the ordered world when their wrath is aimed against the
walls of the gardh, but also the strength which makes Thorr so powerful against his
woe- working likes. Thurisaz is the rune of aimed might, melding, as is the nature
of the thursar, the brute force of fire with the brute being of ice to create a violent
but guided reaction.

At best, this is the striking of the iron hammer Mjollnir aimed outward to ward;
at its worst, it is the mighty fists of the thursar beating in the walls of the world. As
a phallic rune, thurisaz has both the woe-working powers written forth in the rune
poems and the weal-working power to break barrenness and bring fruitfulness. You
must remember that Thorr is a god of the crops as well as a warder, as his being is
shown forth in the Summer thunderstorms which keep the grain alive. In parts of
Scandinavia it is still believed that the wheat will not ripen without the autumn
lightning-the wedding of Thorr and his golden-haired wife Sif, who embodies the
ripening grain. Thurisaz is the might which breaks through shields and barriers
and clears the way for new growth and rebirth.

The "torment of women" and "the sickness of women" of which the rune poems speak may well be the first pains of the loss of the maidenhead and the illnesses which sometimes come with pregnancy-pain which is necessary if birth is to take place, This side of thurisaz's being is shown clearly in the Eddic lay Skirnismal. Freyr, the lord of fruitfulness, has fallen in love with Gerdhr the giant maiden who embodies the frozen winter earth. Her name is derived from gardhr, enclosure, indicating the barriers of coldness and unwillingness which ward her womb. Neither love, nor riches, nor the threat of death can move her; only when Freyr's messenger (hypostasis?) Skirnir carves the rune thurisaz on a wand does she finally yield, as written: "*I carve a Thurs rune for you and three more staves-ergi, madness, and impatience. I can scratch them off just as I scratch them on, if need arises...Welcome now, heroic lad, and take this Rime cup full of hoary mead, though I never thought that I would ever love a Van's son[1]. The first main use of thurisaz is in settings of struggle.*"

It is the *main* stave used for purpose of revenge and harm-mighty warding and is useful in battles of both wizardry and weapons, as written forth in the Havamal. As a rune of warding, it is best set to strike back to another's thrust. In the personal sphere, thurisaz may be used to prick your will awake and to strengthen and aim your use of force. In certain bindings it aids in bringing on the rage of the berserker, which, however, is seldom a good thing in any setting less than open war and not always then. Used carefully, it may break down the barriers of a closed mind and bring the lightning-stroke of new thought.

An understanding of the way in which thurisaz melds opposites into a single point of might bursting forth will make this rune a great source of power for the skilled vitki; for the novice, it is something to approach with caution. The skilled vitki will also find this rune helpful in overcoming blockages of both the soul and the body, especially in certain forms of fertility magic where hindrances are met with. Used with other runes, thurisaz is a worthy warder aimer, and awakener. A common method of enchanting a person in Germanic tradition is to prick that person with a thorn, the Anglo Saxon name for thurisaz, easily seen in the shape of the stave. Odhinn puts the valkyrja Sigrdrifa to sleep by pricking her with a "sleep-thorn"-an enchanted thorn, perhaps with runes carved on it, the powers of which the thurisaz-shape of the thorn would guide into her and prick into action.

This thought has survived in the numerous Germanic children's stories in which the prick of a thorn, pin, or spindle casts a charm upon its victim. In the tales of Sigrdrifa and Sleeping Beauty, the thorn of awakening is the phallus of the hero who wakes the enchanted maiden, the act of sex being discreetly symbolized in later versions by a kiss. Thurisaz can be used in the raising and guiding of thunderstorms, either as a ward against the wrath of the storm, or in aiming the lightning, if you must, though this would not be wisdom's rede. All in all, working with thurisaz is like picking up a thorny branch barehanded. If you are careful and skilled, you can use it well; if not, you can do yourself much harm. Agate is associated with the warding side of thurisaz. The Anglo-Saxons used this stone to guard against thunder, demons (thurses), witchcraft, and the venom of snakes, all of which Thorr is mighty against. Bloodstone is fitting for this stave, having been a traditional ingredient in the raising of thunderstorms.

It gives its wearer strength and courage in battle. The iron oxide hematite can be used well with thurisaz, being a tattle-help like bloodstone. It is, further, said to be a shield against electromagnetic energies. The point of a terminated crystal works with thurisaz in its ability to meld energies and send them outward. You may notice the likeness between the shapes of the stave and the crystal's tip. This shape is a large part of the power of terminated quartz crystals as a focus for active workings. It may be worthwhile to meditate on this in conjunction with the forth-rushing nature of thurisaz.

Thurisaz Meditation

You stand on the side of a rocky mountain, near a glacier of black ice. The earth around you is covered with jagged gray boulders. Nothing grows here except thistles and tangles of thorn bushes. The ground is hard and icy beneath your boots; the sky above you is heavy and dark. The mountain begins to shake beneath you, grinding as it moves. The rumbling earth knocks you down. You fall painfully among the sharp rocks. Suddenly a spurt of fire bursts through the center of the glacier. The brilliant flash of light and the deafening thunderclap strike you together. As you blink your eyes clear of the searing brightness, you see the glacier slowly raising itself from the mountain in the shape of a huge, manlike wight whose skin is the gray of stone or iron. He raises a great club and roars at you wordlessly, striding towards you with heavy steps that rattle the rocks.

You scramble to your feet and run farther up the mountain, never more than a few steps from the stone-shattering blows of his mighty weapon. Fleeing blindly, you run into an impassable barrier of thorns that snag your skin and hold you fast. Desperate, you pluck one of the thorns and fling it at the massive club descending towards your head. The thorn flies straight and true, striking the thurse's weapon and shattering it to bits. He roars in anguish and rushes towards you as you throw a second thorn at him. This thorn hits him with a flash like lightning and his body bursts asunder. Great chunks of stone and shards of red-hot iron fly through the air, but the thorns about you smash them to dust before they can harm you. Plucking a third thorn, you hurl it into the heavy, dark clouds above you.

Its lightning flash is answered by the rumbling of great chariot wheels through the sky and the sound of a man's deep laughter mingling with the thunder. The heavy chariot bursts through the low clouds, drawn by two wild-eyed goats with sparks flashing from their hooves and champing teeth. In the chariot you see a burly, muscular man with fiery red hair and beard, swinging a great iron hammer around his head in an iron-gloved hand. Thorr raises his hammer in a salute and grins at you, then flings the weapon down to strike the frozen ground below with a terrible rending crash. Looking down from the mountain, you can see the furrowed cracks in the icy earth. The hammer returns to Thorr's hand and he throws it again, shattering the stones below to dust. Re cracks his whip and the goats turn and gallop up into the sky. Thorr's third throw breaks the dark bellies of the clouds into jagged cracks of lightning, striking the ground as a torrential rain pours down from the sky. The storm is blindingly intense, but soon over.

When the water clears from your eyes, you see that the sun is shining on the valley beneath you and a thousand shoots of green are already springing up where Thorr's hammer struck. Carefully you disentangle yourself from the thorn bush, breaking off one branch to carry with you. You descend into the newly fruitful valley and back into your own body, feet firmly planted on the earth, knowing that you hold the lightning-might of thurisaz within you.

ᚠ ANSUZ

Galdr-sound: aaaaaaaaaa
(A as in call, a steady rush of wind)
Letter: A

(God / Mouth) is the chieftain of all speech, the mainstay of wisdom and a comfort to the wise ones, for every noble warrior hope and happiness.
— Anglo-Saxon Rune Poem

(Ase) is the olden-father and Asgardhr's chieftain and the leader of Valholl.
— Old Icelandic Rune Poem

I know a fourth, so that if bonds bind my limbs, I can get free.
Fetters spring from my feet, and bonds from my hands.
— Havamal 149

Ansuz is the rune by which the first of Odhinn's powers and root of his being are manifested. The rune-name means "god"; the Anglo-Saxon form is "mouth," showing the side of Odhinn's being which is lord of poetry and keeper of Odhroerir, the mead of inspiration. Ansuz is a stave of opening in every way, as described in the Havamal (above). Ansuz opens the subconscious to receive and transmit artistic inspiration; it opens all lines of communication, earthly and magical alike, and releases locks and blockages of energy. This stave embodies the soft and cunning passing of air, as opposed to the forcible piercing of thurisaz Odhinn's wit instead of Thor's strength.

As the rune of air, an element which blends both manly and womanly qualities, it shows Odhinn's endless power of changing to fit the world around him and disguising himself as needed, as well as his hermaphroditic nature. It also shows his endless, restless wandering in search of new knowledge and his work of learning, integrating new wisdom, and teaching it in turn to those who can understand it. Ansuz is the rune which rules the power of galdr-magic: the might of the spoken and chanted word and of the breath of life which Odhinn breathed into Askr (ash) and Embla (elm), the first humans.

This breath, ond, is the actual spirit, analogous to the Hebrew ruach which means both "soul" and "breath." As Lord of the Winds, Odhinn is himself the embodiment of this idea of "spirit" and of all the magical might within, as his title Galdrfadhir, "father of magical songs," shows. The highest mastery of the magical breath is, of course, the magical song which melds the ecstasy of poetic inspiration with the guidance of power. In the shapers trance, one has reached a state in which one can receive the truths of the hidden thoughts of the world (collective unconscious, also implied by the nature of Mimir's Well) and transmute them into forms which show their might in the deepest layers of the hearers' minds. This is the gift of Odhinn through the rune ansuz, the gift of the mead Odhroerir, one of the three great roots of Odhinn's might.

As well as embodying Odhinn's powers of inspiration and thought, the rune ansuz also shows the side of Odhinn's being which is the Lord of the Wild Hunt, leader of the dead. As the passing soul is often felt as a breath of wind, the ancient Germanic people also sensed the nearness of restless ghosts in the stormy autumn and winter nights, knowing the fury (wodh) from which this god takes his name in the rage of the wild winds. It is thought by most that this is Odhinn's oldest shape: leader of the horde of rushing ghosts and embodiment of the might of madness which is shown through his followers as both poetic inspiration and berserker rage.

The rune ansuz is the rune of Odhinn as the lord of life and death alike: of wrath, wisdom, and mighty words; of the godly melding of greatness and madness. The rune ansuz is used for creative inspiration and reception of Odhinn's might. As a rune which works on the deepest layers of the mind, it brings the ability for magnetic, even hypnotic speech-a power which can be used for weal and woe alike. The most extreme example of this can be seen in the oratorical trances of Adolf Hitler, who seemed to have tapped into this might unknowingly and used it to mesmerize a great part of his nation. (For the interested, H.G. Baynes' contemporary study, Germany Possessed, goes into this instance of archetypal/ mythological breakthrough in great detail.)

Ansuz unblocks the channels of self-expression; it can be used to overcome the blockages of body and mind caused by fear or trauma and to deal with bindings and restraints of every kind. Through meditation on ansuz and the side of Odhinn's being which is the Lord of Death, you can come to a fuller understanding of death and thereby overcome the terrors it holds. Ansuz is used in all forms of receptive psychic ability and magic. It ought to be called into the vitki's own sphere before any act of galdr-magic. Should you be trusting or fool enough to lend your body to a spirit-being, ansuz could be used for channeling. This is not, however, a wise thing to do at all, as most of the walkers between the worlds are no more trustworthy than the average human stranger and frequently less so. A good stone to use with ansuz is lapis lazuli, which has traditionally been seen as a link between the human and the godly. The name "lazuli" is derived from the Arabic word for "heaven"- fitting for a rune so close to the lord of wind and sky. Lapis is said to be a mental and spiritual opener, aiding one in receiving both the messages of the hidden mind and the inspiration of the gods.

Ansuz: Meditation

You stand in the center of a barren plain. Everything around you is utterly still. Locked into your stiff stance, you cannot move or breathe; even your heart does not beat. Slowly, a faint breeze begins to blow around you. As it rises, you hear a deep, wordless singing far away, growing louder as the wind strengthens. You see a tall, hooded man in a dark blue cloak gliding swiftly towards you from the north, his graying beard and dark garments tossed by the might of the blast that moves him along the plain. He stops before you, his voice mingling with the howling of the wind as he leans forward and begins to chant, his words ringing through your whole being. "Sense you have not I soul you possess not / being nor bearing I nor blooming hue. I Sense I breathe into you I soul I breathe into you I being I breathe in you I and blooming hue."

With his final words, he breathes a great gust of air into your lungs. It tingles coldly through your body as your blood begins to flow, loosening the stiffness that had held you bound and filling you with wild might. The man, whom you now know to be Odhinn, is moving away from you already as swiftly as if he rode on an unseen horse. The restless power that he breathed into you drives you on behind him, eager to learn more of the song-magic that brought you to life; but Odhinn's path is as random as the wind, and he never stops or looks back. You follow Odhinn from the barren plain into a region of green foothills and from there into the pine-forested mountains, along the craggy granite overhangs and through the dark trees that shadow the purplish-black peaks.

Brilliant red toadstools flecked in white spring up where Odhinn has passed over the wet needles carpeting the forest earth. You dare not stop for fear of losing sight of him, but as you run you reach down and pluck one up, its damp white stalk thick and firm in your hand. The sun is setting behind a mountain peak. The wind is colder and sharper now, and heavy black clouds roll across the light-bloodied sky like a stormy avalanche. Desperately as you pursue Odhinn, you fall farther and farther behind him until at last he follows the twisting path into the shadow of the pines and you can see him no more. The harsh wind spatters raindrops across your face as the storm clouds shut out the last fading light. You hear the storm rushing through the treetops like a great river, moaning and howling through the pines.

A sudden fear comes over you as you hear the human voices crying in the wind, ghostly huntsmen hallowing back and forth in wild despair and abandonment, the blowing of a deep horn and the hungry howling of great dogs on a track. You walk more swiftly, keeping your head low. Over your head, a wind-tossed branch breaks. Glancing up, you see a train of dark shapes against the blackened sky-cloudy men on horses and their red-eyed dogs running before them and the cloaked figure on an eight-legged steed who leads the Wild Hunt. His arm reaches out, one finger pointed straight at you, and you feel a shaft of ice pierce your heart. You begin to run again, fleeing in terror before the dark horde of ghosts. You twist and turn among the pines, but the Hunt is gaining on you. The cold breath of the dogs is on your back when your foot catches in the writhing root of a tree, and you fall to the wet earth. As the Wild Hunt sweeps down to claim you.

You raise the flyspecked crimson toadstool to your mouth and take a bite out of it. A great rushing of wind fills your skull, bearing you aloft. You shout in furious ecstasy with the wild excitement of the wind that you ride behind Odhinn, and the other ghosts howl in answer around you. The dark madness of the Hunt possesses you wholly as you fly screaming down the wind, over the black-needled treetops. You have no sense of how long you ride but in time the wind slows and the gray light of dawn rises around you. You fare alone with Odhinn again. He turns and looks at you. His dark blue hood shadows his features, but you feel that he is smiling as he begins to chant:

"Well have you ridden I won wisdom-reward / Galdrfadhir's gift the magical mead, I Songs be your strength I words your bright weapons, I For galdrrnight's mastery I drink now of Odhroerir!"

Odhinn hands you a horn of mead. You raise it and drink it off in one Mighty draught, your head spinning with the sweet drunkenness of the poetry you can feel whirling up from the depths of your soul. When you look up, Odhinn has gone, but the wild ecstasy of his nearness still roars from his gift within you. You ride downward to return to your own body, feet firmly planted on the earth, knowing that you can call the might you have reached at any time through the rune ansuz.

ᚱ RAIDHO
Galdr-sound: rrrrrrrr (a rolled r, as in the Scottish brogue or like the sound of a motor starting)
Letter: R

(Riding) is in the hall of every warrior easy, but very hard for the one who sits up on a powerful horse over miles of road.
— Anglo-Saxon Rune Poem

(Riding) it is said, is the worst for horses Reginn forged the best sword.
— Old Norwegian Rune Rhyme

(Riding) is a blessed sitting and a swift journey and the toil of the horse.
— Old Icelandic Rune Poem

I know a fifth. If a foe shoots a shaft into the host, it cannot fly so fast that I can not stop it, if I catch sight of it.
— Havamal 150

The name of this rune has been interpreted variously as wagon,chariot," and "riding." It is closely tied to the ancient Indo-European images of a horse-drawn wagon or chariot carrying the sun, and also to the practice of burying the dead with horses, wagons, and/or ships.

As a solar rune, raidho writes forth the cycle of the day, the solarhiringar (ring of the sun). This ring was divided into an eight-spoked wheel matching the eight points of the compass and determined equally by the passage of the sun (midday, midnight, etc.) and by the daily rhythm of social life (hours of rising and going to bed, mealtimes, etc.).[1] When solar measurements rule social rhythms, time is always seen as a relative phenomenon. The legal measurement of time written forth as the hour in which the sun stands just over the shaft of an upward-pointing spear will point out a different "objective" time at different places and seasons, but it will always be the same in relationship to the actual length of the hours of daylight. Raidho is not a rune of absolute measurement but of proportionate and appropriate relationships. Above all, raidho is a rune of ordered movement-movement in space, movement in time, and the relationship between the two.

The Norse concepts of direction and distance were not based on objective points, but on the movement of people between points. Space was measured in terms of motion and time: the main unit of distance was the length of a day's faring on horseback, which might vary wildly in absolute terms according to the soft of land one crossed but which in fact precisely indicated the space and time needs of one's faring.[2] Raidho rules the rhythms of movement in all ways, melding the temporal and spatial with the personal needs of action. As the rune of measurement of time and space, raidho is also the rune of social boundaries as reckoned by the movement of the calendar and physical location in regard to other individuals or communities. The chief events of the Norse calendar were the three Things taking place in the summer half of the year, which was thought of as the best time for dealing out justice and making the greatest social decisions.

The Althing, the greatest gathering of justice and government was also the center of each year's time-reckoning. It was in the course of this gathering that the calendar for each year was determined and spoken forth. Legal boundaries were, like boundaries of measurement, determined by motion rather than objective space: a man using another man's horse or boat without permission had not committed a major crime until he had passed three farms or more in a given direction; a court of banishment had to be held "within a bow shot" of the fence around the lands of the accused man.[3] As the rune of rhythm and faring, raidho maybe felt in the beating of the drum or singing which carries the spakona (female shaman/prophet) or spamadhr (male shaman/prophet) on the vision- quest.

The "horse" of the rune poem is both the fylgja or fetch, which is spoken of further under ehwaz, and the rhythm of the faring itself, which, if you are acting rightly, will bear you along on its own. Raidho is also the rune of the final faring, the faring of death or rebirth in the manner of the sun's course. In the personal sphere, raidho makes you aware of both the rhythms of the natural world and the right times for ritual and social action as they fit with the turnings of nature (separation between these not existing in the Germanic world-view). The line in the Old Norwegian Rune Rhyme, "Reginn forged the best sword," shows the power of awareness of the right time and setting: the shards of Sigmundr's sword could only be forged into a weapon of true might when the hour of Sigurdhr's first great deed had come.

Raidho can also be used to bring you the wisdom to pace your efforts so as to be sure of finishing your task. Raidho is used to bring about justice and harmony as relative things within a society; it is the rune of judgment according to perspective and mitigating or incriminating circumstances. Raidho is the soul of the law, as tiwaz is the letter of the law. It also works in melding the individual with the folk within the normal bonds of society. In ritual work, raidho rules ritual forms, gestures and movements, especially circle-walking and the use of music, dance, knocking, and number.

It should be used together with ansuz in writing or readying for a ritual and in creative work when rhythm and proportion are needed. Raidho can be used to ward you while traveling in the realms of either spirit or earth; it may be inscribed on your vehicle to keep the faring smooth and swift. Raidho controls movement of all sorts, as described in the Havamal. It can be used to aid your aim. A stone to use with raidho is turquoise, a traditional warder of travelers and also traditionally used to improve marksmanship. Jacinth may also be used with this rune; it, too, is a warder of travelers and it relates to the social order of raidho by supposedly ensuring that the wayfarer will always be treated with fitting hospitality.

Raidho: Meditation

You sit silently with your eyes closed. Around you and you hear a soft, rhythmic thumping. At first you think it is the beating of your heart, but as it grows louder and clearer you can tell that it is the regular pounding of a drum. The sound grows louder and louder, drawing all your thought into it. When you open your eyes, you see that the drumbeat is actually the pounding of a horse's hooves and you yourself are riding the horse, a beautiful chestnut. Looking down, you see that it has eight legs, although it is well proportioned and the beating of its hooves against the dirt road is perfectly regular. The land you are riding through is mountainous and rocky, silent in the cold gray light of dawn.

The sun rises as you ride, moving at the same pace as your steed, so that its place in the sky is never any farther or nearer to you. The day grows warmer as you ride down from the mountains over a rocky field to the coast. You can see little thatched farmhouses in the distance and people dressed in plain tunics and breeches beginning the day's work in the fields. Your horse bears you down to the seashore, its hoof beats as regular and rhythmic in the damp sand as they were on the road. A crisp breeze is blowing off the ocean, stirring up the waves. You can see a small boat keeping pace with you over the water, rising and falling in a measured pattern.

Circling up from the shore, you ride past rich and fruitful fields. The wheat is high and just beginning to ripen, green tinged with gold. As you turn towards the western coast, you see the farmers going in for their midday meal. A cool, damp breeze blows from the sea ahead of you; the little boat is rounding the curve of the land, still keeping pace with you and the sun. As you ride up towards the northwest the land begins to become rockier again. You can hear things slithering and moving be- hind the boulders, and every so often a dark tail or paw whisks swiftly into a hole, but none of the hidden creatures dare to come near the road. A cold, sharp wind cuts through the lingering warmth of summer as you ride.

The day is beginning to darken as the sun sinks and the farmers go in for their evening meal. You are beginning to grow tired, but the pounding rhythm of the horse's hooves beneath you strengthens you and carries you onward. A wolf's howl rises from the mountains around you, answered by another and another. Several gray shapes slip out of the rocks behind you. The wolves follow you along the sides of the road, waiting for your horse to miss a step. Past the wolves are other things, murky black shadows waiting and whispering. Their voices get louder, calling your name. You hear the voices of your parents and of friends from the past in the darkness, begging you to turn aside. Staring down at the faintly glimmering path before you and you guide your horse along without turning or breaking the rhythm of its hooves. Clawed hands reach out along the side of the road as if to drag you down. You see glowing green eyes in twisted faces and foxfire glinting off shark-sharp teeth as the thousands of nameless dwellers in the dark howl and yammer around you.

You know that to turn from the road or break the rhythm of your riding is to be lost forever among this horde of dark things. Over and over you chant the name of the road-rune to ward yourself: raidho, raidho, raidho. Ahead, you can see a faint gleaming; your road has brought you spiraling upward into the air, so that the jagged dark peaks are shadows in the night far below you. The creatures following you begin to drop back as you draw nearer to the source of the light. At first you think that you are coming towards the sun; but as you get near enough to see through the golden gleaming, you see that it is a silver-roofed hall upheld by glowing pillars of gold from which the light and summery warmth radiate.

The walls are open. Within you see a fair-featured man with golden hair and beard, seated on a raised throne before a clear spring of water. He holds an oaken staff in one hand, beckoning to you with it. He does not speak as you come before him, but dips up some of the water in his free palm and drinks of it. You do likewise, dismounting and drinking of the spring in holy silence. This man, whom you now know as Forseti, god of righteousness, smiles at you and traces the rune raidho over your heart with the tip of his staff. He points to a second path from his hall, which leads straight downward through the light of the sunrise. You bow in respect and thanks and mount your horse again, riding down to your body on the earth. Closing your eyes, you hear the hoof beats of your horse soften to the beating of a drum, until you can hear nothing but your own heart beating. You are back in your own body, your feet planted firmly on the earth, holding the power of raidho with Forseti's blessing.

ᚲ KENAZ

Galdr-sound: Keh-Keh-Keh (The K sound is hit hard, volume tapering down like the sound of a sharply struck bell. The galdr-sound is neither prolonged like those of most of the runes nor chopped off like that of thurisaz, but fades swiftly to a natural end.)
Letter: K, hard C

(Torch) is to every living person known by its fire it is clear and bright it usually burns when the athlings rest inside the hall.
— Anglo-Saxon Rune Poem

(Sore) is the curse of children Grief makes a man pale.
— Old Norwegian Rune Rhyme

(Sore) is the bale of children and a scourge and the house of rotten flesh.
— Old Icelandic Rune Poem

I know a sixth.
If some thane attacks me, with the wood of a young root, he who says he hates me will get hurt, but I will be unharmed.
— Havamal 151

The source of the meaning behind kenaz is one of the most deeply shrouded in the runic system. The rune's two names, "torch" and "sore, boil, or swelling," seem utterly unrelated to each other. The answer to this seeming dichotomy may be found in the changing burial practices of the early Germanic peoples. At first a corpse was kept in an unsealed mound and left to rot until the flesh had disintegrated to the point where it could easily be separated from the bones and (possibly) used in the burial rites.[1] This is the "house of rotting flesh" referred to in the Old Icelandic Rune Poem. The Anglo-Saxon poem, on the other hand, tells of the later time when fire had largely replaced decay as a means of freeing the bones from the flesh.

Both meanings of kenaz speak of the readying of the corpse for mound-burial. On the esoteric level, this readying deals with the initiation inside the mound, an initiation written forth in the image of a smith flaying the candidate to pieces and reforging his bones. The alfish smith as initiation-master is a well-known Germanic figure. Echoes of this dismemberment/initiation ritual can be seen faintly in the lay of Volundr (Wayland) in which, however, the ritual usage is only mistily remembered among the details of the smith's revenge. The initiation-by-fire is an initiation on different levels for both king and shaman, as may be seen in outline in the Volundr tale and more clearly in the Eddic poem "Grimnismal" in which Odhinn, tortured by fire for nine nights, chants the ritual knowledge which empowers himself and raises his hearer, the young prince Agnarr, to the kingship. Kenaz governs the primal craft of the smith and all works of knowledge crafted into action.

Its work is that of cleansing followed by transformation, as the verse of the Havamal writes forth, telling how the energy of a woe-working spell can be reshaped to work woe to one's foeman and weal to oneself. Although the smith/king initiation seems to be a work of males, the workings of the mound belong to the necklace-adorned earth-goddess who was originally called Nerthus and later became Freyja, "Lady." This goddess ruled the twin workings of death and fruitfulness, as will be spoken of later under Berkano. The rune kenaz shows the fire of Freyja's sexuality (fehu) given shape by the wit and craft of the smith. This relationship is best written forth in the tale of Freyja's buying of the necklace/girdle Brisingamen (Fire- necklace), center of much of her might.

Freyja saw four dwarves forging the necklace of gold and bought it from them at the price of four nights of her love, which is to say that she gave them the fiery might in the form of sexual power with which they were able to bring forth the necklace to its final being. Kenaz is the power of fehu controlled and used for shaping. It is the rune of unmaking for the sake of remaking. It is used for all acts of artistic shaping, in which the vision, or fire, must break down the raw gold of the earthly material and reshape it into the vision-image set forth in earthly being. Used by the experienced magician, kenaz is the rune which releases the spirit into the realms of power, as written forth in the lay of Volundr and Grimnismal. Kenaz is used for mastery over the sexual energies, often in conjunction with the other fire-runes.

It may also be called upon for guiding emotional power to achieve a goal and to shape the feelings of others. Being closely tied to the inherited right of kingship and the mound in which the dead ancestors dwell,kenaz is one of the runes useful in testing and bringing forth those powers which have passed down to you either from the ancestors of your body or from earlier lifetimes. This use is written of in the story of Ottar, in which Freyja makes the cave-dwelling witch Hyndla tell all the names of Ottar's line so that her lover may gain his rightful might. Kenaz is the source of the bright charisma burning like a torch within the true leader,[2] the rune of the king.

As the rune of the fire within the mound, kenaz is also associated with the dragon or wyrm, the coiling wight of Wyrd's hidden workings. The woe-working side of kenaz's being is disintegration without reintegration, or unguided shaping, shown forth as rotting sickness or as tumors and cancer. In ritual workings, kenaz may be seen as the torch or candle which is a sign of the controlled fire of the vitki's will through all the realms in which he/she is working. Used with other runes, kenaz aids the vitki in shaping their power and selecting the sides of their being on which she/he wants to call. The stones associated with kenaz are flint, the primal source of human craftsmanship and mastery over fire; the fire agate and fire opal which aid the control and use of sexual power and raise creativity; and smoky quartz, also used with eihwaz.

Kenaz: Meditation

You stand on the northern side of a mound at sunset, dressed in a white tunic and carrying a round shield and longsword. At your right hand, the sky glows red and gold around the sinking sun; at your left, it is already dark. One star shines brightly from the deepening blue above you. It is the evening star, the star of Freyja. The mound is not much taller than your head, a rounded heap of stones overgrown with thick grass. As the last rim of the red sun sinks below the horizon, a dark opening appears before you. The hole in the mound is barely large enough for you to crawl into with weapon and shield held before your body. The stones lining the way are harsh and cold as death against your bare knees.

At the end of the long passage you see a glow as of red gold lit by fire. A steam like hissing like an overheated bellows sounds around you. As you near the end of the passage, you see that it opens out into a great round chamber, filled with all sorts of cunningly worked golden treasures: cups, bracelets glittering with rubies and emeralds, necklaces, and statuettes, each gleaming in the light of little flames which leap about them. In the middle of the mound is a great iron anvil and the fire pit and bellows of a forge. The huge river of coins coiling through this hoard moves restlessly as you enter, and you see that what you had thought were gold pieces are the scales of a great dragon, who lifts his crested head and opens eyes glimmering with many-colored fire. Wary of the wyrm's power to enchant, you do not look straight into his gaze, but rather at the flame like tongue flickering in and out of his razor-toothed mouth.

"Who are you, and what do you seek?" The dragon asks in a voice like water hissing off molten metal.

Knowing that you should not tell this beast your true name, you answer, "I am Child-of-Good-Kin and I seek the goddess gold bright, Brisingamen's well-known wearer. Away, wyrm, or die by my blade!"

The dragon rears up like a huge snake, firelight glittering off the great golden shield-scales across his belly. There is a dark spot about the size of your palm where two scales do not quite join in the middle. "Flee now, mortal, or fall to my flames!" He roars.

A great gust of fire spews from his throat, but you duck under it and drive your sword deep into the naked place on his underside. His thrashings tear the weapon from your hand, whipping the length of his serpentine body against the stones of the chamber. You crouch down beside the anvil, trying to keep from being battered to death by the death throes of the dragon. When only a few shudders run down the length of the wyrm's corpse, you pull your sword out and cut his heart out of his body, burning blood welling up over your hands as you pull the dark, throbbing piece of dragon-flesh forth. Spitting the heart on your sword, you roast it over the fire of the forge, drops of blood sizzling onto the flames.

The first bite of meat burns your tongue, but you know that you must eat it all. It tastes like wild game, but stronger, fiery and yet with an underlying sweetness. When you have swallowed the last bite, you feel a terrible flame in your belly. You sag against the iron anvil falling as the flames roar through you. They scorch your flesh from your bones until your skeleton lies clean upon the worked gold. You can still see and hear; it is as though your soul still lay beside the white remains of your body. A crippled dwarf hobbles into the mound from the west. He walks with two crutches. As he moves around you, you can see that he has been hamstrung. His face is horribly scarred with burn marks and his ragged, scorch-holed tunic is smeared all over with black soot.

His arms are hugely muscled, but his gnarled fingers are delicate as he picks your bones up and lays them upon the forge. One by one, he heats the bones of your body until they glow like iron, then smiths them back together. You feel each battering blow, each touch of fire and blast of the bellows, but in spite of the intensity of these sensations, there is no pain. As the smith strikes you again and again with his great hammer, he stands straighter and becomes more and more comely, the burns and smears of coal on his face vanishing, his back untwisting and his legs healing, until he stands before you in a fine white tunic as a handsome alf with long blond hair, clear gray eyes, fair skin and noble features.

"Hail to thee, Child-of-Good-Kin!" The smith says, and puts a heavy gold crown into your hands. This crown is worked into the image of a boar's head with eyes of glowing fire opal golden snout open, and tusks set for battle.

The smith leaps into the air and is gone. You get off the forge and stand, feeling new strength rush into you as you look towards the southern side of the mound. A tall woman appears before you, red-gold hair curling thickly down her back, her arms spread out to embrace you. She is slender but her hips flare sweetly and her breasts are large and full. Her face is breathtakingly beautiful. She wears only a great collar of four amber-inlaid gold rings connected by a great golden tree in the middle. The tree is surrounded by four amber pendants in each row, carved into the shapes of a sow, a cat, a mare, and a woman. You recognize her as the goddess Freyja, ruler of the mound and wife of the human king. She embraces and kisses you, and the sweet fire of making roars through you at her touch. The two of you rise through the top of the mound, passing easily through stone and earth. At the mound's top stands a stone chair facing east. Freyja guides you into it then places the heavy golden crown on your head. As the fire of the sun's rim rises into the pale blue and gold of the eastern sky, she sinks back into the mound. You stand and walk towards the sun, slowly melding back into your earthly body with the wisdom and might of the fire-rune kenaz within you.

ᚷ   GEBO

Galdr-sound: geh-geh-geh (as in get; an even, cyclic repetition, swelling smoothly into the eh-sound and diminishing just as smoothly)
Letter: G

(Gift) is for every man a pride and a praise help and worthiness and of every homeless adventurer it is the estate and substance for those who have nothing else. — Anglo-Saxon Rune Poem

The name of this rune has been, variously, "gift," "hospitality," "generosity," and "wedding." Both the name and the stave-shape of this rune show its being as the embodiment of the equal exchange of those energies which, as shown by fehu, are set forth in earth as wealth. To the Germanic people, the act of giving was a highly meaningful one, the process of exchange also being a binding of loyalty. A common kenning for a lord was "ring-giver" speaking of the duty of a lord to give freely of his wealth to his followers.

By accepting a gift, one pledged one's trueness. It was, indeed, thought of as shameful for a man to live past a battle in which his ring-giver was slain. The breaking of this holy bond is always followed by disaster, as shown by the end of Beowulf, in which the hero's death is caused by the cowardice of his men, who abandon him in his fight against the dragon. Widsith, the only man who remained faithful, reproaches the others with the gifts which were the outward sign of the binding between themselves and the lord. Hjalti's speech in the Bjarkimal shows the same understanding:

In foul winds as in fair, keep faith with your lord, he who withheld
no hoard for himself but gave us freely of gold and silver.
Strike with the swords he bestowed, and the spears in helmets and
hauberks you got from his hand let shine the shields that he shared
with you thus honestly earning the wealth he gave.1

Gebo also relates to the practice of sealing alliances between clans by either marriage or an exchange of hostages, usually the sons of the lords who would then be fostered by the families of their earlier foes and slain if treachery took place. This is the reason for the presence of Freyr and Njord among the Aesir, they being the hostages who ended the war between the Aesir and the Vanir, their Aesic counterparts being Hoenir and Mimir. This understanding of loyalty-through-exchange works on every level, as described in the Havamal:

Friends should share joy in weapons and clothes that are evident to
one another.
Those who share gifts stay the fastest friends,
When things go well.
A man shall ever be a friend to his friends, and give gift for gift,
laughter for laughter, but give lies for lies...
He who gives gladly lives the best life and seldom has sorrow, but the
unwise suspect all and always pine for gifts. [2]

Generosity in every wise is one of the chief Teutonic virtues, whether it is expressed as gifts, as hospitality, or as the blessing of sacrifice. The ability to give freely is the only way to gain, not only the loyalty created by the act of giving but also the hamingja-might which comes from right action. The strict Teutonic code of hospitality is grounded on this understanding, as spoken of in the rune-poem. The homeless wanderer relies on this code for the food and shelter which, in the icy northern lands, often meant the difference between life and death, while the host gains the weal of working rightly as well as the growth of his/her good reputation. The setting of Grimnismal writes forth the workings of gebo.

Odhinn has gone to settle a wager with Frigga by seeing whether it is true that King Geirrodhr is stingy towards his guests; Frigga warns the king of the approach of an ill-meaning wizard and he thus questions Odhinn, who refuses to talk, then strings him up over a fire. Finally Geirrodhr's son Agnarr brings Odhinn a horn of beer, to which gift Odhinn replies, *"Eight nights I sat between the fires. / No man dealt me food, except for Agnarr alone, / the son of Geirroth / he alone shall rule the land of the Goths. / Hail, Agnan! Veratyr bids you greetings. / You will never get / better payment for a single drink."*[3]

Odhinn's gift to Agnarr is the chanting of mystic wisdom, which, as described in the king/shaman initiation of kenaz, raises the subject to the kingship and frees the worker. Odhinn ends by turning the woe-working power of gebo on King Geirrodhr, returning woe for woe by causing him to stumble and die on his own sword, paying Geirrodhr back and bringing Agnarr to his inheritance. Gebo governs both the religious work of sacrificing to the gods and the mystical work of sacrificing self to self, as Odhinn does endlessly in his search for wisdom.

In Teutonic thought sacrifice is more than simple supplication or payment for favors; rather, it is the binding of loyal love which shapes the relationships between individual heroes and their gods. This can be seen with special clearness in the case of Odhinnic heroes: either Odhinn comes against his hero to claim him in his final battle, or the dying warrior must have himself marked with the point of a spear to show that he is himself a gift to Odhinn. In return for the gifts of victory which Odhinn gave them in life, his heroes become members of his troops of einherjar who will fight beside him at Ragnarok. The runic section of the Havamal contains several references to sacrifice, the most notable being Odhinn's telling of his ordeal on Yggdrasil.

> *I know that I hung on a wind-swept tree all of nine nights wounded by spear, and given to Odhinn myself to myself.* [4]
> *It is better not to ask, than to sacrifice too much. A gift always looks for a gift.*[5]

Odhinn's sacrifice on Yggdrasill and his giving of his eye for a drink from Mimir's well demonstrate the sacrifice of self to self which the vitki must always be making. This is one of the roots of the death-initiation: you must always be ready to sacrifice your current ideas and state of awareness and being for the sake of reaching a greater wisdom. Every act demands a payment of some sort; you cannot gain without experiencing loss.

Gebo represents the endless exchange of energies through which all comes into being. In this aspect, it is the rune of sexual magic and the "alchemical marriage" in which each of the single components is sacrificed for the sake of creating something transcendent (see Dagaz). Gebo is used in all cases of equal exchanges of energies, especially those in which a binding is wished. The power of gebo brings friendship, loyalty, and hospitality. In working of woe, gebo may be used to bind someone to an unwanted obligation or to return woe for woe. Gebo is the rune most often used in 'love magic."

Properly used, it creates an awareness of the self-sacrificial and balanced nature of love between two people. In ritual, gebo represents the payments which must always be made: the gift of energy or food made to a plant before cutting it; the blood and life of the vitki which give life to the runes; and the mead or ale poured over the altar to the gods. The initiatory value of gebo is that of Nietzsche's "going under"-giving up all that you are for the sake of becoming something higher, as Odhinn did on Yggdrasill.

When the Christian trappings have been stripped away, you may see the workings of gebo in the Parzival story. Gebo works as a moderator with other runes, especially fehu, the force of which it binds and guides for a balanced weal, warding off the woe that comes when fehu is blocked or misguided. The stones associated with gebo are emerald, which is a traditional emblem of love and loyalty, and jade, which is said to open you to an awareness of the need and fitting times for sacrifice to seal your relationships with the gods and other wights.

Gebo: Meditation

You sit at the head of a long wooden table inside a great hall. The polished wooden seat is hard and smooth under you; the air is cold with winter and rich with the smells of bread and roasting pork. Long haired, bearded warriors line the benches along the tables, talking and laughing. You know that this is your hall-you have provided the great roasts of meat that weigh down the table and the mead that flows in ceaseless streams from the pitchers of the serving maids into the drinking horns of your followers. Nevertheless, there is a certain chill to the hall, and you see several men pulling their cloaks about them and glancing at you uneasily. You yourself are beginning to become uncomfortably warm, as if a fire burned just beside you.

The heat, you find, is radiating out from a large bag by your side. Standing, you pick the bag up. It is very heavy, so heavy that your arms ache after holding it for a few moments. Slowly you begin to walk down one side of the table, stopping before each warrior and taking a heavy gold ring or bracelet out of the bag to give him. Receiving the gift, each warrior draws his sword or ax and turns the hilt for you to touch as a sign of his trueness to you. As you keep walking down one side and up the other, the hall becomes warmer and the unnatural heat fades from your bag of treasure. Your enlivened men cheer and toast you as you pass, returning to their feasting with redoubled vigor, fingers and arms weighted with your gold.

When you have gifted your last man and received his troth, you return to your place at the head of the table. A knock sounds hollow against the far door and one of your warriors gets up to open it. At the door is an old man in a dark and tattered cloak, soaked through and disheveled by the high night winds. One of his eyes is a frightful ruin of scar tissue, and his gray beard cannot hide the livid scars of rope burns on his throat. Your warrior is about to push this old beggar away roughly, but you always mindful of the laws of hospitality, command him to let the old man in.

With your own hands, you bring the unexpected guest a heaping plate of meat, bread, and cheese and a large horn of your best mead, making a place for him in the seat of honor at your right hand. He eats and drinks with an amazingly hearty appetite for such an old man, but there is always plenty of food and drink for everyone in your hall. The time has come for you to make sacrifices to the gods. Behind your seat is a harrow of heaped stones, glassy from the many fires that have been lit by you and your ancestors. On the harrow leis the great gold ring of oath-taking, the hammer used for hallowing the sacrifice, a cold-glittering sax, a stone bowl, and a dark-needled pine twig.

Two of your men lead the sacrifice. A great bull with a glossy flawless white hide, through the hall and up to the harrow. The old man watches you carefully, his one dark eye bright, as you swing the heavy hammer over the bull's head, chanting, *"Holy thou art /gift gladly given / to the gods for good given us/ and good that shall be"*. The handle of the sax-knife is cold and smooth in your hand as you lift it and, with one quick, strong motion, slice through the bull's throat. A rive of hot dark blood spills out over the harrow and the floor. The light of life dims in the bull's dark brown eyes and he falls with a crash that shakes the timbers of the hall.

You lift the bowls of warm blood and the twig, dipping the needles into the bowl and sprinkling the eight directions of the winds, splattering warm droplets of blessing over the feaster and the walls. This done, you pour the blood onto the harrow. It runs and pools in the hollows of the glassy stone. The torchlight glints off it darkly, holding your gaze. When you look up, you see that you are outside in the gray light of twilight. The blood-filled hollow in the altar has deepened to become a stone well. The old man stands on the other side, smiling slightly at you. Despite his gray hairs and scars, there is nothing decrepit about him now; he stands straight and tall, his dark blue cloak billowing about him.

"Well you know how to give to others, and are gifted again with good. Can'st sacrifice self to self?" Odhinn asks. A shudder of cold fear runs through you, but you look the god straight in his single eye.

"I can," you answer. "I will."

Odhinn points to the well. "There is the harrow and bowl."
Looking down into the dark water that half-fills the well, you see what seems to be the shape of the rune gebo, but it is only two crossed lines of black against the darkness, not yet filled with the power of life. When you glance up again, Odhinn is gone. A short spear leans against the well where he was standing. You pick it up and test the edge of the head with your thumb. It is exceedingly sharp, the barest touch leaving a thin line of blood behind.

You lean over the well, setting the spear to one side of your throat. Before you can flinch or turn back, you pull it through in one quick slash, the blade so keen that you feel only a breath of icy cold through your neck. The blood gushes out more slowly than you would have thought. As it touches the rune gebo the stave begins to glow brilliantly red through the gloom of twilight deepening to night. You slump over the edge of the swiftly filling well.

The brightness of the rune grows and grows until its shape fills your whole sight its might pulsing through your frozen body. Something wet touches your cold, numb lips and you taste, as if from far away, the faint sweet saltiness of blood. Warmth and strength pour into you from that touch. The rune gebo shines bright before you on the surface of the full well and you stand, entirely whole, although when you put your hand up to your throat you can still feel the ridge of the scar. You return to your own body, feet firmly planted on the earth, knowing that the power to give and receive, the might of gebo, will always be within you.

ᚹ WUNJO

Galdr-sound: wwwwwwwww (a deep buzzing w, rather like a U with lips almost closed)
Letter: W, V

(Joy) is had by the one who knows few troubles pain and sorrows and who to himself has blessedness and bliss and stronghold enough.
— Anglo-Saxon Rune Poem

The rune wunjo, "joy," rules the virtue of cheerfulness, which is as necessary to the Teutonic hero as strength or generosity. A cheerful mind through all hardship was seen as a great part of courage, as Sigurdhr, the greatest of Teutonic heroes, tells:

> Ever the fearless, but the fearful never will fare well in a fight.
> To be glad is better than of gloomy mood whether all fall fair or foul.
> [1]

This gladness showed forth the strength of will to endure all the sorrows and hardships of a time much more beset with bodily struggles and threats than our own. For the vitki, it is a sign of the ability to maintain her/his enthusiasm for the work in spite of all the disappointments, discouragements, and strife within that come in the process of learning magic. Wunjo is the first rune of the will itself, as well as the rune of a balanced, integrated personality. To reach the goal of wunjo, you must be able to keep your pains and sorrows from looming too large in your life, yet you must know a few troubles in order to understand how to deal with problems when they do arise.

The last line of the rune poem is especially meaningful, when seen in the setting of Germanic thinking in general and Anglo-Saxon thinking in particular, in which the world-view seems to be gloomier than that of most of the Germanic peoples. The only place where you may find happiness and fellowship is the stronghold or byrg of the rune poem. An ordinary person without "stronghold enough" is doomed to sorrow, as the poem "The Wanderer" tells in such wrenching words. Life itself, even in the Christian writings of Bede, is compared to a sparrow which swoops from the dark unknown into one door of the hall, bides for a little while in the warmth and light, and flies out again into the stormy blackness.

Being within the stronghold means both warding against sorrow and experiencing the joy of being with your kin and friends-the only cure for the loneliness which was such suffering for the outcast. Wunjo is the rune of fellowship and the bindings of kin, as distinct from the "social contract" of gebo. For the vitki, wunjo is the rune which melds the different sides of your own being into a whole, relieving tension and binding the sides of the self together as the kinsmen in the hall are bound. The reference to "fortress enough" hints that the vitki is never truly set apart from his/her base of power but is able to keep the unwavering brightness of outlook which is her/his strength through all trials, because there is no weak spot in him/her which would be in danger of crumbling under stress.

Wunjo is used to battle all kinds of despair and sorrow which weaken the soul, especially when these stem from magical struggle. It is particularly useful in cases when emotional healing is needed, as it both strengthens and balances the self. Wunjo is a good rune to use in healing rifts between people, especially between family members, and to unite varying groups of people. It is more powerful if a common threat or goal exists; it raises awareness of similarities and lowers the uneasiness that comes with unfamiliarity between people.

In the personal sphere, wunjo aids the twinned powers of courage and cheerfulness and helps self confidence, bettering the self- image and giving the person a strong standpoint from which to relate to the world. It can also be used to make yourself pleasant and generally beloved. The woe-working sides of wunjo's being are its capabilities to cause overconfidence, complacency, or trust and affection towards an unworthy wight. It can dim awareness of the meaning of problems and lower alertness. The powers that enable this rune to deal with despair also enable it to lull wariness and suspicion; it can attract someone to a person or goal which will work woe to him/her. Wunjo is a good rune if you are a leader of some sort, but the power a beloved leader has over her/his followers can easily work either for weal or woe. Also, magically binding someone to yourself should be thought of as putting that person into a kind of slavery, which without good cause is a work against all right. The being of the rune wunjo is shown forth on one level of the story of Baldr.

Frigga gains the oaths of everything (except the little mistletoe) in the Nine Worlds that they will not harm Baldr, bringing him into their clan, as it were. This warding leads the gods to merrily toss weapons at him, a game which gives Loki his chance to put an arrow of mistletoe into the hands of the blind Hod and thus slay Baldr. Wunjo is good in physical healing because it melds its healing of the mind and heart with the ability to bind the recovery of the mind with the recovery of the body. It works best in warding against contagious disease by strengthening the immune system on all levels.

Ritually wunjo rules the use of scents, which work as a vibrational key to harmonize all aspects of the working, both recel (incense) smoke and the use of oils, which both ward and strengthen the vitki. It tends to be more a passive than an active harmonizer (considered against thurisaz, say), and most useful in creating a charged atmosphere or bind-runes for a taufr meant to have a long-term effect. The best stones to use with wunjo are topaz, a traditional bringer of joy and warder against madness and sorrow, and rose quartz, which is said to open the heart and raise your sense of self-worth and ability to love. The newly found stone kunzite has also been proved to work well with this rune.

Wunjo Meditation

You stand outside a great wooden hall in the night. An icy wind cuts through your cloak and tunic, blowing sleet and freezing rain into your face. You are lonely and miserable, the crushing of despair almost a physical weight upon you. Slowly, hopelessly, you raise your hand, knocking on the door. The heavy oaken door opens, showing you a sight of light and warmth. Your mother embraces you and draws you inside, closing the door behind you. Her hug drives the cold from your bones and looses your heavy mood, filling you instead with a feeling of wellbeing and comfort. All your family sits inside the hall talking and feasting cheerfully.

Your mother gives you a horn of mead, which glows warmly in your belly as you move among your kin, greeting them with joy. After a time, you know that you must leave again. You pass silently out the other end of the hall into the cold and freezing rain of the night. Although the cold is a sudden shock to you after the warmth of the hall, the wind does not bite as deeply as it did before, nor does the night seem quite as dark. Looking down at yourself, you see that you are glowing faintly with a golden radiance, as though you carried the light of the hall within yourself.

Heartened for the next steps of your faring, you walk along briskly, even whistling to yourself a little. The storm clouds are beginning to break up. A shaft of cold moonlight shines down onto the road, lighting up the dark figure that stands directly in your path. You see that it is a man in chain mail, tall and strong. Beneath the plain steel cap on his head, you can see that his features are harsh and narrow, sharply angled and etched with deep lines of sorrow. His skin is grayish, like pale stone, and his eyes are the cold black of dead iron. He raises a sword in one iron-gloved hand.

"Stop," he says. "Turn back. There is no hope for you on this path. This is the land of the dead, the kingdom of dust, and none stay here who have not given themselves up to cold and ice and sadness. If you try to pass, you will fall to the sorrows you bear within you and never leave. Go back to the hall of the living and bide till death brings you here forever."

"I fear neither sorrow nor death; joy is the strength of my bravery, you answer, stepping forward and drawing your own sword. You fight, blades clashing harshly in the chilly moonlight. The warrior of sorrow beats you back and back. Ice seems to flow through you, weighting your heart and your limbs with a sadness that saps your strength.

You wonder if it is worth it to fight, but you remember how the light within you warded you from the cold night. You force yourself to smile, then to laugh raggedly through your harsh breathing as you fight, and your strength comes back to you. Golden light shines brightly around you as you push the warrior of sorrow back to the place on the path where you met him, then beat his blade aside and whip your own around and into his throat. He falls, silently, his body flowing into a gray and icy mist. You begin to walk. It is not long before the warrior before you again.

"Stop," he says. "Turn back."

Knowing now that you can beat him, you leap at him before he can finish his words, thrusting your sword straight through his chain mail and into his heart. You go along the path, walking easily through the mist which does no more than chill your calves and feet for a moment, like a sudden pool of icy water. The third time he appears, looming darkly over your path, you walk straight through him, feeling no more than a shudder. You stride along boldly, cheerful in your knowledge that you can beat back any of the fears held by this country of sadness. It is not long before the sun rises on a very different land.

The gently rolling hills are green and lush, starred with the little white flowers of wild strawberries. As you come over one hill, you hear laughter and cries. Walking downward, you see a fair young man who shines with a golden light standing in the center of a circle of fallen arrows, knives, spears, and rocks, his head thrown back in laughter. The noble men and women around him are tossing a great assortment of weapons at him, but as each one touches his light it falls harmlessly to the earth. A tall, beautiful woman in a dark blue dress adorned with rippling silver embroidery stands by watching and smiling gently. Her silver-streaked black hair forms a crown of braids around her head. Although she wears no ornament of rank, you nevertheless bow in respect as you come nearer to greet her. You do not voice your curiosity, but you feel that her deep blue eyes look directly into your thoughts.

She tells you that she is Frigg, wife of Odhinn. The shining youth is her son Baldr, who cannot be wounded because everything in the world which might possibly do him harm has sworn not to harm him, as if they were part of his own clan. Looking at the bright god, you feel a deep sense of relief at the knowledge that he, the embodiment of joy, is so warded; but you also feel a faint prickling of wariness at the back of your neck, and wonder if it is truly wise for the enchantment to be tempted in fun.

Baldr looks up to meet your eyes and raises a hand to halt the game for a moment, beckoning to you. You go over to him and he greets you as a cousin, embracing you and tracing the rune wunjo over your heart. A mighty wave of joy and strength fills you, and you feel the light within you brightening with his blessing. You would like to stay with him longer, but you know that you must return to your earthly body now. This you do, feet firmly planted on the earth, knowing that the light of wunjo is always within you, strengthening your heart and will, yet never blinding you to woe.

ᚺ HAGALAZ

Galdr-sound: hhhhhhhh (a powerful aspirated breath)
Letter: H

(Hail) is the whitest of grains, it comes from high in heaven showers of wind hurl it then it turns to water.
— Anglo-Saxon Rune Poem

(Hail) is the coldest of grains
Christ (Hroptr = the Hidden One = Odhinn) shaped the world in ancient times.
— Old Norwegian Rune Rhyme

(Hail) is a cold grain, and the shower of sleet and the sickness of snakes.
— Old Icelandic Rune Poem

If I see a fire high on the hall around my bench companions, I can help them by singing the spell.
— Havamal 152

The rune hagalaz, "hailstone," shows the shaping drizzle of uruz frozen into a solid form: the pattern, instead of the patterning force. It is always spoken of as a "cold grain"; this shows the seed pattern of shaping held in this rune. This is the rune of the primal crystal which bears the same relationship to the overall pattern of being that the DNA of a single cell bears to the ideal (unaltered) shape of the body. The reference in the Anglo-Saxon Rune Poem, "then it turns to water," writes forth the relationship between hagalaz and uruz, the essential blueprint and the force which endlessly works to bring it forth, Ymir and Audhumbla.

It will be noticed that the vertical model of the Norse cosmos is patterned in the exact shape of the stave in the Younger Futhark, the literal glyph for the crystalline shape. Hagalaz represents the unchanging structure or set pattern of the Nine Worlds in the tree Yggdrasill through which all living wights move and through which the runic energies flow-the unity of "organic" and "inorganic." You may see this relationship by finding a quartz crystal which is either naturally symmetrical or has been shaped to the six-sided form. Looking at the tip, you may see the younger form of hagalaz inside the solid hailstone, a symbol which contains all the other runes and which continued to be used as a mighty hex sign even in the Pennsylvania Dutch settlements in America.[2]

The crystal is useful in understanding this aspect of hagalaz if you meditate on the relationship between the ordered, unchanging crystal form and the energies which one can guide to flow through it. Hagalaz is a great controller and focuser of energies, as written forth in the Havamal, where it is spoken of as a rune with which to control the wild might of fire-raw active power. The use of crystals in runic magic, while not a part of original Germanic working, can nevertheless be a powerful addition to it, as shown through the rune hagalaz. The very word "crystal" comes from the Greek krystallos, meaning ice, a term ringing close enough to the rune name "hailstone."

Using a quartz crystal in rune work can have the effect of potentiating this rune through the wholeness of hagalaz and bringing it to being in all the Nine Worlds (nine, the number of this rune, also being the number of completeness and bringing forth to full being). In this setting the imaginative vitki can find countless uses for the terminated crystal in rune working. The naturally symmetrical stone is best; next best is one which has been shaped into perfect symmetry by a machine. Asymmetrical crystals are less effective in this context and occasionally given unpredictable results, For hagalaz, the shape of the crystal is very important. Hagalaz, being the rune of perfect and unchanging structure, is a mighty rune of warding when used against entropic forces, as indicated by the line, "the sickness of snakes" in the Old Icelandic Rune Poem.

This line refers to the embodiments of venom which endlessly gnaw at the roots of the World Tree; that is, which try to break down the structure that embodies the order necessary for the preservation of life. This rune is most effective as a rune of warding when used on a building, as has been traditional for hundreds of years. The main effect of hagalaz on the individual life is to bring you into unity with the universal pattern, which often appears as a mighty and seemingly woe-working breakage of the everyday life. The Anglo-Saxon Rune Poem reference shows this process of breakage and regrowth according to the seed of the pattern (hagalaz) through the shaping powers of water (uruz). Above all, hagalaz is the rune of completion and bringing into being.

It may be seen, in one sense, as the passive form of thurisaz, and in another sense as its antithesis. Thurisaz melds fire and ice to create force which breaks down form; hagalaz uses ice and fire to create that form which holds and guides force. Thurisaz is active, more in the way of fire; hagalaz is unmoving, more in the way of ice. Sides of the being of both are destructive or disruptive for the sake of regeneration, and both are associated with Ymir-thurisaz in that Ymir is the proto-jotun of blind force and strength, father (and mother) of the whole race of thurses, and hagalaz in that the androgynous Ymir is the first coalescing around the original seed crystal of the universe and the source of the structure of the World-Tree. It is interesting to note that the terminated crystal holds the shapes of both hagalaz and thurisaz-hagalaz in the pattern and thurisaz in the pointed tip bringing the forces of all the sides together and aiming them. Used with other runes, hagalaz brings them into complete being on all levels. You should remember that nine is the greatest Germanic number of power. Hagalaz may be seen as the equivalent of the hexagram in establishment Western magic, which also represents the unified structure of the universe.

Hagalaz: Meditation

You stand in the center of a small, hex-shaped crystal surrounded by a six-spoked framework that reaches all through the crystal, which is rigid, clear, and cold as ice. You find that you can move easily and at will within this pattern, although you cannot alter it; and indeed you fear to try, thinking that if you should cause one break in the crystal the whole would crumble, leaving you to the darkness outside.

Your crystal slowly begins to grow, the glittering walls moving farther and farther back and light gleaming less brightly from the icy pattern inside as it stretches farther and farther above your head. The solidness under your feet resolves itself into earth from which a wheat field springs up around you. You now seem to be standing on Midgardhr in the late summer, dressed in a simple brown farmer's tunic and breeches. The wheat is just beginning to turn golden; it seems to be a good, rich, harvest. You know that this field is your whole livelihood, and you are glad that it is ripening so well. As you walk along the rows of grain, pulling a weed up every now and then, you feel the chill of a shadow passing across the sun. Looking up, you see the clouds coming in swiftly, huge mountains of dark blue-gray mist sailing across the sky towards you.

You feel no worry as the storm nears; your wheat needs water, and this is the time for it. You can see the leading edge of the storm coming across the fields towards you like a gray curtain, and hear the heavy raindrops pounding against the earth. Suddenly, as it reaches the edge of your own crop, the beating of the rain becomes loud and sharp and the gray curtain turns to a glittering white. You cry out in anger and despair as the hailstorm beats down your grain mercilessly, leaving no stalk standing; you must cover your own head against the barrage of ice crystals raining down on you. As suddenly as it began, the hailstorm is done, clouds blowing onward and sun shining down on the mounds of white ice between the ruined rows of your wheat field. You walk back through it guessing at the limits of the harm done; it seems that nothing can be saved of this year's crop. As you walk, you hear a faint hissing and see steam rising a few feet away.

Going to look, you see something moving beneath a mound of hail, the steam wafting up from the stones in a trail that fades as the thrashings become weaker and weaker. When the movement has altogether stopped, only a little molten ice flowing out onto the ground, you carefully kick the clump of hailstones away with your boot. Beneath lies a frozen tangle of adders, their glinting, venomous fangs bared in anger. The ground beneath them is black and discolored from poison; you can see the ruined wheat beginning to rot blackly in a wide circle around the nest of serpents. You realize that although the hail killed this year's crop, it also saved you from the poisoned grain and from the certain loss of your field that would have come if the snakes had continued to gnaw at its roots. You kick the mess of snakes to make sure they are quite dead. Their frozen corpses snap easily beneath your boot.

The head of one rolls next to your feet, fangs upturned; you see that it holds a small hexagonal crystal in its jaws. Carefully you pry the crystal loose, turning it to see if you can look inside. The walls are milky ice; it melts in your hand, leaving only a small red berry inside. Looking at the berry, you see over it the ghostly image of the needle leaves, scarlet berries, and rough bark of the full-grown yew tree. You walk to the center of your field seeing how, as the ice melts, tiny green shoots are already starting to spring up through the life giving water.

You bend and plant the berry in the rich mud. As you stand, you realize that you are at the foot of a great yew tree, roots stretching out below you and branches above, much farther than you can see. You stand in the middle of its framework, looking at the tiny hexagonal crystal that lies like a seed in the berry from which the tree grew, knowing that the pattern is one and the same. Slowly you return to your own body, feet planted firmly on the earth and the image of the crystal still in your mind, knowing that the power of bringing forth into being and the wholeness of the pattern of being is always open to you through the rune hagalaz.

ᚾ NAUTHIZ
Galdr-sound: nnnnnnn
Letter: N

(Need) is constricting
on the chest
Although to the children of men it often becomes help and salvation
nevertheless I if they heed it in time.
— Anglo-Saxon Rune Poem

(Need) makes for a difficult situation the naked freeze in the frost.
— Old Norwegian Rune Rhyme

(Need) is the grief of the bond-maid and a hard condition to be in and toilsome work.
— Old Icelandic Rune Poem

I know an eighth. It is useful for all who know it. Whenever hatred flares up among warriors' sons, I am able to quell it.
— Havamal 153

The stave-shape of the rune nauthiz shows the bow-drill used in kindling the need-fire from wood without the use of flint or steel. The ritual of the need-fire was generally used when a sickness had fallen upon the cattle of a clan or village. The need-fire would be kindled by the leader of the folk (who was also the godhi, or priest, in pagan times) and the cattle driven through the smoke. The magical meaning of this act is that the extra energy needed to kindle the fire by the means of the bow-drill would also supply the additional power needed to force out the sickness and cleanse the cattle.

Nauthiz is the testing and suffering which brings the hidden magical force of fehu forth. It is the self-generated fire kindled in the time of greatest need. Nauthiz represents the unloosing of potential energy on all levels. This rune is the force of friction and resistance which builds up the individual strength and will. Its being is best written out in the sayings, *"Every battle that doesn't kill you, makes you stronger," and "No pain, no gain."* You may mark that the stave shape resembles that of a gebo-rune with one line straight up and the other canted. This rune, like gebo, embodies the need of sacrifice for results; however, unlike gebo, it is not a rune of mutual interaction, but of the type of sacrifice to self in which all the energy is guided in one path-the power of imbalance, as set against the balance of gebo.

In the earthly body, nauthiz shows forth as the phenomenon of "hysterical strength": the sudden burst of adrenaline which makes ordinary people capable of seemingly impossible feats of strength in desperate circumstances and which is one of the components of the berserker-power. Magically, it is the rune which gives you the strength not only to meet trials but to overcome them. It is most effective when you are working to counter or "write around" that which has already been written in the Well of Urdhr, as may be seen clearly in Odhinn's many workings to overcome the doom of Ragnarok by ensuring that a new and even better world shall emerge after the downfall. The word Wyrd or Urdhr comes from a root meaning "to turn"; the bow-drill is the counter-turning which works around the turnings of Wyrd at need.

Nauthiz rules the ability to guide the great power of deliberate sexual frustration (as opposed to the guided sexual expression of kenaz). Nauthiz is essentially a rune of overcoming in all ways. In its ability to deal with the woe-workings of Wyrd, it is also a rune of counter-spelling, as described in the Sigrdrifumal where the valkyrja Sigrdrifa gives Sigurth a veiled warning about the enchanted draught of ale he is shortly to face, which, by forcing him into love with Guthrun and betrayal of Sigrdrifa (Brynhild) will bring about his death. She tells him to "Learn ale runes eke I lest other man's wife I betray thee who trusted in her: I on thy beer horn scratch it I and the back of thy hand I and the Nauth rune on thy nails".[1] Nauthiz can write around both that which has been written by the Norns and that which has been written by other wights, if you know when to use it. Nauthiz represents the power to deal with all factors of stress, as described in the Havamal.

In the personal sphere, nauthiz should be called upon to strengthen yourself at need and turn woe into weal. As well as sudden bursts of great bodily might, Nauthiz brings sudden bursts of creative inspiration; the cliche "necessity is the mother of invention" writes it forth well. It is the rune that brings forth the full range of your inner might when it is most needed. It also aids in the growth of your self discipline. Nauthiz is the stave of the inner stress which drives you to either greatness or an early grave, sometimes both. It can cause compulsiveness and obsession. The woe and weal of nauthiz's working are so mingled that you can hardly use the one without the other. When it is used on another person, it may give him/her the strength to endure suffering or it may bring about hardships which teach that person an important lesson and ultimately strengthens her/him.

However, whether the stress caused by nauthiz ends in destroying or empowering its object is entirely dependent on that person's inner, hidden strength. Ritually, nauthiz is the rune of banishing and cleansing by fire, especially the need-fire and the smoke of recels. When blended with other runes, nauthiz can be called upon in its being as the rune of counter-spells and writing around written ørlög, particularly in the setting of the many rune-readings which are done before and after each runic working. Nauthiz develops both the will and the self-sufficiency of the vitki. Its hardships must be faced with only your own might, and only the self-generated fire can overcome them. Nauthiz is the rune of trial and testing. The stone of nauthiz is obsidian-glass hardened by intense fire until it can be shaped into weapons which can take the sharp and painful edge of need. Obsidian is said to be a psychological tester which shows you the faults in yourself and the sufferings you must undergo to overcome them.

Nauthiz: Meditation

You crouch in thin, dead grass on a mountainside at night, hungry and alone. A chilling wind sweeps down from the peak, cutting through your wool tunic and patchy cloak as if you were naked, freezing your very bones. The waning moon glitters off patches of frost on the scraggly grass around you and shows your breath as little white clouds of ice in the air. Your cows huddle together near you. They are thin, with scruffy coats, and most of them have the cloudy eyes and running sores of sickness. Spreading your cloak to block the wind, you pick up a block of beech wood with a small hollow cut into it, a small bow, and a stick of wood. Putting the end of the stick against the hollow, you turn it rapidly back and forth with the bow. Your hands grow tired soon, but you keep at it doggedly, shivering as you turn the bow-drill faster and faster.

Slowly the exercise begins to warm you. Your panting rasps hotly through your throat, breathing out great puffs of mist, but your hunger and fear keep you going. You know that if you cannot kindle the need-fire now, before too many of your cattle have died, you will starve this winter. You are beginning to sweat now, your muscles shaking with tiredness. You close your eyes and keep drilling, grimly forcing your trembling arms to move faster, move faster. You do not stop until you feel the sudden rush of warmth from beneath your hands and see the little coal burning. You feed the fire slowly with kindling, putting a few leaves of dead grass on it the frost hissing away as they catch alight, and then a few little sticks. Slowly you build your fire up until you no longer need to protect it from the wind with your cloak.

The wind from the north blows a black stream of smoke straight away from your need-fire. You herd your cows together and move them slowly through the smoke, one by one. They are still thin when they come out, their coats still rough and matted, but the sores are gone and their dim eyes have cleared. Suddenly you hear a deafening rumbling above you. A shower of rocks tumbles straight down the mountainside towards you, boulders bigger than a man falling and ripping a torrent of earth with them. You run as fast as you can, hurling yourself forward in a desperate try to escape. With one mighty burst of speed, you fling yourself just past the edge of the rockfall, but one of the great boulders hits a jutting crag and bounds straight at you. Your body seems to explode in a split second of fire. As your eyes clear, you see the rock lying more than thirty feet away from you, cracked jaggedly in two.

Amazed, you walk over to look at it. Smoke rises from the broken edges; it is too hot for you to touch. A larger rock lies next to it, knocked aside by the might of your blow. Where it had been, there is a dark cavern in the mountainside. When you look straight into the opening, you can see that it is not wholly dark; a faint fire glows from the walls. You step inside and walk along the tunnel. In time you come to a chamber filled with twisting tree roots and serpents slithering among them, chewing at them, their venom eating holes in this root or that. Warily you pick your way along the floor. The snakes ignore you, writhing through the roots; there are no eyes in their fanged heads. Past this chamber is a short passage which leads up to a well of bubbling water, which stands at the foot of a great, dark evergreen.

Three women sit turning a wheel that is half hidden in the tree trunk and dips into the waters of the well. They wear dark cloaks that hide their faces. They do not speak. You know that you are near to the Norns at the Well of Urdhr. They are turning the Wyrd of the worlds, shaping the branches and roots of Yggdrasill. It feels to you as if the endless turning of the wheel is rubbing against your own skin, filling you with pain and frustration and the dry heat of burning friction. You are about to cry out when you feel a tap on your shoulder. Turning, you see a tall, powerful man on a horse behind you.

He is clothed in forest green, his face shadowed by his cloak's dark hood. He does not speak, but you can feel the heat glowing from him as he reaches down and hands you a root that is twisted back over itself, turning till it has completely re-twined its path. Looking through the loop in its end, you see as if you were watching from a great height. Shining men and women battle with creatures of darkness, fire, and stone on a broad plain. A gigantic serpent writhes across the plain, leaving a mile-wide trail of wreckage behind it. From the other side, a mountainous wolf roars, rivers of froth foaming from its jaws. You see Odhinn on eight-legged Sleipnir riding towards the wolf, his dark blue cloak flying behind him in his own wind.

The Fenris-Wolf lurches forward suddenly; the jaws close on the Allfather. Behind Odhinn rides the hooded, silent man who gave you the root: Vidar, begotten of Odhinn's fore-sight to avenge his father's death. He leaps off his horse, running towards the Wolf. Fenris' vast jaws open again; it seems that Vidar has only leapt to his death in the Wolf's great throat, but a sudden flash of light bursts from its huge head.

Vidar steps out, hood blown back and golden hair streaming free. His burst of strength has torn the Fenris-Wolf asunder. A mighty blast of wind blows from the Wolfs ripped corpse, blowing back Vidar's hair and cloak as though he stood in the middle of a storm. The loop in the root clouds again, and when you look up, Vidar is gone. You trace the re-twisting of the root, glancing at the Norns who spin silently on and wondering if the turning of Odhinn's weird will truly end at Ragnarok. You return to your own body with the root, feet planted firmly on the earth, knowing the power within you which you can reach at need through the rune nauthiz.

| ISA

Galdr-sound: ecceeceeccee (as in "see"; sung on a steady, absolutely unwavering, tightly focused pitch, sharp and high)
Letter: I

(Ice) is very cold and exceedingly slippery it glistens, clear as glass very much like gems, a floor made of frost is fair to see.
— Anglo-Saxon Rune Poem

(Ice), we call the broad bridge the blind need to be led.
— Old Norwegian Rune Rhyme

(Ice) is the rind of the river and the roof of the waves and a danger for fey men." — Old Icelandic Rune Poem
That ninth I know if need there be to guard a ship in a gale, the wind I calm and the waves also, and wholly soothe the sea.
— Havamal 155

The rune Isa, ice, is the elemental rune of Niflheimr. As the being of fire is energy, expansion, motion, passion, and change, so the being of ice is solidity, contraction, stillness, calmness, and unchangeability. Although Niflheimr holds the primal life-stuff of yeast and death-stuff of venom, these cannot come forth directly from the ice; it must first be melted into the rushing waters of Hvergelmir. The elemental ice shows complete immobility, which in its ultimate form is antimatter, as without the motion which holds the substance of the atom together there would be complete disintegration. However, as ice works in Midgardhr, together with the fire which is in all things to some degree, it is simply the force which slows energy and causes solidification, concentration, and density.

As the rune fehu embodies warmth, fruitfulness, life-force, and conflict, so does the rune isa embody cold, barrenness, death, and still peace. The reference to the "broad bridge" in the Old Norwegian Rune Rhyme seems to be a reference to a river covered with ice, which makes a very broad bridge indeed. Seen within the shape of the Nine Worlds, it speaks of the bridge to Hel the second line perhaps being a reference to blind Hodhr. You must not forget how closely Niflheimr, the realm of ice, and Hel are bound together in the Northern mind. To reach the realm of Hel, you must lower your own vibrational level; this bridge is broad because this is very easy to do and is, in fact the ordinary way of the soul after death.

This maybe set against the purifying flames (intense vibration) of the narrow bridge Bifrost. Isa, the "I" rune, is also the strength of the ego, and it is a bridge also in the sense that it provides safe passage through the turbulent waters (laguz) of initiation-both because it guards the ego from dissolution by holding the vitki's concentration firm and warding it against the stresses placed on it, and because it provides a sound mental "footing" as you travel through the dark abyss. The rune-poem line "a danger to fey men" shows the perils of trying to travel on this way before you are ready. The ice of your ego may seem thick and strong, but it is often surprisingly brittle and soft beneath the glistening surface, and if you have allowed your ego to deceive you about your magical and mental prowess, the bridge of ice will break. At best, you must tread with utmost care; the power of isa is, indeed, "exceedingly slippery," and any crack in the ice of your concentration will drop you into the dark waves beneath. Isa is the antithesis of fehu in all ways.

It can be used in workings of woe to bring about barrenness, to interfere with prosperity, and to cause depression and lack of the will to act. As fehu is the rune of energy and movement, so isa is the rune of binding. It can be used to set battle-fetter and cause paralyzing fear or obsession; it works to prevent or halt movement, both that of growth and that of disintegration. As a rune of control, isa should generally not be brought into direct contact with fehu except as guided by the workings of thurisaz and hagalaz. As described in the Havamal, isa is a "sea- rune": the unruly powers that it is best at calming and guiding are those seen as wild winds or waters, such as the might of troubled circumstances and confusion. In the personal sphere, isa can be used to strengthen powers of concentration and stabilize the personality.

Care should be taken, however, that you do not render yourself or another dull or obsessive. Isa works to calm hysteria, hyperactivity, and restlessness. In the side of its being which is part of Hel and the ice of death, isa is often used in magics of revenge and defense. In ritual workings, isa embodies the unbreakable will and concentration of the mage. Isa can be used to numb pain of the heart or the body. Together with other runes, isa can be used to bind or to "shield" one rune from another to keep them from interacting, although generally making a separate taufr is simpler and more effective. Stones which may work well with some sides of isa's being are herkimer diamond, which is said to hold thoughts and energies stilt and gem silica, which is calming and relieving, particularly to the pain of female troubles.

Isa: Meditation

It is night. The thin crescent of the waning moon sheds a pale light over the snow-covered ground around you. You stand near the bank of a huge, powerfully rushing black river, its wild waters laced with white froth and tumbling chunks of ice. A strong, freezing wind blows about you, quickly numbing your face and hands. You feel that you need to cross to the other side of the river. It is as if you were bound to a path leading across it, but the river is too wide and its icy waters run too deep and fast for you to even think long about fording it. You walk closer to the edge of the bank, your boots leaving deep footprints in the blue-white snow. As you near the water, you hear a sharp cracking sound and feel your footing beginning to tilt beneath you. You try to scramble away, but the thick ice over the river's edge has already broken off flinging you face-down on one of the larger chunks. You must cling to your piece of ice, embracing its numbing cold tightly.

It tilts sickeningly, one way and another, as the black waters whirl it around and around, sweeping you unstoppable, downstream on the little floe that threatens to dump you into the river at any moment. Slowly, moving an arm or leg to balance yourself every few seconds, you draw yourself up until you are sitting in the center of your piece of ice, which, balanced, no longer tilts so alarmingly. You can see now that all the solid snow on the banks is actually a roof of rime over the wide black sea, holding its rushing wildness back except where the betraying waters sweep you along. Carefully, concentrating on every motion to keep from tilting the ice or sliding off, you rise to your feet and stand in the position of isa, feet together and arms over your head, feeling the stillness of the rune come over you like a shield against the wind.

When you open your eyes, you stand on a fixed island of ice in the middle of the water, a white bridge stretching to the other shore of snow. It glitters eye-catching, like a bridge of diamonds. When you put your foot to it, you find that it is very slippery. Slowly, care- fully, you walk across the treacherous bridge, standing perfectly straight so as not to slip off its rounded edges. Your eyes never waver from the white line ahead of you until you stand on solid ground again. You look out over the blue-white field of snow to the glacial mountains in the distance. Something is moving in the snow, coming closer. Watching, you make out the figure of a dark stag running in a weaving course, followed by a black shape like the shadow of a woman on skis with a bow, her long hair and loose cloak streaming out behind her. A black wolf runs at the woman's heel, its mournful howl cutting through the still air like a needle of ice. The stag is panting hard, little clouds of ice crystals puffing out of its mouth. Its dark eyes roll desperately as the huntress skis nearer.

Although you do not hear the bowstring's twang, you feel the cold streak of the arrow passing you. Its dark length sinks into the chest of the stag without leaving a wound. The hart drops heavily with neither movement nor sound, its fur already rimed with ice. The woman skis up to you, looking you straight in the eyes, and you stand frozen in the cold of absolute fear. Her skin is white as death, eyes black and cold with the ancient cruelty of the rimethurses. Her features are straight and severe, yet harshly beautiful beneath her tangled mass of straight black hair.

You know her to be Skadhi, the icy huntress whose name means "shadow" or "scathe," daughter of the giant Thijazi. After Skadhi has held you frozen in her gaze for some time, she nods sharply once and hands you a black ice-arrow from her quiver, fletchings first. It numbs your hand, sending a sharp shock of cold up the bones of your arm. You bow respectfully as she skis away, the black wolf running behind her. Slowly you turn and walk back over the bridge of ice, which is now a broad, solid path over the waters below, and return to your own body, feet firmly planted on the earth, knowing the power of ice that is always available to you through the rune isa.

ᛃ JERA

Galdr-sound: yyyyyyyyyy (as in "year")
Letter: J,Y (remember that in pure Teutonic languages such as German and Old Norse J is always pronounced as Y)

(Harvest) is the hope of men, when god lets, holy king of heaven, the earth gives her bright fruits to the noble ones and the needy.
— Anglo-Saxon Rune Poem

(Good harvest) is the profit of men; 1 say that Frodhi was generous.
— Old Norwegian Rune Rhyme

(Good harvest) is the profit of all men, and a good summer, and a ripened field.
— Old Icclandic Rune Poem

I know a tenth. If I see ghost-riders I sporting in the sky, I can work it I that the wild ones fare away so their spirits fare home.
— Havamal 155

The shape of the rune jera shows the way in which the Germanic peoples thought of the seasons and their interactions, particularly concerning the ways of farming. The Teutonic year is not divided into four seasons, but two, summer and winter, which work upon each other continuously. The harvest of the summer is food for the winter. At the beginning of the winter, you plant the seeds which must lie under the earth for a season in order to sprout as summer comes near. The rune-name, literally "year" speaks of not only the course of a year, but of a good year with a rich harvest-a year in which all planting, tending, reaping, and soon has been done as was fitting within the outer timetable of the year and its changeable weather and the inner timetable of the plants themselves.

The relationship between raidho and the fulfillment of jera should be plain. Like raidho also, jera is a rune of the sun's cycle, being the cycle of the year as raidho is the cycle of the day. The alternate stave-shape of jera is the same as the alternate form of ingwaz: the glyph indicating the complete male genitalia (as set against the Elder Futhark's ingwaz, which shows the castrated male). This shows one of the workings of the god Freyr in the process of bringing-into-being: Freyr as Lord of the World. Although the pattern of cyclical growth is "feminine," as set against the "masculine" straight line, it needs the masculine force of Freyr to bring it to full being. The alternate stave-shape shows the straight line passing into the circle, bringing out this rune's interaction-of-opposites in yet another way. Jera may be looked at as, in a sense, a "Teutonic yin-yang," showing the interlocking of fire (summer) and ice (winter) not as warring opposites but as interacting complements. Only the raw primal forces of fire and ice are violent together.

Jera shows their weal-working interaction within the ring of Midgardhr, calmed by their manifestation through the secondary elements of water, air, and earth. Jera differs from the eastern yin-yang in that it shows this unity not as a circle, but as a spiral in which each turn brings the whole to further growth. This is related to the thought of every action or happening being layered on the last and shaped by it; you cannot return to the beginning, as in a circle. Jera shows a process of endless cyclical growth and weal-working change, seen in its highest form as the growth of the "seed" planted in humankind by the gods to reach the wisdom and power of our godly kindred. Jera shows the natural development of spiritual understanding, which cannot be hurried or forced. It is a rune of patience and of awareness, of moving in harmony with both your inner changes (the "seed") and the changes of the world around you ("seasons" and weather").

Jera is not a rune of immediate gratification, but a rune of long-term planning and the day-by-day process of bringing your plans to fruit. Magically, jera is used to bring your will into effect slowly and naturally, a process which is almost always more effective and desirable than forcing change on an unready world. Like nauthiz, jera is associated with the original meaning of Wyrd, "to turn"; however, nauthiz is the power of turning around or "counter-turning" Wyrd, while jera is the power of turning with the flow of Wyrd, making slow and subtle changes in it which can only be seen as they come into being. In the personal sphere, jera is used to aid the growth of your own understanding and to guide you in finding the correct times for rituals, especially initiation.

Jera helps to determine the time for increases in the difficulty or power of your magical workings, according to what you are truly ready for. It can also be used to develop the potentials which lie like seeds within everyone and which require long care and daily tending to bring them to fruition. It is used to ensure the success of plans. In workings of woe jera can be used to bring the worst possible layers of someone's weird to fruition or to develop the seeds of self-destruction which also lie within everyone. The spiral of jera can turn downward as well as upward. The spiraling form of jera and its relationship to the movement of nature is what makes it an effective rune of warding against woe- working seidhkonur ("witches"); the spiral current disperses spirit farer and unturns such workings that are not part of the course of nature. Jera is a good rune for workings involving fruitfulness or any sort of interaction with nature.

It also rules the creative process, from the seed idea through the completed concept and the finished work. Ritually, jera represents the series of daily meditations which, practiced faithfully, lead you slowly into higher levels of consciousness and power. Used with other runes, it brings them into being through the workings of nature and the normal turnings of Wyrd. Jera shows the entire cycle of interaction between the earth goddess and fertilizing god: his birth, marriage, sacrifice, and rebirth. This cycle is described more fully by the runes berkano and ingwaz and the conceptual ties between the three runes. Ingwaz is the seed planted, berkano is the earth that receives it, and jera is the growth and harvest. The stone associated with jera is moss agate, which is traditionally tied to the plowman's arm and the horns of his cattle to ensure fruitful fields and breeding. Moss agate aids you in a deep attunement to the movements of nature and the natural cycle which is jera.

Jera: Meditation

You stand in the middle of a field. The sun shines brightly, but there is a sharp bite of frost in the air and the day is turning rapidly towards night. Around you, men and women in plain farmers' tunics of brown wool are harvesting the wheat that grows tall, rich, and golden. Scythes whirl to cut the grain down; behind the reapers follow the gleaners who gather the stalks into bundles, and behind them follow the sowers, planting the autumn seed which must lie in the ground all winter. You join these last, collecting a sheaf of grain from one of the gleaners and picking up a digging tool. The ground is cold and clay like under your hands, and it feels to you almost as if you are digging in grave mold among the beheaded stalks that rustle like wraiths above you.

You bury each seed and cover it carefully, neither too deep in the earth nor too near its surface. When the sun has set, leaving only a stain of blood-red light in the west against the darkening sky, you go into a great hall with the other harvesters. The feast is set with all the fruits of summer's end, bowls filled to overflowing with wild berries and grains and great loaves of bread on the table. A huge pair of roast pigs, boar and sow, grace the middle of the table. At its head sits a tall man with blond hair and beard, dressed in a yellow tunic and sky-blue cloak with a crown of stag's antlers. Behind him is a woman whose deep green dress curves richly over her body, the torchlight catching gleams of red from her long dark hair. The Lady rises and walks about the table, pouring out thick, rich beer. You blow the creamy head off your horn and taste the rich, nutty grain-flavor of its malt.

Laughing, the Lord raises up a scepter as thick as his wrist, chanting, *"May Mornir receive this gift!"* He passes it about the table, each of the farmers repeating his words in turn. It is leathery in your hand; looking close as you chant *"May Mornir receive this gift!"* You see that it is the stuffed phallus of a stallion, fully erect and smelling faintly of herbs. You pass it on to make the round of the table. Snow has begun to fall outside, covering the fields with a soft white blanket. The Lady veils her hair in black, her face still and a little frightening. The winter turns around you, freezing the land to a still, brittle world of ice and snow and the days darkening. When there is no more light, the Lord leads a great snow-white boar, its neck garlanded with rosemary, into the hall and around the table. Everyone leans forward to touch it and voice a vow or boast.

The swine's hide is warm and comforting beneath your fingers; its dark eyes look up at you and you are silent and awed by the might of the god within it. It follows the Lord to the harrow of heaped stones at the end of the hall, standing still as he cuts its throat and the blood springs out in a torrent. As the boar falls to the floor, the Lord sprinkles its blood onto the folk from a bowl. A few drops touch you, filling you with warmth as you feel the year turning upward again within you. The folk move together out of the halt where a great wooden wheel stands, woven with straw and pitch. The Lord brings a firebrand out; you and several others set your shoulders to the wheel, and as he lights it you push. It rolls off, slow and wobbly at first, then picking up speed as it blazes down through the snow-covered fields.

The wheel of fire burns along the dark pathways, flaming and whirling till far, far down the hill it plunges into the icy river with a great hiss, a white cloud of steam rising up. The winter turns around you and gradually the days become longer again and the ice begins to melt leaving bare fields of dry stubble behind. The sun brightens, and finally you see the first shoots of green pricking through the earth. The light shines brightly from the golden hair and stag's antlers of the Lord and the free-flowing auburn tresses of the Lady as they stoop to tend the fields with you and the other farmers. The beginning of summer is an endless round of work, one day much like another as you bend and pull and dig in the earth until at last the wheat is tall and strong.

With summer's height, most of the work in the fields is done, but there are cattle and swine and sheep to tend as you wait for the harvest. The sun reaches its height on a day without night, and you light the Midsummer's fires in broad daylight, dancing around them, drinking ale, and feasting. After Midsummer, the sun starts back down, the nights grow longer and the winds become cold and sharp as the field of grain turns from green to gold. When the harvest-time has come again, the Lord and the Lady come to you in the field. Each of them plucks a stalk of ripe grain and hands it to you, their touch filling you with mellow contentment. You bow in respect as you thank them and bid them farewell. You return to your own body, feet firmly planted on the ground, safe in the wisdom and power you have gained through the rune jera.

ᛇ EIHWAZ

Galdr-sound: ei (pronounced as i in "ride"-prolonged, steady, and powerful, at once stabilizing and uplifting).
Letter: This stave can be used for EI but generally appears as a magical symbol rather than a letter; the phonetic value is not certain.

(Yew) is on the outside a rough tree and hard, firm in the earth, keeper of the fire supported by roots a joy on the estate."
— Anglo-Saxon Rune Poem

(Yew) is the greenest wood in the winter; there is usually, when it burns, singeing."
— Old Norwegian Rune Rhyme

(Yew) is a strung bow and brittle iron and Farbauti of the arrow.
— Old Icelandic Rune Poem

Yew holds all
  — Abcedarium Nordmanicum

The rune eihwaz, "yew," is the rune holding the powers of the most mysterious of the magical trees known to the Germanic peoples. The evergreen that played such a great part in the world-view of the Germanic was, it has been well argued, a yew tree; the magical wand or talisman, when made out of wood, was most often carved of yew. As the all-holding cosmic structure of Yggdrasill, the yew is indeed the tree of magic, for there is no rune whose being it does not hold within itself. Seen in this setting, you may understand one level of Odhinn's runic initiation on Yggdrasill: only through the power of the yew tree could Odhinn learn the runes which are the keys to all of being in their completeness. As the turning point of the runic circle, eihwaz holds the entire futhark hidden within itself.

A "rough tree" on the outside, and perhaps the hardest of all the runes to fully understand, eihwaz is the "keeper of the fire": the hidden, but all-holding might of runic wisdom. As jera embodies the interaction of opposites and the gradual growth of understanding, so does eihwaz embody the melding of opposites and the lightning flash of revealing at the completion of initiation. The yew is known to the folk as the tree of death, having been planted in cemeteries until this day. According to popular belief, the yew tree can "trap" the souls of the dead. This is the simple shape of a much mightier mystery-the central mystery of the rune eihwaz and, it may be argued, the final unspoken secret of Odhinn. On the simplest level, the yew is understood to be a tree of death because it is very poisonous.

It can literally be death to eat of it and even lying beneath it can be dangerous because of the gaseous toxins it emits. As the alchemist and the magician know, however, poison is a sign of power. Alchemy purges the subject of the physical poison to create a healing agent; magic renders the poison, properly prepared, into the vehicle of initiation and immortality, and both depend on the worker as much as on the process worked. The yew shows its power of life equally with its power of death. It is an evergreen, which lives when every other tree seems to have died, yet its poison seems to forbid its power of immortality to humankind. In this one sees the melding of life and death, which is the might of the rune eihwaz. Odhinn's initiation on this tree is the initiation of death in which he gains power over both death and life, returning from the dead as the mightiest of the gods. The stave-shape of the Elder eihwaz does not appear in the Younger Futhark, and it does not seem to have been used for writing at all except as a magical sign, in contrast to the other runes which were used phonetically as well as magically.

By thinking on the nature of this rune it may be suggested as a refutation of von List's assertion that the final secret of the Havamal was shown in either the fyrfos (swastika) or its substitute, gebo.[1] There are sixteen runes in the Younger Futhark; the Havamal lists eighteen spells, implying either that two of the runes of the Elder Futhark survived as magical signs (but not letters) or that other signs were added to the list. Of the last, Odhinn says, *"I know an eighteenth that none know, I neither maid nor man's wife. I It is always better kept secret, I except to the one who lies in my arms, I or my sister."* [2] First Ódhinnn states that he will not tell it, especially to any woman; then he says that he will tell it to a mysterious feminine principle-as he has said, "neither maid nor man's wife." There is a certain hint of sororal incest here, even though Odhinn has no sister.

The answer to this riddle is that the god is affirming within himself the synthesis of eihwaz: the lover/sister is Odhinn's own feminine side who, not being brought forth into being as independently female, can be "neither maid nor man's wife" and yet holds Odhinn in her arms and is also his sister. This is also, perhaps, the mystery which Odhinn whispers into the ear of the dead Baldr, the rune which "no dweller on earth knows."[3] It is the power of immortality, not as an escape from death, but as an acceptance of it and the melding of life with death which the yew tree shows forth in all ways. This is the rune of the will which survives death and rebirth again and again, life hidden within death as the fire is hidden within the rough, cold bark of the yew.

This is the rune by which Lif (life) and Lifthrasir (the stubborn will to live) hide themselves within shoots of Yggdrasill through Ragnarok, after which they can step forth and breed the human race again on the new earth. It is a literal description of the rebirth of power and memory which survives the death of the body. By this rune Baldr, hidden for a time in Hel's protecting kingdom, is able to bring himself and Hodhr forth alive again after Ragnarok. Eihwaz shows the trunk of Yggdrasill which unites Hel and Asgardhr, the dragon Nidhoggr at the bottom of the tree and the eagle at the top. The true vitki draws his/her powers from the roots and the crown of the World-Tree alike, melding, like Odhinn, the mights of light and of darkness into a single power. This rune is also associated with Ullr, god of the winter sky who dwells in Ydal, "Yew-dales." Ullr's weapon is the yew bow. He is called upon to shield the fighter in duels.

Eihwaz is used for making wands and staves, both because of its nature as the all-holding tree of the runic initiation and, perhaps, because of the implication that spells cast through a yew focus will be shot as strongly and truly as an arrow shot from a yew bow. Eihwaz can be used to send messages along the trunk of the World-Tree or to fare up and down it yourself The name Yggdrasil means "steed of Ygg" (Odhinn); the gallows is called "the horse of the hanged." Through this rune, you can speak to the dead and learn wisdom from them as Odhinn does, or call them up if your need should be so great that nothing more will suffice. The Poetic Edda writes how Odhinn has to ride down to the seeress' mound at the eastern gate of Hel to chant her up, and even then she complains of the "fear-fraught ways" he makes her fare.[4] Both the riding and the calling forth are ruled by eihwaz.

It is also a rune of warding when you must fare past the bounds of the gardh, as shown when the movable shield which is associated with eihwaz is compared to the unmovable circle (othala). Making the dead fare to Midgardhr is a sure way to rouse their wrath, as described in the Hadding's Saga, where the angry spirits rend the witch who has called them forth to shreds in spite of her wardings. The woe-working powers of eihwaz as a rune of death and power over the dead should be obvious. Eihwaz strengthens the will. It is the might which holds memory and purpose through death and rebirth, and it may be used to call upon wisdom and might from earlier existences. You can learn from both other dead and the dead whose knowledge and power have been passed on and hidden in your own soul. Control of both the continuation of life implicit in the sexual act and the personal death it encompasses as both the ecstatic loss of awareness and the physical giving up of vital force.

Ritually, eihwaz is a Eihwaz shows its being in the body as the spinal fire,[5] the kundalini force controlled orgasm being the rune of the death-initiation. It also corresponds to the staff-which shows the vitki's steadfastness of will piercing through all the worlds from the lowest to the highest and carries the entire range of her/his magic-and to the wand. It may also be seen as a shield, especially in cases of magical duels, in which Ullr may be called upon to aid and shield the vitki+ You should also remember that one of the greatest sides of eihwaz's being is that of shielding the soul through all hardship. Eihwaz governs deep, mighty, and sudden transformation on all levels. Eihwaz may be used both to store and to send power. A stone which works well with eihwaz is smoky quartz, which, like clear quartz, shows the hagalaz structure of the World-Tree, but adds to that the hidden fire of the natural radiation which has darkened the crystal and gives it its transformational character. Smoky quartz has also been used in raising and guiding the spinal fire.

Eihwaz: Meditation

You are walking through a forest in winter. The trees are gnarled and leafless, their craggy bark gray and black. Dead grass crunches beneath your boots as you walk. In a little while you come out of the forest and into a field where the snow has blown into drifts at the north sides of the stone barrows that rise from the silent earth. You look about yourself uneasily and walk a little faster; you know that a barrows-field is a bad place for the living when evening begins to darken the dull gray sky. Ahead you see a tall, lone tree, red berries bright among its dark green needles. As you get closer, you mark that there is a longbow and one arrow leaning against the low stone well at the tree's foot. The sky is darkening, the barrow-mounds fading into uncanny shadows across the field. Something rustles faintly behind you. You look back quickly, but there is nothing there. You hasten to the yew tree and take up the bow and arrow.

Looking around yourself, you strain your eyes to see if anything is coming through the darkness behind you. Everything is still for a moment, then rock grates on rock and you see a pale, unholy light from one of the barrow mounds. The light glows around a figure-a dry, brown corpse of a large man, whose black fingernails have grown into thick claws. His grave-clothes hang on his sinewy limbs in pale tatters; rings of gold still adorn his bony fingers and arms. The draugr walks clumsily and slowly, but steadily towards you, his moon-eyed gaze filling you with fear. You want to flee but the tree behind you blocks your escape, holding you up. Still a little way from you, the draugr reaches out his arms as if to embrace you. You clutch your bow tightly; strengthened, you knock the arrow and let it fly in one smooth burst. It pierces the draugr's withered skin and sinks between his ribs.

His corpse-light goes out and you hear his bones clattering together as they fall into the icy grass. Amazed by the might of the bow, you pull the string back again, as far as it will go. Suddenly you hear a cracking noise. The bow breaks before you can drop it, sinew wrapping around your neck and choking your wind off as the jagged end punches into your guts with a stabbing, searing pain that spreads through your body like fiery poison. Your feet dangling, you hang onto the spear of yew wood in you with a death-grip as a mighty wind roars up around you. The pain slowly fades into numbness. Your sight darkens and clears again as you look down into the kingdom of Hel far, far below at the roots of the tree on which you hang. The land is all black and gray. Corpses move slowly about like beetles in it, some fresh with the marks of sickness or bleeding wounds on them, some green or black with rot, and some all bare bones.

Serpents gnaw at the roots of the tree like maggots at flesh. You see yourself mirrored far below: a hanged corpse with black face and dead tongue sticking out, circled by ravens who pluck off mouthfuls of meat. Above, you see a shining eagle at the crown of the tree, a noble bird over the roof of a golden hall which glows like a jewel. You hang halfway between, the winds turning your body about. Far down at the root, you see a spark running up the trunk of the tree from the nest of serpents. The spark grows to a great flash of fire, striking upward through your body like a lightning bolt. You cry out soundlessly as the burst of brilliance thunders through you. Against the white light, you see all the runes burning red with power, burning themselves into your being.

The whole length of the tree flames with the might that runs from serpents to eagle and back again. Drawing on the power flowing through you and you easily loose the noose around your neck, breathing in the fire to heal all the ravages of your death. Supporting yourself on one limb with the yew stave that had pierced you and you stand in the shape of eihwaz, arms pointed downward and leg bent up, binding the fire within you and slowly hiding it in the darkness of your body again as the fire running through the tree fades into the darkness of the rough bark. When you can neither see the flames anymore nor feel their warmth, you return to your own body again, knowing the secret might that you will always hold within the rune eihwaz.

ᛈ PERTHRO

Galdr-sound: peh-peli-peh (a full, round sound, neither chopped off nor prolonged)
Letter: P

(Lot-box) is always play and laughter among bold men where the warriors sit in the hall together."
— Anglo-Saxon Rune Poem

The stave-shape of perthro appears to be that of a lot box, which suggests the early Germanic love of gambling, a game fraught with far more meaning than one might guess at first. Tacitus has written that even while sober, the Germanic warriors would gamble for hours until one had lost all his possessions and had to wager his own freedom on a toss of the dice, and that if he lost that throw, he would go cheerfully into slavery, even under a weaker man, because he thought it to be the will of "fate."[1] In this seemingly excessive and pointless game, one of the greatest parts of the Teutonic spiritual understanding may be seen: the deep awareness of the turnings of Wyrd.

While the vitki may sometimes write his or her own weird or at least write around it, the ordinary woman or man can only meet it with courage. Hence you see the typical image of the Norseman laughing as he goes forth to die, as well as the high worth placed on the "luck" of a leader or king, for it was clearly better to fight for someone whose weird was written for success and victory. Perthro is the rune of divination. The dice of the early Germanic tribes show this might in its crudest form-the same method is used for tossing the dice and casting the runes, and the root understanding is the same: that the web of that-which-is and that-which-is-becoming is so woven together that the idea of randomness or "coincidence" is impossible. Thus the dice show ørlög* on the level of personal fortune, and the runes show the shape of this web in all ways. Both dice and runes are tossed out of a cup, which is the earthly embodiment of the Well of Wyrd from which flow all the runes that the Norns have written.

The act of casting the runes thus partakes of the magical law of sympathy. As the runic streams flow from the Well, they must be reflected in the carven staves flowing from the cup with perthro, the rune of the Well, written on it. The act of divination is the willed attempt to reach an awareness of the workings of that-which-is on that-which-is-becoming and that-which-should-be, or an awareness of the contents of the Well in their wholeness. Urdhr's Well is the side of the Well's being which is active and choosing, but this side of its being is necessarily based on the well of "Mimir," which holds all of that-which-is. The name Mimir seems similar to the name of Ymir, the proto-etin, the difference being that the runes mannaz, the rune of thought and memory, and isa, the rune of the ego, are put in the stead of jera, which shows a natural, unconscious process.

Hence, it might be said that Mimir can be seen as the embodiment of the self-awareness of the cosmos. The story of Odhinn giving up an eye for a drink from C Mimir's Well can be understood easily when one realizes the nature of the well itself. By internalizing the entire awareness of that- which-is, Odhinn changed his own sight so that he could at once see the evolving "present" as most are aware of it and the whole structure of the hidden layers which lie beneath and shape it. This is the third root of Odhinn's power: as he gained the runes themselves by his initiation on Yggdrasill (eihwaz), and the power to use them with the might of galdr-magic by the poetic inspiration of Odhroerir (ansuz), so he gained the awareness of the workings of Wyrd, of his own ability to alter it, and the knowledge of what should come of his workings from Mimir's Well (perthro). Perthro has also been interpreted as the grave-mound, which, as Bauschatz points out, is closely bound in thought to the Well of Wyrd, as both contain the concealed might ("treasures") of the past. Literally the ur-layer or proto-layer of Wyrd; used to describe the weird which has been written in the Well.

In later usage, the word ørlög was used for a spell, particularly a curse, implying the relationship between the working of magic and the Well of Wyrd. Perthro can be used for all manner of divinations and for an understanding of all the workings of Wyrd through the worlds, including an awareness of synchronicity and an understanding of the entire pattern of universal evolution. In workings of woe, perthro can be used for intensifying the woe-bringing effects of Wyrd in another's life, or for awareness of another's actions.

Perthro is the rune by which you can gain the wisdom and the awareness to use the runes without unknowingly destroying yourself or another. It gives you the capability to "think runic like"~to see the workings of the forces of the runes in daily life and to under- stand how to use them in a setting which seems to have changed greatly from the time that first learned and wrote of them. Ritually, perthro represents the cup of rune casting and the several-fold process of self-checking by rune casting, which should go with any active use of runic magic. Used with other runes, perthro receives them and sends them out into being.

It is the passive complement of the active uruz in the context of the Well. Perthro can be used to tap into the wisdom of Mimir's Well and to recover knowledge about the runes themselves that has either been forgotten or was never learned by humans. It is the rune of meditation. A stone which works well with perthro is layered onyx, the pattern of which shows the layers upon layers that determine the shape of weird. The onyx has often been thought of as a stone of ill-luck; in fact, it embodies ørlög, the effects of which are often woe-bringing and need the willed resistance of nauthiz to alter or mitigate. By meditating on the layered pattern of this stone, you may come to a better understanding of the workings of Wyrd and the structure of that-which-is.

Perthro: Meditation

You are inside a hall, sitting on a circle of rough wooden benches with a group of long-haired, bearded warriors. The fire burns in a pit in the center of the hall, the smoke rising out of a hole in the thatched roof. Pale winter daylight shines through the hole. Your cloak wards you from the bitter cold behind, and the fire warms you from the front, aided by the thick ale you drink from your horn. The other warriors are garbed similarly, wearing heavy cloaks but light tunics and breeches. A dice-cup is passing around the circle, each man shaking it until he makes either a good throw and can pass it on or a losing cast, in which case he must strip off one of his heavy gold bracelets and pass it with the cup.

You know that this game can keep on until one man has lost everything he owns, even his freedom if that is his weird. When the cup gets to you, you rattle it for a long time, the dice inside clicking against the wood like bones. You sense when it is time to cast the dice. You let them fall knowing that whatever your wyrd is, it is already written. Two of the dice show sixes; the third has become no longer a die but a strip of rough hewn wood on which the rune perthro is graven. As you stare into the rune, it grows and grows until your sight is wholly overwhelmed by its dark and mysterious might. Slowly the rune fades from around you, and you find yourself standing at the foot of the great evergreen Yggdrasill, looking down into the Well of Wyrd.

The three black-hooded women beside the Well ignore you completely, their shadowed faces turned away from you. They dip their hands into the water and sprinkle a layer of muddy white clay onto the tree the touch of their water healing the tattered bark. It seems to you that Yggdrasill grows a little as they do this, the branches and needles stretching out just a bit farther and the gigantic roots beneath your feet thickening by a layer. The air shimmers and you suddenly see that the tree and the world around you are only figures on a vast tapestry that these women weave, the whole quivering at each touch on the thread which they turn and shape skillfully through the layers of weaving. The tapestry shimmers and fades; they are splashing water from the Well onto the tree again, and this time you see that where it falls, it graves runes into the bark in an endless, intricate pattern of interwoven might.

You know that you could follow any of these patterns through the tree, but you are too eager to see more of the power shaping them. You stand for a while, watching the Norns. You would like to speak to them but you know that they must speak first. Their backs are to you as they sprinkle the roots and trunk of Yggdrasill. When you walk around the tree to see if they will notice you, some of the water they toss falls on your head. The world begins to darken around you, fading until you can only see the World- Tree as a great shape in the darkness. There seems to be a faint white light glowing over the Well, and you walk around again to see what it is. 4 The light comes from the bone-white fire of a torch. Standing beside the Well is a dark, stooped figure with the white hair and beard of an old man. Only when you come closer do you see that his body is too thick and powerful to be that of a human, his head too broad and features too low. For all of that, you can sense the immense wisdom in this being. He is Mimir, wisest of the etin-kind and keeper of the Well of Memory by which you stand.

> "Be welcome," he says. His voice is deep and rough but not unpleasant.
> "What do you seek?" "A drink from your well," you answer.
>
> He sighs. "Do you know the price?" He asks. "Once you have looked through its waters, one eye must always remain; once you have drunk from its waters, you must keep drinking forever."
> "Nevertheless I will," you say.
>
> "So be it," Mimir replies, and hands you the wooden cup from which you had been casting dice. You dip it into the dark waters of the Well.

As you drink, the water before you becomes clear. You see Odhinn, cloaked in dark blue, drinking as you drink and standing with one eye gone. Odhinn whispers his wisdom in the ear of a gray-haired, fur clad skald, who sings it again and again fill a younger learns it, passing it down through the ages of men fill another writes it down, passing from mouth to ear and book to book till it brings you here to the same well. The Heruli scatter from Denmark across Northern Europe and back, carrying the runes with them as they ride bloody and unarmored, filled with berserker-fury and the runic wisdom they leave in a trail behind them, carved on stones and staves, on the blades of swords and silver bracelets.

The workings of men and the will of Wyrd come together and turn. Norsemen harry down to Dublin; Sigurdhr falls beneath his raven banner and the tide turns east to Stamford where Harold of Norway meets Harold of England on the bloody field and the Normans, Norsemen, come across the Channel from France, burning England around Harold's ears and laying the next of the great layers that lead to the land you live in. The white dragon of the Saxons coils rune-magic, Odhinn's gifts of wisdom and song, into every hidden layer of your speech and thought, bringing you here to the brink of the WELL that holds it all. Slowly you return to your own body, feet firmly planted on the ground, and look around you, seeing the echoes and might of all that has happened, shaping that-which-is, ceaselessly turning and turning again from the first breath of life and every layer after. You know that you can always reach this wisdom through the rune perthro; that, indeed, you will always look through the Well of Memory with one eye and see the shaping of the worlds.

ᛉ ELHAZ

Galdr-sound: zzzzzzzzzzz (a deep, full buzzing, halfway between Z and R, rather similar to the g in "rouge")
Letter: Z, final A

(Elk's sedge) has its home most often in the fen it waxes in the water and grimly wounds and burns with blood any man who in any way tries to grasp it.
— Anglo-Saxon Rune Poem

(Man) is the increase of dust; mighty is the talon-span of the hawk.
— Old Norwegian Rune Rhyme

(Man) is the joy of man, and the increase of dust and the adornment of ships.
— Old Icelandic Rune Poem

Man in the middle I ycw holds all.
— Abcedarium Nordmannicum

I know a fourteenth
If I talk of the gods before the folk, 1 can speak of Ases and elves.
Few of the unlearned I know these things.
— Havamal 159

    The name elhaz may be derived from the words for "elk," swan, or protection," or possibly, from he Germanic twin-gods known as the Alcis. The reversed stave of the Younger Futhark is called "yew" or "yew-bow." All of these names carry a meaning of both warding and holiness. The rune elhaz is closely related to the rune mannaz; in the Younger Futhark, the stave-shape is given the name mad/ir, or "man."

The two runes are alike in that both refer to the spirit in earthly shape that is the being of humanity, the difference lying in that elhaz rules the pathways between the gods and humans and the drawing/sending downward of godly might, while mannaz is the rune of the indwelling, inherited seed of the godly being in humankind. The alternate shape of this stave, the Younger Futhark's "yew" (I), is also associated with eihwaz, and the primal tree-shape (I) is very similar to the snowflake-shape of hagalaz (I). The difference is that the "branches" are connected to the "roots" by a bridge showing the human awareness of Midgardhr as the middle of all things, "man in the middle."

The rune elhaz shows the awareness of the human that she or he is both a microcosm of the universe and (necessarily, because of the nature of human perceptions) its center. One interpretation of the stave-shape is that it shows a human with head and hands upraised in the Teutonic stance of "prayer"-that is, willed and mutual communication between gods and humans. The full tree-shape shows this communication with both the wights above and the wights below Midgardhr. As the rune showing the threefold bridge Bifrost (made of air, fire, and water), elhaz is also a rune of cleansing and warding. It is the rune by which one may hold speech with one's own valkyrja, the swan-winged bringer of wisdom and messenger between gods and humans.

Bifrost may only be crossed by humans when they are guided by the valkyrja, when the "increase of dust"-that is, the full melding of the highest being of the soul with the living human awareness-has taken place. The rune elhaz is a great rune of warding, as shown by its bond with the shielding might of the valkyrja and yew tree and by other aspects of the stave as well. The stave-shape has been suggested to show the horns of the elk or the hand outstretched in a warding gesture~-both powerful images of defense.

The "Anglo-Saxon Rune Poem" writes of the rune as burning, which shows the being of the warding called upon through elhaz. It is the warding of holiness, the intense "fiery" energy, like that of Bifrost, in the presence of which nothing unclean can abide. In both thought and working the rune elhaz is similar to establishment magic's conception of the pentagram: it embodies the might of spirit as the guiding force within the earthly being; it shows the conscious human microcosm, as contrasted with the hagalaz of the macrocosm; it wards and makes holy at the same time. Like the antlers of the elk, elhaz is both shield and spear: not only does it ward but it also brings woe to the enemy who tries to work woe against its wielder.

The rune elhaz may be used to ward a person or a place, and also to hallow a place, especially if one is about to begin a dangerous working. The power of elhaz to communicate and ward may be seen, in a sense, as a complement to the power of eihwaz; the two yew-staves may be used harmoniously together. Elhaz may be used to fill a space or an item with the power drawn from the higher realms: to make it "holy," that is, both whole and filled with godly might. Elhaz is a guide to spiritual growth and cleansing through calling on the higher energies which gradually raise the personal vibrational level. It both drives unclean energy away and brings in holy might in its stead. At the same time, it holds a balance between the lower and higher faculties, being the bridge of consciousness which at once unites and separates the lower and the higher.

One may use the original tree-form (I) and stance to draw power from all the worlds. Elhaz may be used to cause woe to those who are too spiritually unrefined to benefit from its cleansing fire. It is especially mighty against the dead who have been drawn up to this plane by magical means and also against all beings of the lower worlds. Ritually, elhaz rules all forms of hallowing. It may be used in most cases where the pentagram would be called for in Western establishment magic. Elhaz may be used to fare through the worlds. The reference to "the talon-span of the hawk" speaks of the way in which several of the gods make use of the hawk shape in traveling between the realms of being. Used with other runes, elhaz brings out their highest level of spiritual workings, binding them to the goal of evolution of the consciousness. A stone which works well with elhaz is black tourmaline, which shields against woe-working might and brings power down from the higher realms into earth as well as from the wheel of power at the crown of the head to the lowest wheels (Chakras).

Elhaz: Meditation

You stand in the middle of a marsh in autumn. The sky is gray. A V of wild geese flies overhead, crying mournfully. The ground is squishy beneath your feet, thick mud mixed with dead reeds and cattails. Elksedge grows tall around you. You are careful not to touch it, knowing that the sharp blades of marsh-grass will cut burningly into your hands. As you make your way carefully through the marsh you begin to feel that you are being stalked. You hear splashing and faint sucking sounds behind you but when you look back, you see nothing, and when you stop, the noises stop also. As you move onward, the sounds grow louder; it is as if something is sloshing through the mud behind the hedge of elk-grass, taking great care not to raise its head too far from the salty marsh. Now and again you think you see the quick flurry of a dark scaly tail or limb behind the high sedge. Ahead of you, the hedge that surrounds you ends at the bank of a dark pool.

The pond's surface is roiled, as if something moved just below it. A deep loathing stirs in your guts as you watch the ripples on the water. You back up a few paces, listening to your hidden hunter sloshing closer and closer to the black mere. It moves quickly, breaking from its cover to leap into the stagnant pond. It is shaped like a man, but larger, gnarled and hideous, covered with black scales. Its head comes up again at once and it begins to pull itself out of the water in front of you. Without stopping to think, you pluck a handful of the elk- sedge that had warded you and toss it at the grim thing. It keens, covering its eyes with webbed hands as if burned, while the pieces of elk-grass grow into a thick hedge before you.

The creature slides back into the water. You wait a few moments but it does not come up again. A movement catches the corner of your eye, and you look up to see a great white swan flying slowly overhead. There is something in the powerful beat of her shining wings, the cleanness of her feathers and the freedom of her wind-path that catches at your breath and brings tears to blur your eyes as she circles above you once and flies on. Eyes fixed on her, you hurry quickly after, heedless of the betraying mud beneath your feet. Without stumbling or stopping you follow the path of the swan, who always moves just slowly enough for you to keep in sight of her, until you are out of the marsh and standing at the foot of the great yew-tree that unites Asgardhr, Midgardhr, and Hel's kingdom.

The swan flies straight up to the crown of the tree, dwindling to a bright speck. Imploringly, tears streaming down your face, you raise your arms and head towards her. Her upward flight slows, then stops, and she begins to circle down again. When she is close enough, you see that the great white wings now support a surpassingly beautiful woman, armed and dressed in chain mail and leather. Her features are very like your own but perfect in a way that brings an ache of longing to your heart. She halts halfway down, holding her arms out to you. You see that she stands on a bridge of shimmering rainbow fire, her feet near its end. She beckons to you, but there is no bridge and no way for you to climb the huge bare trunk of the tree.

As you stretch your arms upward, however, you begin to feel a stream of golden power flowing into you from the end of the bridge, a shimmering holiness that seems to lift you up even as it brings the rainbow bridge and the swan-maiden nearer and nearer to you; yet you are aware that your feet still rest on the earth, its solidity balancing the heady wave of power flowing into you from above. At last you are close enough so that the tips of your outstretched fingers just touch the tips of the maiden's. The shimmering light glows around you. You sense the mighty love, wisdom, and guidance of your valkyrja. You set one foot on the end of the rainbow bridge. Its fire does not burn you, but it is so strong that you cannot yet go any farther up it. Your valkyrja bends down to kiss the top of your head. Her touch is a crown of warmth, enfolding you in her power and wise warding. You return slowly to your body, feet firmly planted on the earth, knowing that guarding and guidance which you may always reach through the power of the rune elhaz.

⚡ SOWILO

Galdr-sound: sssssssss
Letter: S

(Sun) is by seamen always hoped for when they fare far away over the fishes' bath until the brine-stallion they bring to land.
— Anglo-Saxon Rune Poem

(Sun) is the light of lands bow to the holiness.
— Old Norwegian Rune Rhyme

(Sun) is the shield of the clouds and a shining glow and the life-long sorrow of ice.
— Old Icelandic Rune Poem
I know an eleventh: if I am to lead old friends I into the fray, I sing under the shield and they fare into battle mighty and whole, they fare from battle whole, they are whole, wherever they go.
— Havamal 156

The rune sowilo is the rune of the sun, an active power which either shows itself forth as the whirling of a wheel or as a thunder- bolt/sword. In either side of its being, the sowilo rune shows the invincible power of the will. You may note that the sun-wheel or swastika is made of two sowilo runes laid over each other, showing the being of this rune as a symbol of holiness and source of power which is recognized even beyond the Indo-European world. Unfortunately, this archetypal symbol has had a great deal of ill thought attached to it as a consequence of its use by the Nazi regime, and hence is used only in private today because of the distress it causes in those who are unaware of its true meaning. It should be mentioned that a good number of metaphysically aware people think that the swastika is meant to spin clockwise (reversed sowilo rune) and that Hitler deliberately made it a symbol of darkness by turning it back- ward.

This is not true. The swastika has been an ancient and honorable sign of power among the Germanic people for thousands of years-in both its forms. The swastika "reversed" does not change its being any more than a rune "reversed" does; the ancient rune- workers wrote right to left, left to right, and alternately back and forth. If rune reversal had any meaning, it would be far harder to make bind-runes well. In point of fact, although deosil and widdershins are not without meaning in Teutonic magic, they do not automatically distinguish between works of weal and works of woe. As the rune of the sun, sowilo is the rune of invincibility and final triumph. The Old Icelandic Rune Poem's reference shows its being as a rune which acts both as a warder and in active combat.

As the wheel, it is a shield; as a thunderbolt it is a sword. The Old Norwegian Rune Rhyme shows sowilo as a ruling power and the light of life. This rune has certain conceptual ties to elhaz; you should mark that the sun, like the valkyrja, is always feminine in Germanic thought. As well as guardianship and might the sun is also guidance, as the Anglo-Saxon Rune Poem tells. "To fare far away" is a kenning used either for death or for the journeys taken by the magician in a deathlike trance. In this case, the ocean referred to may be the waters between the worlds-the dark waters of the underworld or the personal subconscious (see laguz). The magical will is the force which brings you through the dark night of the soul and guides you living through the death-passage.

In this setting, sowilo (the sun) is closely related to raidho (the path of the sun) and to laguz (the waters which must be crossed; note similarities in the Anglo-Saxon Rune Poem references). In both the shape and action of sowilo, you may also see a certain likeness to Eihwaz. Eihwaz, however, is unshakable and unchanging the will to endure, whereas sowilo is endlessly mobile~the will to act. Both are runes of transformation. Thorsson identifies sowilo with the Chakras (wheels) along the length of the spine which are vitalized by the spinal fires of eihwaz.1 Sowilo is used to strengthen the active, magical will, making it into an invincible and unstoppable force. Both its shielding and striking capabilities are bound up in this action; nothing can assail the fully developed will, and nothing can withstand it.

The woeworking side of sowilo's being can clearly be seen in Hitler's SS, who used this rune in their insignia. Wrongly used, it is the rune of arrogance, cruelty, and isolation. The will itself is a neutral force, with weal and woe depending on its goals, as may be learned from both the triumphs and the terrible destruction wrought by Hitler, who consciously believed in nothing but his own will. The rune sowilo and the swastika may both be used in understanding the currents of power which swirl widdershins through the earth and deosil through the heavens, coming forth from and meeting at the poles. In ritual usage, sowilo is associated with the hammer of hallowing.

Used with other runes, sowilo activates and vitalizes. Sowilo can be used with meditations on the wheels of the body (Chakras). It brings out the ability for active leadership; that is, the ability to inspire others with your own will. It is not a rune for victory in the same manner as tiwaz, but it is the rune of active triumph and of warding from wounds and defeat. Tiwaz is a rune by which you may overcome others; sowilo is a rune by which you strengthen yourself. The stone most traditionally associated with sowilo is the Norse sun stone (identified as calcite by some, Icelandic spar by others) which, because of its refractive properties, was a valuable navigational aid to Norse seafarers. There is also another stone called sun stone, an orange form of moonstone which reflects light brilliantly and works well with this rune. Also appropriate to sowilo is the diamond which, like the rune, is brilliantly invincible, its very name meaning either "unconquerable" or "hardest steel." The diamond is a great stone of warding and also brings shining might into the wheels of the body.

Sowilo: Meditation

You stand in a grassy field, a little way from the edge of a red sandstone cliff. Beyond the cliff, you can hear the waves beating against the rocks. A strong salt breeze blows cool around you. Gulls and terns circle overhead, calling sharply. You take a step towards the ocean and at once your way is blocked by a horde of dark figures that seem to have sprung up from the ground. They stand before you like warriors' statues carved from black ice. They do not move until you try to step forward again; then their swords and shields are up at once. A few drops of water run off them in the sunlight, but a cloud is already moving across the sun to shield them. Without faltering, you step forward again, tracing the rune sowilo with each hand. In your left hand the rune becomes a spinning swastika-wheel of white light; in your right, it is a thunderbolt-shaped sword. You push your way through the warriors of ice.

As they strike at your shield, the swords melt in their hands; when your sword touches them, they flow into pools of water, soaking into the grass. By the time you reach the wind-eaten edge of the cliff, the icy warriors have all been slain. The sun above you has burned through the clouds, and her bright light strengthens you. Looking over the edge of the red cliff, you see a small boat resting on the stony beach below. Wind and wave have bitten deeply into the cliff so that, ravaged and gouged, it leans over the ocean. You see no way down, but you know that you must reach the boat. With your sword of light you begin to strike at the edge of the cliff, carving out a few steps, then moving down them and hacking away a few more.

The wave- eaten sandstone crumbles away in great chunks, shattering to ruddy sand on the beach below. You know that it could collapse at any moment but are so intent on your blade biting into the rock that you have no time to feel any fear. At last you reach the bottom, standing on the rocky beach. The boat is a simple rowboat, perhaps a bit small for seafaring, but it looks sturdy enough. You push it away from the beach, your feet and calves numbed by the stinging, icy water. When it is floating well free of the bottom, you haul yourself up over the side. The waves catch your craft, flinging it about violently as you try to paddle beyond the surf to the open ocean.

Finally you must toss your shield into the air before you. The sun-wheel whirls over the prow, pulling the boat straight after it, parting the swells before you. You sail like this for some time. Although the sky darkens quickly around a pale sunset, the spinning wheel before you gives off enough light for you to see clearly, glowing over the water ahead of you. Something large nudges against the bottom of your boat, trying to bump it off course or perhaps overturn it, but it cannot shake you from the path of light, and after a while it leaves you to fare in peace. As the sun comes up behind you in the east, you see a dark mass of land ahead of you. You sail towards it until your boat grounds against the beach with a bump.

Taking up your whirling shield of light, you wade ashore. A shining figure is walking along the beach towards you. It is a woman dressed in white, her long golden hair unbound and flowing loosely around her face. Warmth and glory radiates from her. Above her head is a small radiant white sphere, spinning swiftly enough for you to hear its clear note. In her hands she carries a crown bearing a whirling golden sowilo-rune with a glittering diamond in its center. You bow your head before her glory and she crowns you. The intense might of the spinning sun-rune above you glows down through your body, setting the wheels of power whirling down your spine. Slowly you return to your own body, feeling the might that runs through you surround you in a whirling sphere of holiness and warding, though your feet always remain firmly planted on the earth.

↑ IWAZ

Galdr-sound: tiw-tiw-tiw (to rhyme with "few"; short and sharp)
Letter: T

(Tir) is a star, it keeps faith well with athlings, always on its course over the mists of night it never fails.
— Anglo-Saxon Rune Poem

(Tyr) is the one-handed among the Aesir the smith has to blow often.
— Old Norwegian Rune Rhyme

(Tyr) is the one-handed god and the leavings of the wolf and the ruler of the temple.
— Old Icelandic Rune Poem

I know a twelfth: If I see a hanged man swinging high in a tree, I can carve and stain runes, so that the man walks and speaks with me.
    — Havamal 157

The stave-shape of tiwaz shows a spear, the weapon of the sky- father god and lord of victory. The image of the one-handed god lifting a spear is shown in the oldest Indo-European rock carvings and is clearly Tyr or Tiwaz, whose name in its earlier form is cognate to the Latin deus, Greek Theos, and Greek Zeus. Originally, Tyr held the highest place among the gods, as sky-father and lord of law, courage, and war. Only when the runes and their power became known to humans did Odhinn come forth as All-Father, assuming such sides of Tyr's being as were not wholly contradictory to his own nature. Several of the uses of the spear in Odhinnic worship come from this assimilation, particularly the practice of casting the spear over one's enemies to "give them to Odhinn."

Most of Tyr's characteristics, however, were so different from Odhinn's being as to preclude assimilation, and hence though Tyr's place in written myth is fairly limited (owing possibly to the substitution of Odhinn in some places), he remained a powerful force as a religious figure. The rune tiwaz is similar to eihwaz and elhaz in that it shows forth the central column of the world; but where eihwaz shows melding of the lowest and the highest and elhaz shows communication, tiwaz represents the separation of the heavens and the earth. Thorsson identifies the rune tiwaz with the Saxon Irminsul the great pillar holding up the heavens. ~ Odhinn is essentially bipolar; Tyr is essentially unipolar, as shown by his one-handedness-a literal sign that Tyr is bound to a single course of action, as opposed to the ever ~ changing Odhinn. The rune tiwaz is the rune of stability and ordering force. The star of the Anglo-Saxon Rune Poem is probably the North Star, which always serves as an absolute indicator of direction.

One of the greatest sides of tiwaz's being is its socio-religious nature as a rune of law. Tiwaz is associated with the Thing, the general assembly at which justice was done and community decisions made. In this context, it is the complement of raidho. Elements of this may be seen in the story of the Fenris-Wolf. Tyr must take the weight of dealing with the Wolf upon himself because it, as the embodiment of the forces of chaos, is chiefly his enemy at this point (it becomes Odhinn's doom at Ragnarok because the Wolf is essentially part of Odhinn's own nature; it is the ørlög he has laid for himself). In spite of the fact that betraying the oath the gods have sworn to the Wolf is in the best interests of all life, Tyr still must pay for the deception with his hand, as he is the god of oaths, honor, and absolute justice.

Tiwaz is the main rune used by or on behalf of those who were not themselves greatly skilled in rune word. It was usual for warriors to, as the valkyrja Sigrdrifa tells Sigurdhr, "call twice upon Tyr."[2] The rune was inscribed on the hilt of the sword to instill honor and courage in the welder, and on one or both sides of the blade to fill it with Tyr's victorious might. Battle was seen as a judgment (from which the medieval trial by combat developed), and hence the use of the rune tiwaz made the warrior worthy, ensuring that he would be judged the better man and so win the fight. The rune tiwaz is used to obtain absolute justice and to strengthen a person or thing in the physical realm by filling it with spiritual and moral force.

It is, of course, called upon for victory and is one of the mightiest runes in dealing directly with earthly problems as well as magical struggles. In the personal sphere, tiwaz develops courage, strength, and honor. It makes you aware of your duty to others, especially where the social order as a whole is concerned. Tiwaz can be used for stability and to bind the unruly and woe-working forces within until you have developed the strength to meld these sides into your whole being (wunjo). Tiwaz is used to bring about and maintain order. In working of woe, tiwaz instills rigidity, prejudice, and loss of perspective. It may be used directly against another in revenge-defense magic (casting the spear over) if the cause is truly just. Tiwaz can be used to force someone to fulfill an oath or to bind any undisciplined energy. Ritually, tiwaz is represented by the central pillar of the temple or its symbolic representation. The stones associated with tiwaz are bloodstone and hematite~both of which grant wisdom as well as strength in battle and ruby, which is associated with leadership and warrior might. Star ruby is especially appropriate to this rune.

Tiwaz: Meditation

You are floating in what seems to be a pool of utterly formless chaos. All around you, shapes are half pulling themselves from the restless mass and collapsing back into it, their borders flowing and engulfing each other. Strange sounds, gratings, and grunts and sloshing noises float through this realm of formlessness and confusion. You long for something solid to rest your feet on, for more light than the shifting flashes that pulse irregularly through the sea of chaos about you, and for a clearer air than this thick hell-brew of stinking fog and dust. Looking up, you see a single silver gleam through the seething ocean of madness. You expect it to wink out and be lost, but it glows ever more strongly, one fixed single star shining straight down through the shifting formlessness. As it brightens, the writhing liquid slowly solidifies to viscous mud beneath your feet, then to solid ground, as the air clears about you. The single beam of the star has become a great pillar of light, holding up the dark blue arch of the heavens above the newly-formed earth. You breathe deeply of the clear air, staring up at the star and glad of the solid ground under you.

Something growls behind you. Turning to look, you see a wolf as big as a horse bounding over the ground towards you, its teeth flashing in the starlight. It leaves a wake of eddying, shuddering chaos behind it. At the last moment it changes course, and you see that it is about to attack the pillar that holds the sky up. You look around desperately for a weapon, but all you see is a rope at the foot of the pillar. You grab the rope and swing it at the wolf. It backs off, snarling, then charges right at you. Stepping aside, you swing the rope around its neck with one hand and grab it with the other, pulling the two ends tight to choke it. Although it shakes itself mightily, flinging you about, it cannot dislodge the rope or reach you with its teeth. Finally it falls to earth and you finish the task of binding its feet together and its jaws tight shut. You still hear its low growl - impotent now, you think, until you realize that the beast has not woken yet. The growling comes from a pair of fur-cloaked men who run across the plain at you.

They bite at their shield-rims, froth running down into their beards and the wood splintering under their furious gnawing. A spear and a sword now stand at the foot of the pillar. Without questioning the gift, you snatch up the spear and fling it at them. It takes one through the breast and he falls. The other runs towards you, howling like a wolf in his madness. You pick up the sword and step forward to fight him. When the berserker's ax meets your sword, it flings you back and you land heavily against the pillar. He leaps forward and strikes at you again, but the might flowing into you from the faithful star above gives you the strength to meet his blow. You fight with your back to the column for a long time, neither of you getting the upper hand. Slowly the strength of his furious madness begins to drain from him, though your power continues steady. At last you strike the ax from his hand. He stands staring at you a moment his chest heaving, as if thinking whether to attack again. You could stab him through, but you know that it is dishonorable to slay an unarmed man. The last of the berserker-strength leaves him and he slumps to the ground, unconscious. You step away from the pillar and raise your head and hands to the star in thanks for your victory.

As you watch, a tall, grim man whose golden beard spreads out over his mailed breast steps out of the pillar of light. He holds a spear in his left hand; his right arm is a bleeding stump. Tyr nods at you, smiling, and gestures at your sword. You hold it out flat before him. With the tip of his spear, he traces the rune tiwaz once on the blade, once on the hilt, and once on your forehead. The runes glow red where the god's power has touched.

ᛒ BERKANO

Galdr-sound: bbbbbb (a deep, very soft hum with lips almost closed; the lips may part and open swiftly to vibrate the sound b-b-b-b-b-b if you find the continuous sound difficult)
Letter: B

(Birch) is without fruit but just the same it bears limbs without fertile seed it has beautiful branches high on its crown it is finely covered loaded with leaves touching the sky.
— Anglo-Saxon Rune Poem

(Birch twig) is the limb greenest with leaves Loki brought the luck of deceit.
— Old Norwegian Rune Rhyme

(Birch twig) is a leafy limb and a little tree and a youthful wood.
— Old Icelandic Rune Poem

I know a thirteenth:
If I sprinkle a young thane I with water, he will not fall, though he goes to battle.
He will not be cut down, by swords.
— Havamal 158

The rune berkano, "birch," is the rune of the Great Mother, the goddess worshiped as Nerthus by the early Germanic people, who became Holda on the continent and was split into Hel and Freyja in the Norse countries. This rune embodies the root of much of the Vanic cult: the earth goddess whose powers of fertility must be renewed by the sacrifice of her consort each year. The stave-shape for berkano may be seen as the swollen breasts and belly of a pregnant woman; it may also be seen as the mirroring and fundamentally identical enclosures of womb and tomb. As Freyja, Berkano is the source of life; as Hel, she is keeper of the dead; as the Aesic Frigg, she is the silent keeper of wisdom who *"knows all ørlög, I though she does not say so herself."*[1] Looking with care, you can see that each of these goddesses bears within herself aspects of the others-they are all maternal, keepers of their share of the dead, and silent seeresses.

Berkano is the rune of the earth who receives the sacrifice/seed and holds it within herself, guarding and nourishing it until the time has come for it to return to the worlds outside again. This is the process of rebirth for those who do not struggle up to Valhalla. As a rune of fruitfulness, berkano particularly rules the birth- process of the spring, when the power of the goddess is shown forth most openly as she brings new life from her womb. In a number of Northern countries it was the custom to dress a young girl in birch limbs and/or flowers and have her travel through the village on May Day or on one of the other spring celebrations. This is probably a survival of the goddess Nerthus' spring procession in which the goddess was drawn about in a wain, spreading her fertile power through the land. Her power was renewed by a human sacrifice at the end of the journey, and students of folklore will at once be aware of a great number of folk customs which are obvious survivals of this practice.

The bringing-forth in the spring is prepared for by the concealment of the fall, and it was at this time that the folk of the Norse countries made their gifts to the land, at the festival called Winter- nights, disablot (sacrifice to the goddesses), or alfablot (sacrifice to the elves). The disir are lesser Vanic goddesses, usually bound to a single family or person. They are often dead female ancestors who watch over the births and deaths of their descendants and advise or protect; they are closely related to the kinfylga and the valkyrja. They have also been described as the "attendant Norns," "those who come to every child that is born to shape its life."2 These beings have survived in children's stories as the fairies bestowing gifts- writing weird-at a baby's christening. As a rune of bringing-into-being, Berkano is mighty as a shaping force in itself, the thought being, as written in the Prose Edda, that the layers laid at birth (coming into being) will remain powerful throughout life. This is also written forth in the "Havamal" passage.

The sprinkling with the waters of life is an old pagan custom; in this case, the magical action taken is that of enclosing the child at birth in the protection of berkano, which remains around him throughout his life because it has been written as his ørlög, his first layer of weird. Berkano is the rune of the mound itself, as apart from the initiation within the mound. It is the equivalent of the alchemist's athanor, the oven or "womb" in which transformation takes place. Berkano may be used for female fertility magic and in working with women's mysteries. It is particularly mighty in all matters regarding birth and bringing-into-being. This rune is effective in reaching your disir to call on their guarding might or asking for their wise rede in some matter, as Odhinn often asks for Frigg's.

Berkano is used for concealment, protection, and nurturing, especially of children. It is a good rune for passive warding. In workings of woe, Berkano may be called upon as the rune of the goddess in her being as the Grave-Mother, the devouring bog. Berkano is the rune of hidden transformation and growth. Ritually, Berkano embodies the need for silence and the dark cloth which covers magical implements between use or in the process of creation. It is best for this cloth to be made of linen, as flax is closely associated with Holda, a later German name for Nerthus. Used with other runes, berkano hides their workings until the unified result is ready to be brought fully into being. The stone associated with berkano is jet a black fossil wood which shows the enclosing and secretive nature of this rune. Jet is said to be used in seeing that which is concealed and in healing female problems.

Berkano: Meditation
(After the poems of Seamus Heaney) 3

You are standing beside a low stone wall, overgrown by blackberry vines, the dark drops of their berries hanging heavily down. Carefully you push the vines aside, hoisting yourself up and over the wall. On the other side you see the low-growing brown cattails and green turf of the bog, laid aside in square black cuts where the peat-harvesters have ripped it away. The peat squishes under your feet as you pick your way carefully through the little white bog-daisies and whispering rushes, following the jagged slabs of granite that show a safe path. A small, clear stream of water winds around the rocks, rising and falling as your weight shifts. The ground here is soft, betraying. The little spring runs into a silent black pool like the mouth of a sacrificial cauldron open to the gray sky. Here and there the green moss is stained brown and ocher, stains like ancient blood held in the bog, fermenting below the earth.

The seeds and leaves fall from the bog-plants, rotting into the earth they sprang from, layered into the thousands of years that lie silent here. By a low, moss-bearded heap of stones, just off the path, you see a green hump. You crouch down and reach out to touch it. The moss comes off in your fingers, showing the peat-stained wooden handle and rust-browned blade of a turf digger's shovel. As you pick it up, the mud that held it splits and opens softly - a tawny rut spreading in the bog. You sink the blade and shaft of the shovel back into the hole and the bog slowly swallows it. The cattails around the cairn tremble. Slowly, as you watch, a tall stick, dark from years of lying beneath the peaty waters of the bog, slowly comes forth. It is forked some way down, the cleft carved in more deeply so that in its dark, slender shadow you see the echo of a tall, long-legged woman's shape.

You stand silent for a moment, gazing at the shadow of the hidden goddess of this place. Slowly you step from the path towards the cleft stave. Your feet sink deeply into the sucking bog that pulls you down into her womb, your tomb. Although you struggle, you cannot break free from her grasp. The cold mud rises past your legs, swallowing you in. A strange, still peace comes over you and you let yourself sink deep into the welcoming peat. As the dark bog closes over your head and your breath stills, you feel yourself melting into someone else, into the body that lies just beneath you, kept by the peaty waters for hundreds of years.

The woman has lain, clad for her marriage, in this water and earth, pinned down by the oaken stake that wed her to the bog so long ago. You feel her long sleep here, beneath turf, beneath the cairn and the stone wall. Dead, you feel the seeping waters working into your skin, darkening it with peat, tanning it to leather. The hoard of life guarded within your pelvis shrinks, preserved like the roots and grains that lie in your stomach; your breasts wrinkle where the soft linen and fur lie over them. A thousand dawns warm you slowly, a thousand nights cool you where you lie beneath, where the grip of sun and snow cannot reach. Your brain darkens in sleep, its hoard fermenting slowly in your peat-stained skull, nestled in the dark coils of your hair, beneath the golden circlet whose jewels have dropped, one by one, from their settings.

Held within the bog's endless darkness, softness, your body is slowly changed, skin dark and grained as bog oak, everlasting as amber and jet. Another winter passes, cold and slow, and again the new sun begins to warm all of the bog slowly, setting some of the seeds within to ferment and sprout. You, too, feel its stirring, rising up from the still body in the bog, through the black peat and slowly out into the brilliance of the sun. A birch tree stands above you, and the dark pool before you reflects your image like a mirror.

You are a young, golden haired maiden clad all in birch leaves and flowers. Where you stretch out your arm, the bog, brown from winter, sprouts into a mist of green. You pass through it, your little bare feet springing lightly over the betraying turf and hidden pools as you spread the new life you have brought forth over the land. When you have completed your round of the bog, you stop again before the slender, dark, cleft fork of the goddess. A few drops of bright water spring forth from the top of the stick, landing on your head in blessing as you bow respectfully to her. Slowly you return to your own body, feet firmly planted on the earth, knowing the power of concealment and birth that is always yours through the rune berkano.

ᛖ EHWAZ

Galdr-sound: aaaaayyyyyy (prolonged sound, as in "day")
Letter: E

(Horse) is, in front of the earls the joy of athlings, a charger proud on its hooves; when concerning it, heroes-wealthy men-on warhorses exchange speech and it is always a comfort to the restless.
— Anglo-Saxon Rune Poem

The horse is the most magical and honored animal in the Teutonic tradition, melding the power of godly wisdom with the earthly might of fertility and the power of bearing the soul from world to world. It is closely identified with the cult of the Twin Gods or Alcis among the Germanic tribes, a pair of deities whom Tacitus described as close analogies to Castor and Pollux; in fact, the stave-shape of the rune is very like the crossbeam which was the sign of the worship of the Twins among the Spartans.

It may also represent a pair of horsemen riding joined together, which was a part of the worship of the Alcis among the Germanji. This is probably related to the Germanic dual kingship: A number of Germanic royal houses traced their ancestry back to a pair of royal brothers or twins, and the practice remained in use through the Saxon invasion of Britain, which was led by two brother-kings named Hengest (stallion) and Horsa (horse). An echo from this root can be seen further north in the prelude to the Eddic lay "Grimnismal" in which, however, Geirroedh dispossessed his brother and co-heir early. The Alcis are also etymologically tied to the rune ehwaz through its alternate name - algiz, or "protection." In this you may see the working of ehwaz as a rune of receiving prophetic wisdom. As a sacred animal, the horse, like the valkyrja, was capable of communicating between gods and humans, and in fact was so used in the divination of one Germanic tribe.

Ehwaz is the rune of the "fetch" or fylgja: that part of the being which appears as a beast showing the inner nature of the person it serves and which may be ridden between the worlds. Like the valkyrja, the fetch can receive and transmit wisdom which is not otherwise available to the vitki's mind. Unlike her, it can be controlled and used by the vitki. The most common forms of the fetch seem to be the bear, stag, and wolf; but mice, whales, dragons, and even thursar and troll-women have been written of. The fetch is in a sense the "totem animal" of the vitki, although it is actually more of a guardian spirit. It can be sent forth separately or ridden. This is discussed further in the chapters on the soul and seidhr-magic. The horse is particularly sacred both to Odhinn and to Freyr, the Lord of Wisdom and the Lord of the World respectively. Hence, the rune ehwaz is very fitting for uniting mystical inspiration with earthly being. In this rune, you may read the mysteries of the alliance between the Hidden One and the Lord.

Ehwaz is used in all matters concerning the harmonious union of dualities, either in the manner of equals, as in the dual kingship, or in the manner of guiding intelligence and manifesting might, as with the human/horse and god/human dualities. As the bonder of equals, it may be used in all matters of friendship and marriage. It is useful in forming ties between two people on all levels, including private telepathic and empathic linkages. It may be useful as an aid to sympathetic magic. Ehwaz is a good rune of fertility, especially in those forms of fertility magic where conception is desired for a magical purpose or to bind a certain being or power to the fetus or newborn. Ehwaz brings power under the guidance of wisdom. In workings of woe, ehwaz may be used to enslave another person's might or thought to your own will. Ehwaz may be used in religious divinations for the purpose of understanding the will of the gods. Comparison with the relationship between god and human in Santeria may be valuable -the person possessed is called the horse, the possessing spirit the rider.

It is also said that "a great god cannot ride a little horse," words of caution which you might be wise to heed in opening your mind. In ritual use, ehwaz is used in relationship to the fetch and, together with the other runes of travel, for faring between the worlds. This is the rune to use in creating and dealing with thought-forms and other conscious or sentient extensions of your own power. Ehwaz is effective in building up a rapport with any vehicle of motion, whether living or magical or mechanical. Used with other runes, ehwaz unites the streams of power in a manner opposite to that of thurisaz. Where thurisaz creates reactive force for the purpose of breaking, ehwaz creates active force by melding for the purpose of integration. You must not forget however, that ehwaz is an essentially mobile energy. The stones associated with ehwaz are turquoise, which builds up the rapport between horse and rider, and sand onyx, which is said to ensure a faithful marriage.

Ehwaz: Meditation

You stand in the middle of a grove of oak and ash trees at sunrise, the new light coming brightly through the leaves that move in a gentle breeze. A little way ahead of you, you see a great white horse grazing quietly. It wears a golden saddle and trappings of gold and turquoise. As you walk nearer to the horse, it looks up and you see the wisdom of the gods in its great dark eyes. It stands gazing at you silently for a moment, then lowers its head and scrapes its right forefoot through the dewy grass. You sense that the horse wants you to mount and this you do as it stands quietly. Mounted on the horse, you are filled with a great feeling of the strength beneath you as its powerful muscles move it into a trot.

You guide it out of the sacred grove with only a little push from your knees; although you hold the reins very loosely in your hands, you know that the horse's might is bonded to your will. You ride out into a wide, grassy field where wildflowers grow thickly, rich with color. Looking ahead, you see another person on a white horse riding towards you. In the sharp light of the risen sun, you see your own image and wonder how the whole plain could be spanned by a mirror, until the other pulls out a rope and you realize that this is your own double riding towards you. Your twin uncoils the rope and tosses one end over to you. You catch it and fasten it around your waist. No words are needed between you, you ride bound together, matching each other move for move and step for step as you urge your steeds into a gallop. As you race, the rope between you becomes shorter and shorter until you are almost touching, yoked so closely that a misstep by either of your horses would bring you both down.

You breathe together, your horses' hooves striking the ground in perfect step and the sharp puffing of their breath so close together that you cannot tell which is which. Slowly your double and your mount merge into you until it seems that you ride alone again. You travel from the field up the side of a mountain, directing your horse over the treacherous, rocky trails. It has an uncanny balance and gait often stepping around pitfalls that you do not see until afterward. Although you are guiding it always upward, you give it enough freedom to let it choose among the paths that it seems to know better than you do. The weather is growing colder, clouds passing across the young sun. You climb through patches of thick white mist on your way up the mountain.

By the time you have reached the top, the sky is gray and the field below has disappeared into an ocean of fog. Your horse halts and shakes its head, stamping its hoof on the rocks to show that you should dismount. You get down, uncertainly watching the horse for another sign. Its dark eyes fixed on yours, it slowly begins to melt into a cloud of white mist which hangs in the air before you. The mist whirls about and starts to take shape again, forming into an foggy animal.

Slowly it resolves itself, individual features appearing from the heavy fog until you look into the eyes of the animal which is the beast-shape of your soul. You know that this is your fylgja standing before you. The saddle and reins which bound you and the horse together are still upon your fetch, though they are in a form suited to it. Moving forward, you take the reins lightly in your hand and seat yourself upon your fetchs back, urging it on with a thought.

Your fetch bears you from the top of the mountain out into the sea of fog below, moving easily and surely through the seething mist between air, water, and earth. You know that you could turn it to ride through any of the worlds now, but it is time for you to return to your own body in Midgardhr again. You ride down through the fog to your earthly shape. Both you and your fylgja merge into it as one, your feet firmly planted on the earth, knowing the power and the part of your being that you can always reach through the rune ehwaz.

ᛗ MANNAZ
Galdr-sound: mmmmmmmmm
Letter: M

(Man) is in his mirth dear to his kinsman although each shall depart from the other for the lord wants to commit by his decree that frail flesh to the earth.
— Anglo-Saxon Rune Poem (see also Elhaz)

The rune-name mannaz is a close cognate to the god Mannus of the Germanic tribes. Mannus was the son of Tvisto, who had sprung up from the earth, and the father of the three races of humanity (slaves, the freeborn, and the noble), The same story is told of the Celtic Mannan mac Lir and of Agni in the Rig Veda. In the Norse legends, the place of Mannus is taken by Heimdallr under the name Rigr, which is the Celtic title meaning "king." Whether the story was passed from the Irish to the Norse or grew independently from Indo-European roots, it still tells the tale of humanity's descent from the gods as well as from earth ("the increase of dust," as mentioned under elhaz).

As the warder of Bifrost Heimdallr is also the linker of humans and the gods, both genetically and consciously, as described in the Rigsthula. After Heimdallr has fathered the three races of men, he returns to teach Earl, first of the line of nobles, and to show him the way to conquer his inheritance. In Germanic mystical tales, the reference to nobility is a code speaking of those people who are able to awaken and use the might within themselves.

Thus it was written that *"Walking Rigr came, taught him the runes / and granted his own name, saying it belonged to his son. / Rigr bade him take possession of Udal Vales and old halls. He rode forth on his horse, swung his sword... Fought for land," "He contended in runes with Earl Rigr. / He battled him in wits, and knew the runes better. / So he came to have for himself / the name Rigr and rune-lore."*[2] The key to this inheritance is the power of the mind, especially as shown through the runes. Note that Rigr's true heir in the second generation is not the first of Earl's sons, but Kon, the youngest. This is an inheritance that can only be won by those who are worthy. Mannaz is the rune of the rational mind, of the intelligence which is the greatest might of human beings.

It shows the interaction of Huginn and Muninn, or Hoenir and Mimir, both embodiments of the faculties of hugr, "thought" and minni, "memory," left brain and right brain respectively.3 Mannaz is the rune of the perfected intellect which melds reason and intuition. As the rune of consciousness, it is particularly associated with Mimir, odhinn's maternal uncle and teacher, and in particular with the story of Mimir's severed head. The tale of Odhinn preserving the head with herbs and spells and getting redes from it in his hours of need is actually a hint towards a ritual of reaching and learning from your "race memory," the transmitted wisdom of your ancestors. In this aspect mannaz is closely related to othala, as hinted by the reference to the "udal lands" (entailed by primogeniture) in the Rigsthula.

The god Heimdallr is, in one sense, the ordering and weal- working side of Odhinn's being as AllFather and teacher, as set against Heimdallr's foe Loki, the embodiment of Odhinn's capricious and woe working nature. Heimdallr is spoken of as highest- minded and brightest of the gods.4 He may be likened to the ever-watchful eagle at Yggdrasill's crown, and Loki to the ever-gnawing serpents at its roots Odhinn, of course, melding the mights of both. Mannaz is the rune of this high-mindedness, emphasizing the highest elements in the human nature as the goal and source of the vitki's self-knowledge and self control. Mannaz is used in all matters of the mind, both in strengthening intelligence and memory and in awakening and guiding the force of psychic abilities.

This rune makes you more aware of the hallowed inheritance you share with the rest of the human race and brings you into relationships with other wights who not only partake of this kinship but also have actively taken it up and are setting out to claim its full might. In workings of woe, mannaz can bring a sense of being "chosen" or somehow better than other beings simply by the fact of birth or potential power. You must remember that although the "myth of inheritance" is always ultimately true, it is an inheritance in which all humans can potentially share. In ritual workings mannaz is the rune of the vitki her/himself. Mannaz represents the perfect human being, balanced and self- guided with a full knowledge of the workings of his/her own mind-for only a person who is in complete control of her/himself can work magic successfully, especially the magic of the runes, which depends so greatly on the shape given it by the spoken galdr as well as on the runes themselves. Without full and complete self- knowledge, the subconscious will twist your workings to fulfill drives that may lead to self-destruction as easily as success.

Used with other runes, mannaz guides their workings into the realm of the mind or, at need, to affect the brain. The stone associated with mannaz is amethyst, which of all stones is traditionally the most powerful concerning reason, memory/intuition, and the capability to effectively meld the two. It brings clearness of mind and aids in the guidance of passion by reason. Its name means "without drunkenness" (Greek), and it shows its might as a moderator and balance~ which is among the best of wisdoms, according to the "Havamal," and well shown forth in the nature of Heimdallr. Amethyst is a sky-oriented stone, fitting for this rune whose stave-shape shows the marriage of heaven and earth.[5]

Mannaz: Meditation

You stand in a dark cave by a stone well. Drops of moisture drip from the tree-roots writhing through the cave's walls. A faint white light glows from a ledge at the rim of the well. As your eyes grow used to the dark, you see the low brow, broad-skulled head of Mimir on the ledge, his white beard stained with streaks of brownish red and white hair faintly discolored by madder and other preservative herbs. His withered eyelids are closed. A circle glows faintly around the head, an interwoven pattern of bind-runes written within. The only one you can make out clearly is the rune mannaz on the outer border of the circle. You draw a small knife from your belt and prick your forefinger with the point. As the blood wells, you trace over the rune with it, intoning the rune-name mannaz.

Where your blood touches it the rune begins to glow dark red, warm with power. Mimir's wrinkled eyelids lift and his deep, ancient eyes stare into yours. He does not speak, but you can feel the wisdom flowing silently from his mind to yours. At last he closes his eyes again. Acting as you know you should, you walk around behind the well. A small wooden door opens from the roots and their twisting shadows in front of you. You pass through it, walking up a long spiral of stone steps, up and around for what seems like hours. Finally you can see light above you, the faint glow of late day. You hasten up the stairs. Coming out, you see that you stand alone on the peak of a high mountain. It seems that all the world is visible below you, cities and towns spread out over the land. Some are hazed by smog or clouds, but none are hidden from your all-seeing gaze.

You find that you can narrow or widen your sight at wilt looking down to watch the movements of individual humans or up to see the patterns of motion that shift around the earth with the slow course of the sun. You see two black specks flying up towards you; looking at them closely, you can tell that they are two great ravens. One moves more swiftly, but often wavers off course; the other flies steady and straight, though now and again it droops a little. Each time it drops, your heart catches with fear. You know that these are your Huginn and Muninn, your thought and memory, and that if one or the other should fail, you are doomed. But they fly straight up to you without fail, swift Huginn landing on your left shoulder and Muninn on your right. You feel the streams of might flowing between them, through your head, an X of energy with the cross-point in the center of your forehead. The nexus becomes warmer and warmer, tingling with awareness; you feel your sight turning inward to that point.

You know that you are actually looking into yourself to see your origin. You recognize the place where your parents lived when you were conceived. A man walks up to the door. He is well-dressed and handsome. You see a radiant nimbus like a silver crown about his head, and just beneath his skin you sense the hidden brightness of the fairest of the gods. He knocks on the door; your parents invite him in and feed him well, clearly charmed by this bright stranger. When the lights go out for bed, he lies between them. You sense the moment when he plants the spark of godly might in your mother's womb like a seed in the nurturing earth.

He stays three days, then walks on again. In the course of nine months, your mother delivers Heimdallr's child. You watch the birthing. As the child comes forth, red and wrinkled but shining with hidden might, you know that it is yourself. Turning your eyes outward again, you are dazzled by the blinding white light around you. Only slowly do your eyes pierce the veil of brilliance to see Rig in his full glory, the White God crowned in silver with a great amethyst at the center of his forehead. You realize that this is your godly father and begin to bow to him, but he stops you with his hand, embracing you instead.

"You are my child and heir," he tells you. "It is time for you to go forth and win your father's power, the udal lands and ancient manors of wisdom and might."

He places a sword in your left hand; in your right he sets a wand with the runes carved around it. Lastly he raises a plain circlet of silver with the rune mannaz graven in the middle.

"I give you this as a sign of the might within you, my child," Heimdallr says. *"You must earn the greater crown for yourself."*

He sets the circlet on your head, the rune over the tingling center of your forehead.

The shining god embraces you again and disappears. As you look out over the earth again, you see a few other faraway mountain peaks, each bearing a single woman or man who, like yourself, bears the sign of their god-father. You know that these are the siblings, with whom you long to meet and talk as friends. The signs of kinship cannot be mistaken; you are sure you will know them again when you meet in the flesh. Slowly you descend the mountain and return to your own body, feet firmly planted on the earth, knowing the power of your holy heritage which you can always reach through the rune mannaz.

ᛚ LAGUZ

Galdr-sound: lllllllll
Letter: L

(Water) is to people seemingly unending if they should venture out on an unsteady ship and the sea-waves frighten them very much and the brine-stallion does not heed its bridle.
— Anglo-Saxon Rune Poem

(Water) is that which falls from the mountain; as a force; but gold objects are costly things.
— Old Norwegian Rune Rhyme

(Wetness) is churning water, and a wide kettle and the land of fish.
— Old Icelandic Rune Poem
Water the bright
— Abcedarium Nordmannicum

I know a fifteenth, which Thiodhroerir the dwarf sang before Delling's door. He sang might to the Aesir, power to the elves, and understanding to Ódhinn.
— Havamal 160

The rune laguz is the rune of primal water, the rivers flowing from Hvergelmir which hold both yeast and venom. In the Teutonic cosmos, it is the water flowing up through the well itself, as distinct from the well (perthro) or the path and action of the water (uruz). Laguz is essentially an undifferentiated force which uruz cleanses, shapes, and guides. You can see this dual nature in the great ambivalence with which the Germanic peoples viewed the waters of their world. Water is the bright waters of life and the dark waters of death. The ocean was a great source of the Norse people's prosperity and their easiest road to travel (Njord), but it was also the greedy devourer of ships and men (Ran) which only one skilled in magic could protect against.

Although the rivers and streams were, quite literally, the waters of life for those who dwelt near them and could not live without them, the Germanic people have more tales of ill-meaning wights in the waterways they depended on than any other people. The most famous of these, of course1 is die Lorelei on the Rhine, luring sailors to their deaths; but her sisters inhabit almost every stream and marsh of the North. Standing water where venom collects and ferments was thought of as much more dangerous than running water, which was active, life-holding, and holy. Grendel and his mother are good examples of the woe-working powers of laguz as it represents the festering subconscious, Grendel is the chronic symptom of the monster-brood hidden beneath the waters of the pool.

When he is slain above water (the symptom is suppressed), his mother wreaks a slaughter several times worse than his had been. Only when Beowulf, whose heroic reputation has been grounded on his abilities as a swimmer, goes down into the pond and slays Grendel's dam in her home do the killings cease. This tale shows the need for the mage to be able to find hidden sources of woe and deal with them in the layer at which the woe was written-able to fare through the lightless waters of the subconscious and the hidden worlds in which magic works alike. Laguz is the rune by which you may search back through the layers of that-which-is and move through its structure at will to read ørlög. As well as being a rune of concealment and the unknown, laguz is a rune by which life is brought forth from darkness and the hidden is brought forth into the light.

It is the "waters of life" which are sprinkled on the newborn child if it was not to be left to die, in order to show its acceptance in the circle of the living. It is also a rune which shows and/or combats poison. The alternate form of the rune's name, laukaz, means "leek," and this is the rune to which Sigrdrifa refers when she tells Sigurdhr, *"You shall sign a blessed drink with these to ward against danger, / and put a leek in the brew. / Then, I know, your mead will never be blended with harm."* The working of the rune in this manner is shown in the saga of Egill Skallagrimsson who, suspecting poison in a drink that had been given to him, scratched a rune several times on his horn, stabbed the palm of his hand, and reddened the runes with blood, whereupon the horn burst asunder-as a result of the sudden inflowing of life- force and yeast acting on the venom-and the drink fell out onto the straw.

All the plants of the allium family, including onion and garlic, show the working and nature of laguz: while the bulb stays hidden, the great life-force in it shows itself by the swift upward growth of the green stalk, and all of these plants are powerful strengtheners in both the physical world and the hidden realms. Laguz is a rune of the transitions between life and death-the awakener at life's beginning and the water to be crossed at its end. You should remember that Odhinn often appears as a ferryman to claim the dead. Laguz is used to fill yourself with life-force and to send that force from world to world. It makes your sensitivity to shifts in the flows of power around you greater, especially when hints of danger may be felt. This sensitivity may also be applied to the magnetic fields of the earth.

Laguz is used to probe the subconscious and the unknown, and mastery of this rune is needed to deal with the problems you find in the realms it governs. In working of woe, laguz is the rune of seduction, deception, illness, and poison. It may be used to worsen chronic health problems and cause longstanding problems of all kinds to surface. Ritually, laguz represents the mead or ale used in rites. It rules all magics of brewing and drinking. It is also seen in the magical use of spittle and blood, the body fluids which carry the life-force. In the personal sphere, laguz may be called upon for physical and magical strength and psychological insight. It is the complement of the conscious mind, mannaz.

Laguz brings out the effects of past workings. Used with other runes, laguz is a strengthener; it may be used in sending runes between worlds. If you wish, you can use it either to set runes to work in secret or to bring them up from their root in the hidden realms of being. A stone that works well with laguz is malachite, whose alternating bands of dark and light green show the twofold being of this rune. Malachite is filled with powerful life-force, a healer with might that flows like the wave. Its layered structure also shows its nature within the Well of Wyrd, a hint towards the use of this rune for sinking to the point of origin and claiming the power flowing from your roots.

Laguz: Meditation

You stand at the bottom of a great waterfall, white spray splashing up into your face from the churning river. A little green boat is tied to the drooping branches of a willow tree on the bank, tugging against the rope in the grip of the current. You step into the boat cutting the rope loose and taking up the oars as your craft skims swiftly downriver, jerking this way and that as you skillfully guide it among the rocks that whip the water into white froth. You sense rather than see the sharp edges below the surface of the water, pushing your boat away from the hidden boulders that could tear its bottom out at any moment. After a while, the water deepens and you move smoothly along with the current down through the twisting of the river through the high, craggy mountains above.

You pass through a region of vineyards and rich farmlands along the side of the great hills, watered by the streams that flow down from the tops of their peaks to feed the river. Although the water you ride on is dark, every now and then you can see the glint of gold in its depths, and the pale flashing of fish. High above the sounds of the river, you hear the faint crystal sound of a woman's voice singing wordlessly. You strain to hear it more closely, but it is cut off as the river turns around the curve of a mountain's foot. When you have rounded the mountain, you hear the voice again, clearer and more compelling, like the sweet voice of a silver bell rippling over the water in shimmering waves of sound. Entranced, you let your oars fall, drifting closer to the hidden singer as the river runs along.

You round one last curve and see her sitting on a rock in the shallow backwaters, her legs hidden beneath the rippling stream. She wears a wet, loosely woven green dress which is half-slipping off one shoulder; long black hair streams around her face and down her back. Her face is beautiful and delicate, innocent but somehow melancholy, as her song is melancholy beneath its beauty. You want to embrace and comfort her; your boat drifts more slowly as you stare at her, lost in her high, clear singing. The sense that warns you of something wrong is the same that warned you of the hidden rocks upriver. Half-entranced still, you put your oars into the water to steer around the peril and strike hard against a jagged line of rocks that would have shredded your boat in a few seconds.

Looking hard at the dark water beyond, you see that the river runs deep and hard around the maiden's rock; if you had followed her call any farther, you would have been drowned. She stops singing, rising up on her rock. Instead of legs, she has the black, scaly tail of a great fish, dripping with moss and water weed. Her mouth opens in a snarl of anger and you see the sharp layers of a shark's teeth within. Hastily you shove out into the main current and let it carry you away from her. You glance back anxiously to see if she has slipped into the water behind you, but she is waiting for her next meal, tail hidden beneath the river and delicate lips curved in a sweet, melancholy smile. As you move along, the earth about you begins to shake, the tremors rocking your boat. You steer as close to the middle of the river as you can.

Slowly the earthquake dies down, but the ruins of a farmhouse to your left tells you that the land has suffered much worse, and not long ago: the broken bricks are freshly whitewashed, and the pool of blood to one side of the rubble is not completely dry. The river runs along swiftly, cutting through high, wave-eaten sandstone cliffs to flow out into the ocean. From behind, you hear a deep rumbling. Looking back, you see the land beginning to shake again, moving more violently until one of the bluffs collapses into a great slide of sand, cracking away in huge chunks that shatter on the beach or topple into the ocean. The high waves catch your little boat and fling it about until something lifts it into the air from beneath, turning it over and casting you into the cold, dark salt water.

Suddenly frightened, you draw your sword and stab out through the water until the blade cuts into something solid. You see the gleam of teeth in the water and feel something large thrashing beside you. Stabbing again, you connect solidly and the thrashing stops. You think about swimming back to the surface, but you are used to the water now; you breathe it easily and your sight is clearing till you can see through the dark green layers of ocean with no more trouble than looking through fog. As the very edge of your vision, large shapes move and circle. You sense a threat and swim deeper, letting the darkness of the water hide you. There are more shapes below, nine water-nicors [water sprite] twice the size of a man but roughly man-shaped, finned and dark- scaled with heads that round into thick ridges of bone running from their eye sockets across the tops of their skulls.

They swim up to you, shark like jaws opening and shutting and sparks of green gleaming from their black eyes. You stab out again and again, fighting the creatures until the waters around you run black with their blood and your arms and legs burn with tiredness. Small fish come to begin tearing the corpses apart, followed by larger fish. You dive quickly before the sharks can reach the scene of the battle. You breathe deep breaths of water, letting its power flow into you and fill you with life until your new strength shines faintly green in the black depths of the sea. At last you come to a great dark wall of underwater rock and the blacker hole of a cave in it. You swim down the narrow passage for a long time, your arms and legs scraping against the slippery moss that lines its walls. You can sense the masses of earth above you; you know that you have come well under the land by the time the passage opens out into a huge cavern. The water here is foul and stagnant. You can see nothing, but as you float in you brush against a huge wall of something solid yet smooth and slimy.

The wall twitches and ripples gigantic muscles, and you realize that this is the huge water dragon whose thrashings have shaken the earth above. Careful not to disturb it, you edge warily around, your back scraping against the high rock ceiling as you move over the mountain of slimy black flesh, feeling your way by the faint flow of water rippling in and out of its gills and the currents stirring around its body. Its long, coiled neck is thicker than an ancient oak tree, its snakelike head wider than a man is tall and twice as long. You reach the place where you can feel the faint curve of its closed eye and breathe in the water's power, gathering yourself to strike.

You sense the tightening in the dragon's muscles, and before it can waken or move again, you plunge the sword in through its eyeball and into its brain with all your might. Its final convulsion jerks the sword out of your hands, flinging you upward and through a hole in the roof of the cavern. The water rushes straight up, carrying you with it through the mountain's last quake. You burst out of the darkness and into the light above the cascading waterfall, the new geyser spurting above you to fling a shining torrent into the air, filling you with a great burst of light. Where the bright drops fall on the ground, a carpet of leeks springs up, their green stalks almost bursting with brilliant might. You bend to pull one up, then return to your own body, feet firmly planted on the earth, knowing the might that you can always reach through the rune laguz.

◆ # INGWAZ

Galdr-sound: Iiiiiiiinnnnnnggggg (bright and clear; the ng sound held as long as possible)
Letter: NG

(Ing) among the East-Danes
was first beheld by men,
until that later time when to the east
he made his departure over the waves,
followed by his chariot
That was the name those stern warriors
gave the hero.
— Anglo-Saxon Rune Poem

The rune ingwaz is the male counterpart to berkano -as berkano is the great mother who receives, conceals, and brings forth, ingwaz is her sacrificed consort and the seed she keeps within her until it is ready for birth. The rune poem may refer to the spring pro- cession of Nerthus in the wagon. As described by Tacitus, and in the Norse equivalents of this procession, the mortal consort of the deity rode in or ahead of the wagon carrying the god's statue, and it is plausible that what is described here is Nerthus' consort mg riding ahead until the goddess' return to the sacred island, when he might very well be slain.

The god mg, of course, would be re-embodied in each year's male sacrifice, and during the days of the procession the incarnation of the god would be encouraged to impregnate as many women as he could. This may be the source of the beliefs of many of the Germanic royal houses that they were descended from mg or Freyr; their ancestors had indeed been fathered by the god dwelling in the body of a man. This may be seen as a Vanic likeness to the ideas shown by the Rigsthula and the rune mannaz unites the divine descendant with the heavens and spiritual wisdom of the Aesir, ingwaz unites her/him with the earth and the nature-wisdom of the Vanir.

The stave-shape of ingwaz may show either the castrated male or the seed: both are appropriate to the rune, as the feminine principle receives the life-force of the masculine principle through both blood and seed, then holds it through gestation and brings it forth into being. This is written of in the story of Freyr and Gerdhr: to win the maiden, Freyr must give up his horse-the symbol of phallic fertility in Vanic rituals and his sword, the symbolism of which is obvious. One of the names of Odhinn is also Jalkr, or "Gelding." This may refer to Odhinn's initiation into the art of seidhr-magic, which, along with some of the Vanic rites of worship, were considered by the general Norse public to be "unmanly."

The reason for this was that to assume the feminine powers of vision and understanding or to give himself up wholly to the feminine principle, a man had to be capable of entirely giving up his masculine identity, even to the point of dressing and living as a woman for a time-a practice common to many forms of Shamanism, and something which Odhinn is implied to have done in his practice of seidhr-magic, as well as something done frequently by his trickster-aspect, Loki. In this manner a man can create in the realms of spirit as a woman does in the earthly world. This is the magic by which the horse Sleipnir, a major vehicle of Odhinn's power, was conceived and born by Loki in the shape of a mare. Ingwaz is the gateway by which a man can achieve a full understanding of the mysteries of women.

The true vitki is, like Odhinn, both wholly bipolar and even hermaphroditic. Ingwaz is the rune by which power is stored, a gateway to the hidden realms. It is the rune which converts active power to potential power. In workings of woe, ingwaz may be used to deprive another of vital force for your own gain or to harm a man's masculinity. In ritual usage ingwaz represents the creation of a "place of power' or any magical reserve which is built up as a storehouse of energy. Used with other runes, ingwaz "stores" their powers until needed; it is therefore a good rune to use when creating a talisman or doing a working upon someone the powers of which can be called upon at need but should not be in effect at all times. In this case you will need to re-color or chant ingwaz after each use, in order to return the active might to its potential state. The stone of ingwaz is ivory, which is essentially masculine but which is said to enable spiritual self sacrifice, showing forth the way in which ingwaz combines virility and passivity.

Ingwaz: Meditation

You stand at the outskirts of a small farming village, just within sight of the little thatched cottages among the muddy fields. The wind is sharp with the ice of early spring; the seeds have not yet sprouted, leaving you in the middle of a sea of brown earth. You watch along the sodden, earthen road until you see a procession of horses and wagons approaching. The sun gleams from the golden head of the first rider, whose great brown stallion trots ahead of the group. Behind the wagon, a faint ripple of green runs along the muddy ground as the power of the hidden goddess within brings the seeds forth to life. People are beginning to crowd around you to watch them approach - farmer-folk thin from the long winter who greet the goddess and her consort with the joy of knowing that their fields will be fruitful and food plentiful next harvest.

Ing leads his stallion to the center of the village, the mare- drawn wagon of the goddess rumbling behind him. The fresh spring breeze tosses his golden hair and beard, his sky-blue cloak streaming out behind him. The old women of the town lead out the maiden who has been chosen most worthy of the god. She is dressed only in birch branches and flowers, her long brown hair rippling down over her half hidden breasts. The wagon stops as the Lord drops his breeches and takes her in full view of the town as his stallion mounts the wagon's mare. Should she bear a child of the god, it will be a sure sign of his lingering blessing. At first she is frightened and shy, but as the grasses sprout around her in the wave of might from Nerthus' wagon and the strength of the god fills her, she cries out in her joy. Ing remounts his satisfied stallion and the godly procession rides onward, Ing before the wagon and a riderless mare behind it.

With the other farmer-folk, you follow it to the edge of the village. The empty backed mare stops before you there, waiting for you to mount her. You ride behind god and goddess as Nerthus spreads spring through the meadow, grass sprouting and trees budding as she passes. The procession travels to the edge of the ocean; a ferry waits on the white beach. You follow mg and the wagon over the sand and onto the ferry which, unmanned, slides out onto the rolling swells and bears the god, the goddess, and yourself to the shore of a small marshy island. As you ride off the ferry, you see that the coat of your mare is dulled and that she plods along as if she were about to collapse at any moment. The mare pulling the wagon can barely set one hoof in front of the other. The power which brought the earth back to life is entirely drained. Only Ing and his stallion are still strong and vital. His steed trots along, tossing his head from side to side as though he scented danger on the wind. The wagon stops at the edge of a boggy lake.

You and mg both dismount and you lead your horse up beside the wagon's mare. A veiled woman steps from the wagon, her head and body wholly covered by draping of dark green and brown. She holds a long knife in her hand. Ing's stallion freezes into silence when she touches him, standing still as Nerthus reaches beneath his belly and slices away his great penis and testes. A river of blood spurts forth into the bog; the stallion drops, splashing heavily into the mud. Nerthus gives his gonads to the two mares, who devour them eagerly. Their coats become shiny and healthy again as they eat. They whisk their tails about, raising their heads with new brightness in their eyes.

You can see now that both of them are very pregnant bellies widening and teats swelling. Ing draws his sword and gives it, hilt-first, to the goddess. She casts it out into the bog, the soft mud swallowing it without a splash. Ing takes off cloak, tunic, and breeches, standing before her in his flawless nakedness. Nerthus wraps a twisted rope like a torc [metal neck ring] around his neck, pulling it tight as she cuts his genitals away. His seed and blood spurt into the open bog together. Nerthus lets go of the strangling cord and Ing's body topples. The goddess, now pregnant like her mares, steps into the bog and is gone. You move forward carefully, pushing the naked corpse deeper into the cold mud and scooping mud up with your hands to cover his fair skin. You can feel the power thrumming just below the surface of the earth, refilled with the life-force of the Lord. Slowly you return to your own body, feet firmly planted on the earth, knowing the mysteries contained and reachable through the rune ingwaz.

ᛞ DAGAZ

Galdr-sound; dhaaa-dhaaa-dliaaa (dhi pronounced as thin "the."
Slightly prolonged; loud and clear with a sharp moment of silence
between each sound)
Letter: D, Dli, Th (as in "the," rather than the th of "thorn")

(Day) is the lord's messenger dear to men the ruler's famous light:
Mirth and hope to the rich and poor useful for all.
— Anglo-Saxon Rune Poem.

The Teutonic day should not be confused with the current Western idea of day as simply the period of light. The Norse counted the twenty-four-hour period by nights and measured it by the solar lighting (see raidho) which was divided into two "days" - sunrise to sunset and sunset to sunrise. Hence the idea of "day" holds the idea of transition between the time of light and the time of darkness. This thought is also shown in the story of the birth of Day in the Prose Edda. Night was the dark daughter of a giant called Norfi. Her first marriage was with a chthonic being named Naglfari (ship of the dead) by whom she bore a son named Audh ("the wealthy"; fitting when you think of the association of the world beneath the earth's surface with treasure).

KVELDÚLF GUNDARSSON

She was next married to Annar ("The Second"), whom other references hint was Odhinn in one of his many disguises. Their daughter was Jord, the Earth, the mother of many of the gods and goddesses including Thor and Frigg. Her last mate was Delling ("the Shining One") who fathered Day on her, after which both Night and Day were set to ride through the sky, Night on the horse Hrimfaxi (Frostymane) and Day on the horse Skinfaxi (Shining Mane),

This progressive synthesis with leads from the chthonic to the heavenly realms shows the waxing power of synthesis. Night's first husband is of a nature not far removed from her own giantish heritage. Her second husband, Odhinn, is more of an opposite and hence their child is higher and more powerful than the first. Delling is Night's exact polar opposite, and their union not only creates the transcendent being Day but 'Hi the original participants to the same level of transcendence. Dagaz is the completion of the processes of gebo and elhaz. The synergy gained by the active exchange of energies shown in gebo - the "alchemical marriage" - reaches its transcendent substance in dagaz. This rune may fairly be compared to the spiritual philosopher's stone. In sexual alchemy, dagaz is the moment of orgasm in which the goal of the working is made real.

As the completion of elhaz – the moment of unity with the valkyrja and the higher realms- dagaz is written out in the Sigrdrifumal in which Sigurdhr must pass through the barrier which is described variously as a fire and a wall of shields (elhaz) to awaken his valkyrja Sigrdrifa, whereupon she chants the *"Hail to day."*[1] Dagaz is the rune of the achievement of transcendent consciousness, in which the participant becomes one with the universe in a flash of blinding awareness. It is the moment of awakening, the eternal moment of being reached through Hegel's process of thesis - antithesis-synthesis. Dagaz is chiefly useful as a rune of meditation. It transforms consciousness and being on all levels.

Magically, dagaz can be used to bring something to completion, particularly in the settings described above. It is useful in all workings of an "alchemical" type, whether they be practical or solely concerned with consciousness. Ritually, dagaz represents the moment of power at sunrise and sunset. Used with other runes, dagaz synthesizes their might into a single transcendent awareness. It is generally most desirable when you are dealing with runes of inspiration and wisdom. Dagaz is a rune of triumph and new beginnings on a higher level; it can be written to bring these about. The stone associated with dagaz is fluorite, which is said to balance the mights of light and darkness within the mind. You will notice that, when viewed from above any point, octahedral crystals of fluorite show two interlocking dagaz shapes.

Dagaz: Meditation

You sit on top of a mountain. It is night, faint stars bright in the black sky above you. You are clad in a heavy robe of black which weighs down your limbs. Your thoughts and movements sluggish, slowed by the dull cold of night. Slowly, almost imperceptibly at first, the eastern sky before you begins to gray. You can see the black shadow-shapes of mountains around you, faint against the first paling of morning as the eastern stars grow dimmer. The day strengthens, rimming the black peaks with paling blue, faint light pushing against the heavy blanket of night.

The layers below are still sunk in dark, black firs, lost in an ocean of blackness, but the lightening east begins to show the mountaintop around you-jagged gray boulders stud the dry earth, and sparse grasses sprout like the coarse pelt of a wolf. The sky above you is dark blue, fading to the paleness of morning in the east, where the first yellowness begins to tint the colored sky with light. Behind you the west is still black, the morning star shining through the brightening heavens.

The east grows brighter and brighter - showing the jagged edges of the black pines below you. An ocean of light flows slowly into the dark night-blue above, gold and pink rising with the sky- blue of day. As the first burning edge of the sun rises behind the gray mountaintops around you. You leap to your feet; the dark metal that had weighted you falling away. Your head is filled with a dizzying rush of lightness. You take up your horn of mead and drink off the golden liquid, honey and fire flowing exultingly down your throat. You seem to be floating in midair, suspended between the day before you and the night behind you in the moment of their greatest flow and power. Joyously you toss the horn away a- cross your arms over your chest in the shape of the rune dagaz, feeling day and night meet within you.

Ecstatically you cry out;

> *"Hail, day! Hail, ye day's sons!*
> *Hail, night and the daughters of night! Look down upon me here*
> *with friendly eyes And grant victory to the one here.*
>
> *Hail the Aesir! Hail the Asynjur! Hail, him on the giving earth!*
> *Goodly speech and human wit may you grant to me, the mighty, and*
> *hands of healing1 while I live. Hail!"[2]*

Slowly you return to your own body, knowing that the transcendent power and wisdom of dagaz will always be within you.

ᛟ OTHALA

Galdr-sound: oooooooo (as in "oath")
Letter: o

(Estate) is very dear to every man if he can enjoy what is right and according to custom in his dwelling most often in prosperity.
— Anglo-Saxon Rune Poem

The root idea of othala is that of the boundary separating the innangardhs from the utangardhs, the known and guarded from the unknown and dangerous. This boundary naturally came to define the land which could be inherited, and in due course, kinship, social position, and even law and custom. For example, othala establishes the degrees of relationship within which one might avenge a wrong against a clan member by killing or claiming money from the offender.1 The boundaries of law were clearly defined in almost every case, and usually this was according to inheritance and birth. Although the Teutonic people were not awed by noble or royal parentage, there was a strong distinction made between those born of free parents, those born of bond servants, and those born of thralls. Exceptions came in the cases of those born of unwed free persons or certain types of mixed-class unions in which the father, if the kin agreed, was required to hold a rite of adoption to bring the child within the boundaries of the kin.

Also when a child of any social class was weak or deformed, it was not slain outright but rather, b& mg unworthy of the support of the clan, was left outside the boundaries of its land - circumstances under which even an adult could hardly survive, as seen by the high degree of severity attached to the punishment of outlawry. The Norse were no harsher in this respect than any other people of their time, and far less so than the Spartans, for instance; however, their circumstances were such that they could not afford to support a drain on their resources. It was considered that the child did not have a soul until the ninth day, and was thus not entirely human. The naming ceremony bound the soul to the child and brought it within the circle of a clan, after which exposure would be seen as murder. As the rune of inheritance, othala rules not only the bounds of the clan itself but also the mysteries of inherited power.

This rune is tied to the wisdom of the kinjylgja, a guardian power who bears a resemblance to the fylgja, the valkyrja and the disir. The kinfylga is a feminine personification of a particular family's might who usually attaches herself to the head of the clan, although at times she will pass to a younger member who is better fit to wield her might. Othala rules both that might which is inherited from the genetic ancestors and that which is inherited from the ~ancestors" of the spirit-that is, your previous existences. Either, or both if they are harmonious, may be the determinant of the nature of your personal power. In the end, this leads back to the "udal lands" of the Risgthula, the divine inheritance shown in mannaz. This is the rune of Odhinn's might as Allfather: by his inheritance of the might of both jotuns and gods, he has become identified with the roots of power for every living being.

His assumption of this heritage makes him the fit leader of every clan. Although othala is an enclosure, it is not an isolated enclosure. It may be gainfully increased through the powers of gebo expressed as marriage, as the giving of hostages, or as the relationship between ring-giver and warrior, although the ties of inherited blood usually prove to be stronger than the legal inclusion within the clan. As the final rune and completion of the futhark, othala holds all the runes; the power of the runes is our own mystical heritage. The rune othala is used to strengthen the ties of clan, especially those which relate to family customs and practices. This encompasses all those of similar physical and/or spiritual ancestry, the sibs of blood and soul. Othala is used to bring out wisdom and power from all sources of your heritage, including past-life knowledge and talents.

It is particularly useful here in conjunction with mannaz and ansuz (mark the numerical correspondence also). It may be used to gain an earthly inheritance in cases of legal questions, or to bring you back to the homeland of your ancestors and roots into family history. Othala is used to gain wealth in the form of possessions and immobile property, as set against the mobile wealth of fehu. It also protects that which you rightfully own. Othala shows both inclusion and exclusion; in workings of woe, it may in certain combinations and settings be used to cast an individual out beyond its borders, the borders of human society. It may also create a sense of racial or cultural prejudice.

The vitki working with this rune must always be careful not to let her/himself be bound by it! In ritual workings, othala shows the circle or ritual enclosure. The outer circle is the ordinary space of society (Midgardhr); the circle of the vitki is the holy circle, corresponding to Asgardhr. It also shows the mysteries of the ancestors and the blood-and-soil of the homeland as the truth held in all the beliefs about "native earth." Used with other runes, othala defines their sphere of working, particularly in those cases where the matter at hand is a boundary of some kind-magical, social, or physical. It is good as a part of warding. It may also be used well in meditations to learn more of your past. A stone which works well with othala is petrified wood, which is particularly known for its capability to bring out the memories and talents of past lives, and which can also be used to awaken the slumbering dragon of ancestral might.

Othala: Meditation

You stand outside, in a valley, at sunset, inside a fence which encloses a wide diamond-shaped yard around a house. You recognize this house as your childhood home, set alone in this bit of fertile land surrounded by high, rocky mountains. You begin to walk the long stretch of the fence around the field, tools in your hand to repair any breaks in it you might find. The sky darkens quickly when the sun has sunk behind the dark mountain peaks. The wind from the heights moans and howls eerily, sweeping down through the rocks in a whispering blast of cold. As the night settles into windy blackness, you see that the fence is beginning to glow with a faint golden light. You sense that wild things are moving beyond its border. You can just see the shadows of their misshapen forms.

One of the wild things lopes up to the fence, moving now on four legs, now on two, lifting its face up to sniff at the boundary. It seems to be a manlike wolf or wolf like man, with flat face and long limbs covered with coarse gray hair. The wolf-creature howls, a mournful, desperate sound that sets the hairs prickling up on your arms and down your back, and runs back into the night. You know that you have seen a vargr, an outlaw, cursed to live as a wolf beyond the bounds of kin and clan, and shudder in both pity and revulsion. Finally you have completed your rounds of the fence. Certain that nothing can break through it, you enter your house. Your family is eating dinner inside; it is warm and bright, and you are glad to join them. As you eat, you see a faint brightness out of the corner of your eye.

You turn your head and see the rune othala in bright gold upon the floor. Inside it stands a woman in golden robes. Her hair is streaked with gray, though she is strong and tall; her eyes are bright with wisdom. Although you do not know her, you can tell by her features that she is a member of your family. Your kinswoman beckons to you. You push back your hair and go to her, entering the enclosure of the rune through the crossed lines at its base. As you step in, the rune grows until it seems that you and your kinswoman are standing inside a small cottage-a cottage such as your northern ancestors lived in hundreds of years ago, with hard-packed earthen floor, thatched roof, and a fire in the middle sending a trail of smoke up to dim the stars that shine through the smoke hole.

You feel power thrumming up into your bare feet from the earth; you know that it is part of you, earth filled with the bones and blood of your forefathers and fore mothers for generations. Their might is passing into you from the ancestral soil filling you with their magic and strength. You feel that you bear the waxing power of a thousand generations within you, might like a great wave sweeping through you and filling your mind with secrets, wisdom hidden in the blood and soul that has ghosted down the ages from father to son, mother to daughter, your true heritage coming forth at last. Your kinfylgja places a wand in your right hand. On it is carved a great othala-rune with the whole futhark written within. She bends down and scoops up a handful of earth, pressing that into your left hand until it melds into your flesh. You stand still as she steps forward, her being and might passing into you. Slowly you return to your own body, feet firmly planted on the earth, filled with your own ancestral might and wisdom, which you can always reach through the rune othala.

8 RUNIC RELATIONSHIPS

There are two chief types of relationships between runes: structural and conceptual. Structural relationships are those determined by placement in the futhark order, including division into aettir, Schneider's "futhark pattern of manifestation," = and all relationships discovered through number. Conceptual relationships are those in which the basic idea of a rune is closely tied to the basic idea of another, either overtly through name and references in the Rune Poems or through linkages of nature and function. Because of the manner in which all of the runes are woven together, one may, and should try to, find an endless number of ties between them.

One may see here a model of the universe as a whole and of the human mind at work, keeping in mind that even the most contorted chain of logic will come up with truth when working to prove something true-in this case, the dependence of every part of the universe on every other part and the infinite web of connections between them. One may observe how well the Qabalists have done by the use of gematria (numerical calculations in which each Hebrew letter is assigned a number and words of the same value are assumed to be equivalent in nature) . . . or even by discovering Qabalistic truths in the rhymes of Mother Goose.2 Although the latter may sound exceedingly silly, the discipline of looking into everything-no matter how frivolous or ordinary-to see the workings of the runes is an excellent form of meditation, strengthening both one's capabilities to use the runes practically and one's ability to read the cast runes aright.

STRUCTURAL RELATIONSHIPS

The greatest complex of structural relationships, which was the best-known of traditional (pre-Christian) runic theory, is the division of the futhark into aettir, a curious term which may mean either "eights" or "families." This term is also used for the eight divisions of the compass and their winds. The division of the futhark into aettir was retained even after it was reduced to the Younger form and no longer made up of three literal "eights."

The first aett is formed of the essential elements and abilities which the vitki must have developed within her/himself: magical force (fehu), vital shaping power (uruz), dynamic/active force (thurisaz), inspiration and galdr-skill (ansuz), rhythm and timing (raidho), control of energies and skill to craft them (kenaz), the ability to give and receive power (gebo), and self-confidence in an integrated personality (wunjo). This is called Freyja's aett because it be- gins with the first rune of her name and is largely defined by the runes associated with her, beginning with the basic energy of fehu and continuing with the ability to control, form, and use the power in Midgardhr and the immediately surrounding worlds in< which the might of Freyr and Freyja mainly works.

The second aett is alternately called Hagal's aett and Heimdall's aett. (* Schneider proposes an unknown god Hagal, possibly associated with the creation of the world, as an explanation for some of the mysteries of hagalaz; there is no reference to this being in any other source.) This aett holds within' itself the runes writing forth the shape of the cosmos, those being also the runes of the vitki's initiation into the higher levels of consciousness. It begins with the wholeness of the universe's structure (hagalaz) and continues through testing to awaken the inner fire (nauthiz), primal ice and the bridge of consciousness (isa), the cycles of the year and the growth of the seeds of power within the vitki (jera), the vertical trunk of Yggdrasill and the initiation by ordeal (eihwaz), the Well of Wyrd and the vitki's ability to understand and use its power, the yew-tree/Bifrost bridge and the communication between vitki's and valkyrja, and the wheel of the sun and the vitki's magical will (sowilo).

Both the hailstone (hagalaz) and Heimdallr are found in the naming this aett, the one marking it as the aett of cosmological structure, the other as the aett of rising awareness and expanding consciousness, as Heimdallr, the guardian of the bridge, also hears everything that happens in the Nine Worlds. The third aett is called the aett of Tiwaz because of the rune that begins it: the spear is the emblem of Tyr in his oldest aspect as Sky-Father, and it is this aspect to which the aett-name refers esoterically. For this reason some moderns have chosen to rename this the aett of Odhinn, as appropriate to his later status and the character of this aett as the aett of the gods and the fully initiated vitki.

Tiwaz is the Sky Father/victory rune; berkano the Great Mother, birth, and death; ehwaz the Twin Gods and kings; mannaz the godly might of men, laguz the power over life and hidden sources; ingwaz is Yngvi-Freyr and the god's sacrifice; dagaz the rune of transcendent completion; and othala the inheritance that encompasses all. Within the aett-structure are the eight triads formed by the division of the futhark into aettir. These combinations often prove to be among the most practical of structural relationships in runic workings. Meditating on their interrelationships is a most valuable source of insight into the more hidden sides and uses of each rune. They further offer another guide to the reading of cast runes, should runes of a triad come up together.

> *Fehu force Hagalaz form.*
> *Tiwaz force directed by form.*
> *Uruz cleansing and transformation by water.*
> *Nauthiz cleansing and transformation by fire.*
> *Berkano vessel of cleansing and transformation (athanor).*
> *Thurisaz dynamic/disruptive unity.*
> *Isa immobile/integrative unity*
> *Ehwaz mobile/integrative unity.*
> *Ansuz Odhinn's gift, the seed planted   .*
> *Jera growth of the godly seed in humanity*
> *Mannaz the vitki claiming the full godly inheritance.*
> *Raidho solar journey/death.*
> *Eihwaz mystical journey/ death.*
> *Laguz watery journey/death.*

Mark that this also forms a perfect conceptual triad linked by the horse of raidho, the "brine stallion" of laguz, and Kenaz hidden shaping/creation of the svartalfar [dark alfar/elves]. Perthro well hiding the workings of Wyrd which shape the worlds of being Ingwaz power sent into the hidden realms for the sake of creation.

Gebo sacrifice/exchange binding loyalty between humans and gods.
Elhaz communication between humans and gods.
Dagaz transcendent unity of human and godly awareness.
Wunjo harmony/unity of will.
Sowilo magical will triumphant.
Othala inheritance of being and stronghold of the will.

The interrelationships of the aettir structure are followed by Thorsson's "futhark pattern of manifestation": the pairing of runes in the futhark row from the center outward, usually in contrasting or complementary conceptual patterns.

Eihwaz vertical/instantaneous illumination
Jera spiral/gradual growth compare the straight sushumma and the dual spiral of ida and pingala in kundalini yoga
Isa contraction/immobility
Perthro interactive evolution.
Nauthiz resistance, self sufficiency, internally generated fire
Elhaz acceptance, attraction towards valkyrja
Asgardhr, godly cleansing fire of Bifrost.
Hagalaz determinant immobile form
Sowilo determinant mobile force
(Sowilo is also universal structure and individual will).
Wunjo social harmony/balance achieved through love.
Tiwaz social harmony/balance achieved through law.
Gebo mutual exchange, growth through interaction.
Berkano reception and retention, growth through incubation.
Kenaz control achieved through technical skill.
Ehwaz control achieved by mutual trust and union.
Raidho structure of society.
Mannaz structure of the human microcosm.
Ansuz conscious inspiration transforming subconscious awareness (laguz).

Note the ties between the Odhroerir mead of ansuz and the identification of laguz with yeast and the magics of brewing.

Thurisaz direct aggressive force, phallic male
Ingwaz sublimated/passive force, castrated male.
Uruz evolving separation/creation.
Dagaz timeless, transcendent synthesis/being.
Fehu mobile power, strife among clan.
Othala immobile power, clan enclosure.

Beyond this point, numerical analysis of runic patterns becomes both endless and ever more highly individualized, being really most useful either in meditations or when one is doing an analysis for a certain ritual. For instance, in a rite to draw on the wisdom of one's ancestors, you might take into account that numerically mannaz (20) holds within itself the powers of ansuz (4) multiplied by raidho (5), both of which are also structurally and conceptually tied to mannaz and hence will greatly enhance its workings; further, mannaz (20) plus ansuz (4) equals othala (24), which is obvious in this context. Needless to say, this will work better in some things than in others. The art of the vitki consists, among other things, in being able to tell which method of association is most effective under which circumstances. Regular experimental meditations are good for this purpose, and various numerical patterns may offer a guide to beginning these meditations.

CONCEPTUAL RELATIONSHIPS

Conceptual relationships are, by their nature, harder to classify than structural relationships; however, they turn out many times to be somewhat easier to work with. When one has seen the process of identifying conceptual relationships by different means, one should quickly be able to find a host of correspondences and build up one's personal work with them on one's own. Perhaps the most obvious of conceptual relationships are those which fall into clear elemental categories. Among the fire runes are fehu, kenaz, nauthiz, eihwaz, and elhaz; fehu may be used to strengthen the working of any of the others. The runes of ice are isa and hagalaz.

In the category of water are laguz, perthro, and uruz, the relationship between which has been discussed at length. Ansuz and tiwaz (as the Sky-Father) are the runes of air. The runes of earth are berkano, ingwaz, jera, and othala. Outside of these categories, the remaining runes are those that show the interactions between the elemental powers. Indeed, all the runes do this to some extent, being different aspects of the primal forces working through the universe; but a distinction can be made between the runes that clearly characterize a single element and the runes of synthesis.

The rune poems are also a good guide to conceptual relationships: sowilo's use in guiding one over the sea as written forth in the Anglo-Saxon Rune Poem clearly shows it as an answer to the perils of the sea written of in the verse for laguz, for instance. The relationship between ehwaz, the horse, and the three different types of horses mentioned in the raidho/eihwaz/laguz triad should be clear; ehwaz, the fetch, is the vehicle of the farings written forth in the runes of traveHing1 while the understanding of ehwaz in connection with one's earthly vehicle is needed if one is to be able to use raidho to keep it going and protect it on the road.

Whenever one finds the name of one rune or a reference to its action in the verse of another, one should meditate on the ties between the two and the use of the one in complementing, controlling, or mitigating the workings of the other. The most traditional conceptual divisions of runic action are written forth in the Sigrdrifumal. These are victory runes, ale runes (for dealing with the turnings of Wyrd), help runes (in birthing, or bringing-to-being), sea runes, limb runes (for healing), speech runes, and mind runes. Obviously most of the runes fall into more than one of these categories, although they may seem stronger in one aspect than another. Rather than trying to break down the futhark, the rede here would seem to be to learn all the various workings of each rune and how to use them effectively in all the possible ways, discovering which work together in which categories and manners.

The rune poems and the Havamal will, again, be excellent guides at first for association in this way. Runic relationships can also be found in the shapes of the staves. This is particularly clear when one stave is put in the place of another, as in the case of the Elder elhaz replacing mannaz in the Younger Futhark or the alternate Elder ingwaz set for the Anglo- Saxon jera. One of the better examples of the use of shape-determined relationships is the alu formula, a common runic inscription which calls on the flow of magical energy, vital force and inspiration.

Laguz is the life-force flowing upward; ansuz shows the same shape effective on and transformed through both the conscious and the subconscious; uruz shows this power flowing through every level of being as a vital, shaping energy. The formula laukaz, "leek," also begins with this combination of like-shaped staves, adding the craft of kenaz and the guarding might and upward-reaching spiritual power of elhaz to the basic idea. The fact that each word also has a fitting meaning; alu being a drink that both strengthens and inspires, tied to the source-thought of laguz by that rune's use in brewing magic, and laukaz being the quick-growing, vital leek which was also used in kennings for "warrior"-adds a further dimension of might to these inscriptions.

9 READING THE RUNES

Reading the runes rightly is perhaps the most difficult of the runic skills, as it calls for a deep and thorough knowledge of all the runes and their interaction with each other, as well as considerable insight and the mental training not to be swayed by your desire for a certain answer. You must know how the runes work for woe as well as for weal and always be on your guard against the tendency to put the most favorable interpretation on every rune that falls Unlike the Tarot, reversal of runes has no meaning; their aspects depend entirely on position, interaction, and the context of the question. Perhaps the best way to learn how to read the runes is to do it daily in the morning, writing down the runes and your reading of them, and then at night writing what occurred in the course of the day and comparing it to the runes of the morning. As so much of the practice of this lore has been lost, it can only be reclaimed through practice together with contemplation.

MAKING THE RUNES

The most traditional method of making the runes is to carve them individually on twigs, small wands, or slips of wood. This should be done as if each were a taufr, except that rather than using a galdr-spell to shape the force into the use one wants, you should strive to fill the stave with the wholeness of its being, both for weal and for woe. You may make runes for longterm use, or, in matters of great importance, carve a set of twigs for a single casting, after which they are burnt. If you are unable to make your own runes, you should cleanse, charge, and color a bought set as if you had made it yourself. In empowering the casting runes, after the Circle Rite, you should call on the power of Odhinn and on Urdhr, Verdhandi and Skuld. For a single-use ritual, this calling should also include your question. The steps of concealment and bringing forth after the carving and coloring may be left out altogether, or you may replace them with these steps:

Wrap the runes in a black cloth, binding them about nine times. Chant:
"Within the dark waters of Urdhr's deep well Wait all Wyrd's runes the world there written Nine nights in the web the knowing Norns weave".

Walk the circle nine times deosil, your body turning widdershins. Trace the rune perthro around the wrapped runes with gandr or sax, singing its name.Unwrap the runes, intoning:
Runes written forth to work from Wyrd's well
Flow forth from the darkness to be read a right
Written by Urdhr Verdhandi and Skuld
Show me what is what shapes and shall be!

In a single-use ritual, the staves may be cast now; otherwise, say, *Wrought is the work. So shall it be!*

See the runes enclosed in a shining sphere of might which holds the power in them, ready to show the streams of their force flowing forth from the Well when they fall. Place them in their pouch or casting cup.

Absorb the energy of the circle into yourself or return it to the universe.

CASTING THE RUNES

The simplest method of rune-casting is the three-rune spread. Holding the pouch or casting cup, you should face north with closed eyes, meditating on the Well of Urdhr and the streams of power flowing forth from it to shape the tree Yggdrasil (some of the images from the meditation on perthro may be helpful here). You now concentrate on the shape of your question and try to feel the streams that are flowing into it. When you feel a strong connection, you should trace the rune perthro around the pouch or cup and say,

> Flowing now forth from Wyrd's world-well
> Staves shall show all
> Set into being
> Urdhr who is Verdhandi becometh
> Shadow-Skuld should be!

Cast the runes onto the cloth. Eyes closed, pick up three runes, whispering "Urdhr-Verdhandi-Skuld," and lay them out in that order. The first will show that which is-the roots and layers shaping the situation you asked about. The second will show that which is coming into being now, and the third will show what should result from the interweaving of Urdhr and Verdhandi if nothing is done to change things. The three-rune reading may, if you wish, be expanded into nine, which will give you a more complete view of the factors interacting in each phase of being.

A more complex method, which is much more likely to be accurate and easier to judge with regards to weal-working and woe- working aspects of the runes, is to follow the ritual up to the casting, but rather than picking three or nine runes up, to leave them all untouched on the cloth and interpret them from there. Only those which have fallen face-upward should be read; those which are face down are the runes of forces that are either too deeply hidden to affect the immediate question or are absent from the situation. The positions in which they fall will help you to determine both meaning and degree of importance.

You should try to see the overall pattern of the runes first, tracing out the major lines or clumps of runic power, which will represent the chief factors at work in the reading. Generally lines will show you a progression of force, moving from the rune nearest the reader outward; clumps will indicate that the runes in question are working together simultaneously. When the runes fall in relatively straight lines, the next thing to look for is smaller lines that cross the greater ones at perpendicular angles. These lines are lines of blockage; the runes in them will work woe, reacting badly with the runes of the greater progression. They are hazards which must be crossed or written around. Lesser lines that slant into the greater lines may be seen as "feeders." They are lesser factors that contribute to or rise from the larger progression.

They will more often work weal than woe, although not invariably. Some runes do not work well together in any position, while others almost never work weal in any ordinary situation. A sudden decline of energy in a linear pattern (say, from fehu or sowilo to isa) or a rune of disruption (such as thurisaz or hagalaz) should in most cases be taken as a warning. In clumps you should look for interactions within aettir divisions and conceptual interaction to determine which aspects of each rune will show through.

Berkano together with ingwaz or jera, for instance, will in most cases show a good result, while berkano next to isa would show great inactivity, silence, and perhaps even death. Runes that touch interact more strongly than runes that do not. Slight overlapping may be a sign of unity: one rune hiding another shows either concealment or blockage and woe-working, depending on whether the topmost stave is one that normally indicates concealment or not. Unfortunately, the market is flooded with texts on what is alleged to be runic divination, written by people with little knowledge of magic and less of Teutonic tradition (one book even calls the runes, which are almost purely Germanic in origin and solely Germanic in use, the Celtic Runes!). You should beware of "experts" who cannot backup their expertise with legitimate historical research and knowledge of the Teutonic mind.

10 TOOLS OF TEUTONIC MAGIC

The ritual implements of Teutonic magic are somewhat simpler in conception than those of traditional ceremonial magic, although the correspondences, materials, etc. can be elaborated upon to the limits of the vitki's ingenuity.

THE SAX

The most important tool used in runic magic is the sax-knife with which the runes are carved. For a skilled runic worker, this is the only tool necessary, as described in the Egil's Saga wherein the hero Egil Skallagrimson, works a number of magics at need simply by carving and coloring the runes. The sax is edged on one side only, slanting sharply down from the dull side about an inch back from the point; It is exceedingly important that this knife be kept sharp, both for symbolic purposes and for ease of cutting and shaping wood for tines, carving the runes, and drawing blood if that is the means of coloring used. The sax can be used in every case where the gandr is called for.

Unlike ceremonial magic, Teutonic magic uses the knife for invoking and sending force as well as for banishing. The only magical purpose for which the knife should almost never be used is the cuffing and digging of magical herbs, because the touch of cold iron is considered to break their power. This may of course be wished in certain cases where you are breaking an enchantment. The point of the sax is also useful in laying pigment into the runes, although if blood is used you must be very careful about cleaning it after to avoid corrosion. Some vitkar prefer to use a thin triangle of wood for inlaying the pigment and a special carver or ristir for etching runes into various surfaces. Fitting gods to call upon in the hallowing of the sax are Odhinn (who, as Lord of the Runes, should be called upon in all rites dealing with the runes in general), Tyr, and Freyr. In all hallowing of runic tools, it is also well to call upon Urdhr, Verdhandi, and Skuld, the three Norns.

THE GANDR

The gandr, or wand, is used for calling up, sending, and charging objects with runic force. The exact thickness and length will of course be the personal choice of the vitki, depending on your circumstances; if you want to carry it in a purse or a pocket, it will clearly need to be fairly small, whereas if you have a full harrow (altar) set up, it may be quite a bit bigger. Generally, the gandr should not be thinner than a finger nor too thick to wrap your hand around; a measurement often found is the length from elbow to either the tip or the base of the middle finger. It is good, if you can, to keep all of your tools in relative proportion to each other and to yourself, thinking of them as extensions of your own being. The gandr is traditionally made out of either wood or bone.

Hazel and yew are perhaps the most traditional; ash and oak are also good, and if you feel a particularly strong pull to a certain tree, you are best advised to go with that rather than crippling your own magic for the sake of a system. In the case of bone, it should come from an animal that the vitki knew and considered strong and worthy or else from one that the vitki fought him/herself on equal terms: slaying a full-grown buck with a knife or a wolf with bare hands, for example. Using a gun in this case is unfitting and cowardly. If you should otherwise come upon the bones of a suitable creature, it is best that the animal have died naturally.

If not, it must not have been killed for sport but for a needful purpose such as food, and you must perform a fitting rite of thanks and lay the animal's spirit to rest before attempting any other hallowing. When the raw wood for the gandr has been taken from the tree (see the chapter on Rite of Tree-Gift), it is necessary to strip the bark off, preferably using no tools other than the sax, and sand the wood smooth. You may at this time make an oil by carefully heating (though not boiling!) Appropriate herbs in linseed oil, straining it clear through a coffee filter, and charging it with the force of the futhark either in a single rite or nightly from New Moon to Full.

The wand should then be rubbed with this oil until it gleams. This technique can be used in the making of talismans as well. The runes carved upon the gandr can range from a simple carving of the futhark to whatever the vitki's mind can come up with. It is suggested that the numerical value of the inscription be either a multiple of 24 (the futhark) or 9. Adding the vitki's own name to a runic inscription was frequently done and it is fitting to work it into the carving on the gandr, as that tool is a representation of the vitki's will. In hallowing the gandr, you should call upon Odhinn Galdrfadhir (father of magical songs) and the Norns.

THE HORN OR CUP

This tool is used to hold water, ale, or mead as fitting to various rites. A natural horn is best, as this by its very being refers to the aurouchs of uruz, the shaping life-force which works from the horn. If you find a natural horn which has not been prepared, you will need to sand it down and polish with steel wool, then jeweler's rouge. To clean the inside it is best to pour boiling water down the horn and let it sit till cool, then repeat several times to sterilize and clean out debris. During this process, you should intone the rune uruz and trace it over the horn, visualizing the waters of the rune flowing through, cleansing it and filling it with power.

Finally, you should melt paraffin in a double boiler-being very careful not to let it catch fire, as it is highly flammable-pour it into the mouth of a horn, and swirl it around until the entire inside is coated, pouring out any excess wax before it can set. The runes can be scrimshawed onto a horn fairly easily with the sax. Depending on the material of the cup, professional etching may be needed. The runes laguz, uruz, and perthro should be prominent in the inscription. A sample might be UR ALU URUZ POUR URUZ URDHR URUZ POWER URUZ, written around the rim of the vessel, which adds up numerically to 216 or 9 x 24, the futhark multiplied by the number of wholeness, and also contains 9 uruz-runes. Thorsson also recommends that the vitki have a horn or cup with the word Odhroerir (the mead of poetry) etched on it, in runes and drink mead out of this for Odhinnic inspiration.[1] This can be made into a mighty rite on its own.

THE STAFF

The staff can be seen as a larger gandr, being made and hallowed in much the same manner. It is useful in drawing power from and faring through the higher and lower worlds. It shows the vitki's unshakable will piercing through all the realms. At the most elaborate extreme, you might carve an eagle at the top and a dragon at the bottom in reference to the World-Tree. This tool is not however, as necessary as sax, gandr, or horn/cup; use of it will largely depend on individual preference.

FIRE POT CANDLES

A fire pot with coals is good to have, if possible. It signifies the quickening power of Muspellheim.2 Recels (incense) is burned on the coals. Also, a newly hallowed item may be passed over the coals or through the smoke to increase its power. The fire pot should be set within the southern point of the circle. Candles are used largely as focuses at the beginning of a ritual, representing the vitki's might shaped by will. If you regularly charge your ritual candles, kenaz is the appropriate rune to use. A candle may also be fully charged in the same manner as a talisman and burnt in a ritual to free its full might into the working.

Candles are needed for light in nighttime workings, since having an electric light on is disruptive to the more delicate flowing of energy. The candles should, if possible, be lit directly from the fire pot with an appropriate line of galdr and then set on the harrow before the vitki. Alternatively, candles can be set within the borders of the circle at either the four or the eight points of the compass. If you wish, candles used in this manner can be charged with the fires of elhaz and worked into the warding of the circle. Candle colors are dependent on the intuition of the vitki and the purpose of the rite. Red candles serve well for almost everything; white and blue are also good general colors which may be preferred in certain meditation and religious rituals. Otherwise, see the guide to Colors in Chapter 11.

MORTAR AND PESTLE

These items are used for grinding pigment and recels. Magically, only iron or steel are unacceptable materials. Practically, you will do best with a small stone mortar and pestle (available at many herb stores and/or head shops). Wood is more difficult to grind roots and bits of wood in; earthenware tends to be rather breakable. If graving runes on these items is possible, a good simple formula is eight wunjo-runes spaced evenly around the rim of the mortar and a ninth on the top end of the pestle.

The runes around the rim blend the forces from the aettir of the heavens and the divisions of the runic circle, while the ninth shapes and completes the harmony, bringing the numerical value up to 72(3 x the futhark count a particularly powerful number in traditional runic workings). It is necessary to clean the mortar and pestle thoroughly after every use, as it is both sloppy and disruptive to have bits of the last working's energies interfering with those of the next. As you scrub the physical residue out under running water, you should also see the cleansing power (uruz) of the water running all through the mortar and pestle to remove all the magical residue.

THE HAMMER

The hammer is really more religious than magical in nature; however, inscriptions exist in which Thorr is called upon "to hallow the runes." Magically, it is used to drive out all wights and forces which are detrimental to the working and to fill the place or thing in question with holy might. Should you be magically assailed, the hammer can be used in rites of defense. The sign of the hammer should be painted or carved on or above the doors and windows of your house to ward it and bring "luck"-the weal-working of the energies within. The hammer should be all of iron or steel or else have an oaken handle; the head should be symmetrical, like that of a mallet, rather than a carpenter's hammer. It should be as heavy as the vitki can comfortably handle. If possible, a swastika should be graven on each end. A good inscription for the haft might be THORR VEURR (Thorr the Hallower) (96=8 x 12 - organic wholeness, power of the winds brought forth into the earth).

ᚦᛟᚱᛉᚹᛖᚢᚱᛉ

To use the hammer in hallowing, you should swing it three times deosil over the object or person being hallowed, chanting a galdr such as "Veurr hallow vitki's might" or "Hammer hallow these holy runes," envisioning a great rush of shining might whirling into your object from the swinging hammer.

THE HARROW

The harrow, or altar, should be the center of your place of working. This place may be either outdoors or indoors; if outdoors, in the center of a grove is preferred, but hardly necessary. If you can do your workings under the open sky, it is important to be assured of your privacy and freedom from distraction. Trucks and airplanes roaring by hardly enhance concentration, while some people (and police) become very upset when faced with any form of magical or pagan working. The most traditional form of harrow is one made of heaped stones under the open sky.

If you should find a large natural boulder set in an appropriate place that feels right for your working, so much the better. In this case the circle, rather than being drawn or embroidered, should be cut into the earth around the harrow with your ritual knife. If a stone harrow should be impractical, the next best choice is one made of oak or ash. A small flat-topped cabinet in which the ritual tools can be stored when not in use is excellent for this purpose. This harrow can be rubbed with a charged oil in the same manner as the other wooden tools. If you so wish, the futhark ring can be carved upon it along with such other inscriptions as seem fitting, depending on whether it is used more for worship or for magic, or equally for both.

11 LAWS OF TEUTONIC MAGIC

POETICS OF GALDR-MAGIC

The essential goal of ritual is to provide a focus by which the magician can most effectively raise and guide power. This is of particular importance in rune work because of the many-sided being of the runes, which requires firm and specific concentration on the side of a rune's being and the result wished if you want to avoid unforeseen consequences. Control is of the greatest importance: a miscast or unguided spell is far more likely to cause woe than weal. Despite the current romantic attachment to "wild magic" among those who are more familiar with fantasy novels than with real life, the true mage must be able to rule everything she/he does, or it is very likely to destroy him/her. Ritual can generally be divided into two major categories: physical action and verbal incantation. To work a spell is literally to en-chant; the word galdr comes from a root meaning "to sing."

Unfortunately, the writing of the poetic part of the ritual is often difficult for the ordinary person, as it calls for a good understanding of poetics as well as magic. The more powerful a rune song is as a piece of poetry-as something which both stirs the heart and shapes a clear image in the mind-the more power it will draw up from the depths of the vitki's being and the better it will guide that power. Poetry's effectiveness depends on four elements: rhyme, rhythm, image, and sense. The last of these is simply the message encoded in the poetic work; the more deeply you feel the reason for your working, the more strongly the sense of the galdr will affect you.

If you can find correspondences for your working in the larger universe, this will also increase the might of your galdr both psychologically as you feel the greater forces with which you are working and magically as you call their might into the ritual. The idea of rhyme covers not only the end-rhymes which are thought of by most Westerners as a distinguishing characteristic of "poetry," but all the consonance of sounds which can be achieved in a poetic work. These include alliteration (initial letters the same), assonance ("rhyming" vowels, different consonants), and consonance (same consonantal sound within words)-all of which are of great value in runic work, as the vitki can weave the sound of the runes he/she is using into her/his incantation, thereby strengthening the power of their vibration at every level of his/her being and focusing her/his subconscious along with his/her conscious. An excellent example of how this works can be seen in an exerpt from Dylan Thomas:

> *The force that through the green fuse drives the flower*
> *Drives my green age; that blasts the roots of trees Is my destroyer.*
> *And I am dumb to tell the crooked rose*
> *My youth is bent by the same wintry fever.*

Although this stanza has little overt rhyme, the consonantal pattern of flower-destroyer~ever creates the same sense of impetus and unity that a standard rhyming pattern would. The rr-sound, creating a feeling of rushing motion is emphasized over and over: "The force that through the green fuse drives the flower," etc. In Teutonic magic you will do best to stick to the patterns of Teutonic verse, in which "rhyme" appears only as alliteration, placing the emphasis on the alliterated words. This is particularly powerful in runic work. If you, for instance, were to chant: "By raidho I ride the road a-right," you would not only gain the benefit of the repeated sound of the rune but also direct that rune fully into your intention, strengthening the sense as well.

The use of rhythm in incantation serves several goals. As an element of poetry, rhythm sets a great deal of the tone and character of the poem. You can compare the slow, funereal beat of Foe's "The Raven," for instance, with the galloping hoof beats of "Paul Revere's Ride." The rhythm of the incantation, as much as the words, shapes the quality of the energies it raises. The best gaidrar, of course, are chanted or sung rather than spoken, with each word given its full vibrational and rhythmic value. When this is done right, the rhythm of the spell will also regulate the breath of the vitki, putting her/him into a state of trance like concentration. It is best if this can be done with the rite of hallowing the circle; Thorsson's Hammer Rite (Futhark), with its slow incantation of each of the runes and necessary breath control, is a good ritual for this purpose.

Rhythm unifies the physical and the mental being. If the spell can be accompanied with drumbeats and dancing, so much the better. If the setting does not permit this, the vitki should strive as greatly as possible to create a rite which has a similar effect on the consciousness of the worker. The most important words of the galdr should of course fall on the emphasized beats of the incantation rhythm, which, in Teutonic poetry, are usually those that share the wished-for rune sound in alliteration or, if necessary, consonance. Image may be thought of as the means by which the sense of the galdr is translated into mentally and emotionally striking terms. This is also some of the purpose of symbolism: a candle lit may show the fire of a person's life; the candle snuffed out is that person's death, the fire of life gone from his/her eyes and her/his body cooling.

If this is done in the proper way and under the proper conditions, it will cause the like happening in the target who has been identified with the candle. The use of image and symbol in your galdrar should be done so as to give you a full emotional and mental awareness of the might with which you are working and the end to which you guide it. A couple of lines of poetry should be able to create the same effect in the prepared mind as an entire guided runic meditation. The power of poetry lies in its compactness: through sound and image it can encode a vast amount of passion and magical power in a very little space, filling the mind with the wholeness of a concept that would have taken a thousand ordinary words to communicate.

Also hidden in the use of image is the thought behind "the power of the true name"-that which is no less that the absolute understanding of a person or thing expressed in a single word or image and which can be reached only through immediate mystical experience or by the power of skaldcraft to communicate(and at the same time gain power over) it (ansuz). This is also one of the ideas behind the Germanic riddle-poetry known as kennings o demonstrate the fullness of your knowledge and hence of your power. By calling a warrior "oak-of-battle," the skald communicates the warrior's strength, her/his endurance, his/her unyielding courage in a fight, and her/his rulership over other warriors, as the oak is usually the tree of rulership in the Indo-European tradition. With this understanding, you might strengthen the oak's trunk with tiwaz and set the sun-wheel of sowilo to shine through his/her branches for victory; or you might blast the mighty oak with the lightning-stroke of thurisaz. Those kennings which refer to kinship - calling Thorr "son of Jord (Earth)," for instance-are effective because, knowing a person's kin, especially forebears, you know more of the layers which have shaped that person and hence more of that-which-she/he-is.

You can see this in the sagas, which usually start by telling about the grandparents and parents of the hero in question. Certain elements of this power may also have been borrowed from Finnish magic, in which, to enchant someone, you must know that person's full lineage-all that has gone into creating the person of the moment and that still works within that person's being. The image in magical poetry both encodes an idea or force in magically understandable and hence usable form and gives it the capability to impact upon all levels of the Mage's awareness, concealing it and bringing it forth at the same time. For both of these reasons it is important in Teutonic magic to keep as closely as one can to words with Anglo-Saxon roots. Firstly, monosyllables have more gut-level impact and are more immediately descriptive than polysyllables, being usually the first words associated with images in a child's mind. This is especially noticeable and powerful when you are dealing with onomatopoeic words-roar, crash, etc.

Generally speaking, the more concrete and basic an image is, the easier it is to visualize and the more powerful its effects will be. Secondly, every word in a tongue is a product of the unconscious thought-system from which it has stemmed, and hence it carries certain implications about the workings of the universe. Thus, words grounded in the Germanic world-view will be more powerful in runic work because these words come from the same framework of thought that produced the runes as we know them. An exact etymology is not as necessary for poetic work as it is for scholastics; nevertheless, you should be able to tell the difference between words of Germanic and words of Romantic origins, and likewise between words with Indo-European and non-Indo-European roots, the former in both cases being greatly preferable. Older, even archaic, words tend to be more reliably Anglo-Saxon faring for "journey" or "travel," for instance.

The serious student will do well to find at least a brief guide to the Anglo-Saxon language, which is not too difficult for anyone who reads both English and German, once you grow used to the vocabulary. Failing this, the translation of the Poetic Edda by Lee M. Hollander and the works of J.R.R. Tolkien are good guides to the use of "Teutonic English," Tolkien being perhaps the ultimate example of a Germanic linguist recovering the vitality of Anglo-Saxon speech and Germanic legend in modern English. Of course, certain words simply have no current Anglo-Saxon based equivalent; the choice in this case is between using current Latin-based words or reviving Anglo-Saxon/Old Norse forms for one's personal use.

TEUTONIC RITUAL AND LAWS OF MAGIC

Certain basic laws hold true and virtually unchanged throughout all forms of magical workings. Others vary in both expression and effectiveness from culture to culture. As Teutonic magic works somewhat differently than the more familiar Western ceremonial magic or those neo-pagan traditions which have been created in the twentieth century from archetypal patterns, it is important to know the major elements of this form of ritual work well; only a fool does a magical rite which she/he does not understand.

THE VITKI IN RITUAL

The greatest part of magic is the vitki him/herself: her/his confidence in self and personal power, belief in the effectiveness of the rite itself, and complete absorption in the work during performance. An insecure magician cannot master any energy or other being effectively. One whose mind is split between belief and skepticism or concentration and self-consciousness will be unable to use his/her full power and hence dilute the effectiveness of the rite. Complete certainty and confidence are absolutely necessary. For this reason, spells from all traditions often include statements of power and confidence at the beginning and the end of the working.

Related to this is the creation of the magical persona for any given rite - one of the secrets behind the many disguises of Odhinn. An example of this use may be seen in the All-father's theft of Odhroerir: As Odhinn could gain the mead of poetry only through betrayal and workings of woe, he disguised himself under the name of Bolverk, Evil-worker, and began his work with the murder of several field thralls, building up the magical energy and the identity of the persona he needed to use. The use of the magical persona charges the rite with an added certainty and intensity, as can be seen in several rune stones in which the vitki has identified her/himself by a name which is fitting to the purpose of the inscription, thus filling the enchantment with the totality of the person performing the runes and such godly aspect as she/he has taken upon him/herself.[1]

CREATION OF A MAGICAL PERSONA

Draw or trace your circle. Standing outside the circle facing north, concentrate on filling it with the energy appropriate to your rite. The example here will be a rite of warding. The vitki will of course substitute colors, names, descriptions etc. as appropriate. In this case, the energy will be gold with a faint rainbow shimmering. When the space within the circle is so thoroughly charged that you can see the rainbow-gleaming gold with your open eyes, visualize the energy drawing together into a human shape, which may be male or female depending on the purpose of the rite.

In this case either is fitting, though the female may be slightly more so. She is tall and very fair, with sky blue eyes and long hair so blond it is almost white streaming from beneath her elk-antlered helmet. Great white swan's wings arch up behind her. She wears a golden byrnie [tunic of chain mail] and carries a golden sword which shimmers with rainbow fire. Her golden shield has a burning rainbow elhaz graven on it, and she holds both shield and sword up in a defensive position. When you can see her clearly, you chant:

"Hail to thee, Brightshield! Hail, heaven-bright warder!"

Step forward into the circle, moving into Bright shield's place and take up her defensive stance, merging with her as you do so. You feel the elk-horned helmet on your head, the weight of shield, sword, and byrnie, and the strength of the great white wings which arch out from your back. You are created as a defender, shining with holy fire. Your sky-blue eyes see through all the Nine Worlds; you are ready to meet and overcome any threat. You cry out, hearing your voice ring through all the realms of being,

I am Bright shield, heaven-bright warder, My might shines in shield and sword. My worth shall throw back all workings of woe, Where the secret staves I write, shall ward.

Not wight nor witch, not etin nor alf, shall withstand the strength of works I wreak.

I am Bright shield, heaven-bright warder!

Set up and proceed with the rite as normal, including the initial drawing of the circle and creation of the ritual space, as your crossing its bounds broke the first circle. All of this shall be done in the persona of Bright shield. When the ritual has been completed, including the breaking of the circle and re-wrapping of tools (except gandr or sax, whichever was used in creating Bright shield), draw a second circle around yourself and assume the original defensive stance of Bright shield. You, the vitki, will then walk out of Bright shield, leaving her standing inside the circle. Close the circle behind you and stand for a moment, being sure that your visualization of the persona inside is clear. Say, "I am (your magical name) the vitki. Bright shield, thy work is wrought!"

See her slowly dissolving into her component energy, until her form has melted altogether into rainbow-sparkling golden light within the circle. Break the circle and return the energy to the universe. Alternatively, you may choose to store each persona in an item of jewelry or ritual dress so that you may assume each one by simply putting the article on, rather like the way in which one changes shape in seidh-magic.

SILENCE

Silence in preparing for the rite is important because it helps one to focus on the ritual and avoid dissipating energy. Mundane words and unnecessary actions distract the vitki's mind and weaken his/her power. In magic, every action must be deliberately willed for a specific effect. In Teutonic magic it is necessary to go to and from the place at which you perform any magical act in silence, no matter what you see or who tries to talk to you. This silence should be maintained in all ways when garbing and setting up the harrow. During the rite no words other than words of magic should be spoken, and you must be thoroughly silent when cleaning up afterwards and putting one's tools away.

RITUAL GARB

The ritual garb, like the rule of silence, reinforces the fact that everything about a ritual is set apart, concentrated in power, and willed. Some prefer to work sky clad; however, it is generally thought that clothing put on solely for ritual work is better, because the act of donning this garb aids in concentrating the mind on both the conscious and the subconscious levels. The exact type of clothing used is not as overwhelmingly important in Norse magic as in high ceremonial workings, but it is still meaningful. Traditional Norse clothing-tunic, breeches, hooded cloak-is easy to make and comfortable to wear.

The breeches are traditionally red, the cloak dark blue. A simple robe may also be used at need. One should bear in mind when choosing colors, designs, etc. For ritual clothing and jewelry, that the more supporting correspondences one can find in the Teutonic universe and the runes themselves, the more power one will be able to call into these things. In a sense one can say that the use of ritual garb and a magical name works in much the same manner as the creation of a magical persona, the difference being that rather than entering a persona for a single rite or type of rite, one is expressing the wholeness of one's true self with power in all things.

THE CIRCLE

The use of a circle in magic appears virtually worldwide. It is every bit as traditional in Teutonic magic as in Western ceremonial workings, serving several essential purposes. First, it separates the vitki from the mundane world, creating an area which is an all-encompassing microcosm ruled by the vitki's will. It blocks out both mental and magical forces, concentrating the vitki's mind altogether on her/his purpose. As an impenetrable boundary, it is a necessary warding against the multitude of hostile/ reactive forces which the use of magic always draws. It also serves as a focus within which power can be raised effectively. The design of a circle can range from a simple ring to an exceedingly elaborate structure, according to the knowledge and inclination of the vitki.

A good simple circle is the rune-ring divided by the aett of the solarhringarh. If circumstances keep one from drawing or painting a circle on the floor, or if one travels often, a good alternative is the embroidering of a circle on a large piece of cloth which can be spread on the floor. Nine feet is the traditional width; the circle can be smaller if necessary but should be at least slightly wider than the outstretched arms of the vitki, because you do not want to be putting parts of your body outside it. The circle should actually be visualized as a sphere of shining power. Although it is possible sometimes to stretch it from the inside, this will weaken the circle as a whole, which is not a good idea.

Putting both feet outside the circle, or allowing a break in the physical structure, will break the entire circle. The best way not to have to push against the sphere of power is to make a list of all necessary earthly tools, and to make sure that all these things are inside the space of the circle before you draw it. It is absolutely necessary to retrace a permanent circle before each working, going over its lines with fingertip, gandr, or sax and visualizing its brightness Springing up in light of an appropriate color. One should lie within the circle when faring between the worlds, as it is both a place of power and will ward off hostile forces. Closely related to the charging of the circle is the practice of circle-walking, which raises power in a spiral of concentration.

To draw down heavenly mights or to enact the passage of the sun ("nights" in the Teutonic tradition, the "day" being the half-passage of the solarhringar), walk or dance deosil; to draw up earthly mights, walk widdershins (the direction of the Earth's turning). Widdershins was given its unfortunate reputation because of its association with the magic of Nerthus, Freyja, and Hel and because of the frequent use of chthonic power in curses. It is not intrinsically negative, woe-working, or any sort of perversion of the order of nature. The walking of the circle should generally be done lightly, almost as a dance, although different rituals will of course need different rhythms. It may be found effective to spin one's body in the direction opposite to that of the spiral. At first this will cause giddiness, but once controlled, it will add to the power one is drawing into the circle.

RECELS

Recels, or incense, is used in Teutonic tradition for cleansing a place or thing: "smoking out" those wights and powers which are not wished within.3 It can also be used in the process of charging the working space with the desired energy and levels of vibration. While it is not absolutely necessary for the vitki to make his/her own recels, the scarcity of appropriate scents on the general market will almost force this upon one; and of course, properly made recels will be much more powerful than any store-bought incense, (Chapter 13 may provide a useful basis for composing your recels.) Folk names for herbs, especially those based on Anglo-Saxon or other Germanic beliefs, will be a good guide to their powers, Cunningham's Magikal Herbalism, and Grieves' Modern Herbal are excellent sources for further research.

In making one's recels, one should trace the runes of the working over the materials, intoning their names and feeling the might of each one flowing through the gandr into the recels. One should continue to chant the names of the runes and perhaps a line of galdr describing the purpose of each in the working as you grind, channeling the flow of the runic power through one's body and the pestle into the recels. It may be further charged with a drop of blood when the grinding has been done. It is best to make only enough for one ritual; if excess is left over it can be disposed of in the running water of the sink or else kept in a clean, dry, glass jar with a clear label so that it may be used again in the next rite of this sort one performs. Runes may also be cut, colored, and scraped into recels for the purpose of directing them into a place where visible motions and audible chanting seem inappropriate, or where the force of the fully activated rune is needed and there is no time to cut and color it-though in this case some galdr will be necessary to direct the runic power to its end.

GOD-CALLING; HAMINGJA

It is general practice in almost all fields of magic to perform a brief god-calling after the drawing of the circle and before beginning the active part of the ritual. This furthers the process of banishing unwanted/raising wanted energies. By calling the gods to witness her/his acts, the vitki consciously guides his/her power through all the worlds. This idea is furthered by the practice of calling upon one god at each quarter of the compass, four being a number of earthly completeness and manifestation. It is also possible to call upon one deity for each of the aett-divisions of the solarhringar.

This further strengthens the working in that, by speaking the name of the god, one calls into oneself a little of the hamingja-force (mana) of the god, adding that energy to the rite. It is recommended, however, that if one is making a really serious attempt to pull in the hamingja of a being much larger than oneself, that one have a staff or similar large focus that one can channel the energy into so as to avoid having one's brains stir-fried. The hamingja is the storehouse of magical/life energy which everything possesses to some degree.[4]

It is closely tied to the faculty of shape-changing, being that undifferentiated force which is the strength of the hamr, or hide-that fine body which goes forth, often in the shape of another being, in the faring between worlds. The hamingja, however, can be passed temporarily between one person and another; it was not unusual for a Norse king to "lend his luck" to a messenger or champion. The personal hamingja can be increased by workings of magic and courage. When drained by the expenditure of magical energies, it will refill to its normal level within a period dependent on the strength and activity of the vitki. It is not unusual for magicians to set up deposits of this force outside of their bodies which can be drawn upon when they require more power than their normal capacity.

These deposits can be built up in either objects or places, as wished; they should, however, be well warded against both magical and physical discovery and/or tampering. As well as seeking to augment his/her own store of hamingja force by magical practice and other means, the vitki will also want to be aware of that contained in the items with which she/he works. A great number of the Anglo-Saxon charms give directions for recognizing strong hamingjur in specific cases, generally by some unusual feature showing power: a nettle which has forced its way through a stone wall (called for in a charm against rheumatism) clearly has more strength than an ordinary nettle; wood from a tree which has grown twisted together with two others will make a more powerful rune-tine than wood from an ordinary tree; a stone with a natural hole in it has a great deal of power within, and so on. Most such specifics having been lost with the interruption of the oral tradition, however, the identification of strong hamingjur will in practice be largely dependent on the vitki and his/her ability to draw on the wisdom of her/his racial or personal predecessors.

SIMILARITY AND CONTAGION

Similarity and contagion are the two most general laws of magic. Briefly, the Law of Similarity holds that things which seem alike, are alike; the Law of Contagion rules that things once in contact will remain in contact; and in both cases, whatever happens to one will happen to the other. Similarity is used heavily in skaldcraft and symbolic actions: two things are compared, thus forging the magical link between them, then the vitki works her/his will on the one he/she can directly control. Contagion is generally used either in aiming a spell or in drawing power from something large of which one has a piece.

If, for instance, one wanted to start 6 thunderstorm, one might carve the appropriate formula with runes for lightning (thurisaz), wind (ansuz), and rain (uruz) on a piece of oak wood -hopefully from a lightning- struck oak-then mingle a bit of thunderstorm water with the pigment for coloring and rub the consecrated tine with the water, using the completed tine to sprinkle the water on the ground, and finish the rite by hurling the tine upward with a thunderous shout of "THORR!" The use of thunderstorm water is Contagion, the lightning-struck oak mingles Contagion with sympathetic hamingja force; the sprinkling of the water and throwing the tine up with a shout like thunder is Similarity, and the use of Thorr's name is hamingja-calling.

BLOOD, BREATH AND SPITTLE

The Laws of Similarity and Contagion can be further seen in the magical use of blood, breath, and spittle. As the breath is the sign of life and the source of power for the spoken work, as well as being identified with the spirit, it should be clear to the vitki that her/his own breath is a powerful vehicle for filling anything with life and magical force. Hence it is needful to sing the galdrar as close to the carved tine and as intensely as possible so that the force of the breath and vibration of the words should fill it. This is also effective when using liquid as a vehicle of power. A vast number of Germanic charms are sung over a liquid which is then drunk by the subject. Blood is, of course, the life-force of all animals; hence, by coloring the runes with your blood or with magically charged red pigment, which is equivalent to blood by the Law of Similarity and the power which the vitki has put into it the vitki is filling the runes themselves with life.

Alcohol may also be used in this manner, especially if the runes are to be scraped into a drink. A traditional alchemist would say that the effectiveness of this is due to the fact that alcohol is the life-force of plants and hence works in roughly the same vitalizing manner as blood or its magical equivalent. Spittle carries the personal hamingja-force in the same manner as breath or blood, but to a lesser degree. Spittle is often used in the swearing of an oath, under the Law of Contagion: as it has a bit of oneself and one's power in it, spitting to seal an oath is magically holding oneself hostage to one's word. The mingling of two people's spittle is like the mingling of blood, but the binding created is much less intense, being suitable for legal contracts and so forth. As a vehicle of power, spittle is often used to throw up a quick barrier of protection: one spits three times to block off woe-working energies.

CONCEALMENT; BINDING

There are two types of concealment in ritual practice. The first, temporary concealment, in which an item is wrapped in a black cloth or buried in the ground for a period of time, is used in the creation of a magical item. This is intended as a period of gestation (berkano) in which the powers that have been worked into the item may come into full being. This is particularly useful when coming into physical being is desired. The second, permanent concealment, is done (as a part of ritual outside of practical considerations) for the purpose of making the working more effective in the hidden realms of power. An item may be physically hidden in the earth, beneath the floorboards of a house and so on, or runes may be concealed by numerical encÓdhinng or by other means such as "ice-runes," in which row and placement are indicated by tallies of isa-runes, the larger showing the row and the smaller showing the placement in the row. Other runes have been used in this manner, but isa, being simplest is most common. An example of this can be seem in the encoded name of Odhinn:

The aettir can also be reversed so that 0=1:8 and so on. There are several forms of runic encÓdhinng which work on this principle. The power of secrecy is in some ways similar to the power of silence; it concentrates the energy and attention into the working and separates it from any distraction so that it can pierce more effectively through the hidden realms of being. For this reason it is also a good idea to keep one's magical tools wrapped in black cloth or kept in a special box when not in use. Silk is preferred by many traditionalist Western magicians because of its value as a psychic insulator; linen is preferred by traditionalist vitkar because of its association with Hel/Holda, the Concealing Mother.

Binding and unbinding play a fairly important part in ritual because of the direct control of energy they represent. The act of tying a knot or tracing a circle about something is one of the most immediately powerful ways to achieve mastery and hold force in, while the untying of a ritual knot generates a sudden rush of energy which should be directed at the moment of untying. The traditional example of this is the well-known figure of the weather- worker loosing and binding the winds by tying and untying the mouth or a bag or a knotted string-a "wind" being any rush of power.

FIRE AND WATER; BREWING

Fire and water or other liquids often appear in ritual workings, usually as complementary forces. Both are, of course, tools of cleansing and are frequently used as such, although in runic practice the correspondence would be to kenaz or nauthiz for fire and to uruz for water, rather than to the elemental fehu and laguz. In using a flame or sprinkling water for ritual cleansing, you would want to make that distinction in your mental structure and verbal formula. The elemental forces are used for direct transfer of life and hamingja-force, fehu being the quickening of life and hamingja-power and laguz the basic life energy. The use of air in this setting, of course, would be as the magical breath carrying the life-power of spirit. Running water plays an important part in Teutonic magic.

Whenever the use of water is called for in a ritual, it is best to go out before sunrise and gather running water from either one or three streams, or else to gather the dew off the grass, since both run- fling water and dew have the particular active quality which is so mighty in the Well of Wyrd. They are said to bring life and renew the strength of youth. Running water can be used to either cleanse something enchanted or to simply carry woe-working energies away from you. The use of water or other liquids, especially alcohol, as a vehicle for runic forces is an ancient tradition; both the highest myths and the simplest charms hold drinks of power into which runes have been scraped and over which galdrar have been sung.

Liquid is, in fact, an ideal condenser of energies, being by nature highly receptive and manipulable. If you have access to a shop which sells materials for home-brewing, you will find it vastly preferable to brew your own ritual mead and ale, performing a rite which climaxes with the adding of the yeast to the mixture. Runes may be daily traced and vibrated into the froth of the yeast on top, and appropriate herbs may be added to the drink as well, either by steeping them in it or by making a fairly strong tea with the water which is used for brewing. This may in fact make the brewing of mead easier, as it is sometimes difficult to get honey and water alone to ferment. You should be very careful that the herbs you use for this purpose are nonpoisonous, and also remember that a little herbal taste can go a very long way: half or a quarter of an ounce of dried herbs is enough to flavor a five-gallon batch of strong mead quite thoroughly.

It was common practice among the Norse people to brew their enchantments into ale or mead; you may make small batches for specific purposes, or hallow a general-purpose batch which may be directed towards more specific ends later. Care should be taken if the enchantment itself is directly tied to the ever-growing action of the yeast. It is quite possible to end up with something much stronger than you expect and hence potentially disastrous (rather like intending to smoke marijuana and ending up on a surprise acid trip). If you are unable to actually brew an enchanted drink, scraping the runes into mead or ale and singing the galdrar into it, being sure that your breath stirs the surface of the liquid, is equally as traditional. A more potent enchantment may be set into mead by repeating the rite for three or nine nights. Herbs may be steeped in it as well, though the same cautions apply as do to brewing with herbs.

A single fresh leaf or small dried pinch is quite enough for one bottle. Another alternative to brewing, especially if you wish to use herbal lore in conjunction with runic power, is the creation of herbal tinctures or fluid condensers. These are less traditional than the other two means, being dependent on distilled liquor as a base, but are still within the spirit of Teutonic tradition and can be quite powerful. Herbal tinctures can be made by filling a clean glass jar two-thirds with fresh or dried herbs, then filling it to the brim with Ever Clear or unflavored vodka (methyl alcohol must not be used). This should be done on the night of the New Moon, after which one should trace the runes and sing the galdrar appropriate into the tincture every night of its maturation. If runes are to be scraped into it, this should be done on the night of the Full Moon after the tincture is strained, or else a drop of the vitki's blood should be added on that night in the final ritual of enchantment. A few drops of this tincture may be taken internally (if none of the herbs used were poisonous); otherwise it may be used to charge an item which, for whatever reason, cannot have runes carved into it. The herbs strained out may be dried slowly in your oven and used as recels.

NUMBER

Number is used in Teutonic magic for the purpose of increasing the effectiveness of runic writings and spells. It differs from standard Western numerology in that the Germanic counting worked on a base-12 system (whereby we still have "eleven, twelve" instead of "one-teen, two-teen"). Hence the consciousness of "perfect numbers" is shifted to twelve, its factors, and their multiples. Number in runic inscriptions can be shown by the total of the numbers of the runes in the inscription or by the number of runic staves (bind-runes counting as a single stave). These numbers can be used to multiply the potency of a runic incantation or to guide the sphere through which it works, according to either general Teutonic numerology or the specific numerology of the runes.

ONE: One is the prime source and the end of the synthesizing process; in all Indo-European cultures, a single thing or deity will quite often be divided into three aspects: Odhinn=Odhinn/Vili/Ve, Odhinn/ Hoenir/Lodurr; the Well of Wyrd = Hvergelmir, Mimir, Urdhr, etc. An understanding of this continual process of division and synthesis is important to the working of Teutonic magic, especially as numerical lore is concerned.

TWO: In Teutonic magic, the power of duality is not so much conflict of opposites (which, to be effectively powerful, must be resolved into the synthesis of the triad) as it is the common working of complements (ehwaz). This can be seen in the archaic dual kingship, the Vanic twins Njord/Nerthus and Freyr/ Freyja, and the pairs Geri/Freki (Odhinn's wolves) and Huginn/Muninn (Odhinn's ravens), as well as the other manifestations of dual power discussed under ehwaz. It is associated with active balance.

THREE: Three is the first of the great magical numbers of the Teutonic people. As two is the number of active balance, three is the number of action/reaction. It represents the synthesis of opposites to create directed force (see thurisaz), as fire and ice create the first life. A chant or word of power is often repeated three times to set it into action, and a rune is carved three times to multiply and activate its power. It is both permissible and effective to alter the galdr slightly with three repetitions, being sure to stick to the alliteration in each case. A formula for active defense, for instance, might read "Thurisaz break the woeworker's words / Thurisaz break the woe- worker's works / Thurisaz break the woe-worker's will!" thus multiplying the power and effect of the rune.

FOUR: Four is the number of stability and the completeness of earth. It bears reference both to the four dwarves who forged Freyja's necklace/girdle Brisingamen, the ring of earth-power which is one of the oldest emblems of the Earth Goddess among the Northern Europeans, and to the dwarves Nordhri, Austri, Sudhri, and Vestri (the four points of the compass). It is a number of wholeness and manifestation. It is also associated with the sun in its aspect as the stable source of warmth and light. It is frequently used in rituals which deal with the fertilizing effect of the sun on the earth, especially rituals of worship; it may also be used for localizing and containing a problem.

FIVE: The Germanic week was five days long; the number five appears in the Anglo-Saxon charms as an active complement to the number four. Five is a number of active order and control.

SIX: The number six does not appear often in Teutonic mythology or religion, though the six-sided figure is a powerful emblem. As the unity of the balanced activity of two and the synthesis-activity of three, it is a number of great potential magical power.

SEVEN: The number seven is more characteristic of Oriental and Mediterranean occult studies than of Teutonic magic; it does not appear in the myths or in native charms. Thorsson identifies it as "the number of death and passive contact with other worlds."[4]

EIGHT: As four is the completeness of earth, eight is the completeness of the heavens and the other worlds. It is the divisions of the solarhringar, the eight winds, the eight legs of Sleipnir etc; it is the number of travel between the worlds. Like two and four, it is a number of harmonious wholeness.

NINE: Nine is the greatest of Teutonic magical numbers: There are Nine Worlds, Odhinn hangs nine nights on Yggdrasil, magical songs are taught in either groups or multiples of nine. Holy fires are often made with wood from nine different trees, and nine nights is" a standard period of time between a magical working and its final effect. Nine and its multiples are often used to bring things into being and empower them in all realms. It bears the same sort of active relationship to eight that three does to two and five to four: it is power, direction, and rulership over the organic forces of the even number.

TEN and ELEVEN: These numbers are used seldom, if ever, in Teutonic magic

TWELVE: Twelve is a great Teutonic number of wholeness and being. There are twelve gods and twelve goddesses (24, the most complete number of the Teutonic system), and twelve great halls in Asgard; the use of the quasi-duodecimal system of counting has already been mentioned. Twelve is the number of power brought into earthly being and earthly being strengthened by power. Multiples of twelve are all mighty, the most powerful being the 24 of the futhark and its multiple by three, 72.

THIRTEEN: This is a mighty number of wisdom and magical power. It is considered "unlucky" by the common people because its mysteries are not for the unwise, weak, or untaught. The mysteries of numbers beyond these may be understood by their factors, both as those are seen in general Teutonic lore and in the futhark. Even numbers always carry a power of balance; odd numbers, especially prime numbers, a sense of active will.

COLOR

The most powerful colors known to the Indo-Europeans were red, blue, and white, with red being the greatest of those. Red is the color associated with life, with blood, and with power in general; it is the color most often used in magic. The nature of blue varies with its shade: in its lightest hues it is the daytime sky, the color of hope and revealed wisdom; in its darkest shades it is the sky at night and the dark sea, the color of hidden wisdom and mystery-the color of Odhinn's cloak. The sea or air between the worlds often appears as dark blue. White is the color of intensity of spirit aspiration, and activity; Heimdallr is "whitest of gods," and to be fair or shining is a sign of power. The English word "white" comes from the Anglo-Saxon hvit, meaning "silver-white"; silver and white are functionally identical.

PURPLE: can be seen as a shade of either blue or red; it appears several times in the Anglo-Saxon sources.

GOLD: like red, is a color of power and life. Like white, it is a color of spiritual aspiration and intensity of energy, although more earthy in nature.

GREEN & BROWN: are colors of the earth. Brown is associated with the Dokkalfar.

DARK GREEN: is associated with the Vanic mysteries, light green with birth and the Vanic power springing forth. Green is also associated with the fertility and hidden mysteries of water.

YELLOW: is a color of ambition and fertilization. It may be seen, in one aspect, as the masculine complement to green. It can also be seen as the color of the sun's workings upon the earth, or a very earthy gold.

BLACK: is the ultimate color of concealment and mystery, into which dark blue and dark green both shade. It is the color of stillness and death, and the womb of rebirth.

TIME

The Teutonic use of time in magic is not nearly as strictly regulated as that of ceremonial magic. It is mainly ruled by the position of Moon and Sun, although certain times of the year are more powerful than others. The times of day which are traditionally used in Teutonic magic are sunset, midnight, and sunrise; it is unusual for a ritual to be performed between sunrise and sunset. Sunrise is best for religious rites, some meditation rituals, and collecting of herbs and hallowed water. Sunset is also good for religious rites and some meditations; trials should begin at sunset.

Midnight is best for practical magic, for some initiations, and for divination. These times are by no means the only times at which you may perform rituals of any sort; as always, it will depend on both the individual vitki1s intuition and her/his circumstances. The day of the week is relatively unimportant in Teutonic magic. If it is convenient, the day which bears the name of a god fitting to one's rite may be used for extra harmony of atmosphere, but omitting this detail will not detract from the rite's efficiency in any way. The days of the week correspond thus:

Sunday=Sunna

Monday=Mani

Tuesday=Tyr

Wednesday=Odhinn

Thursday=Thorr

Friday=Freyja (also Freyr or Frigg).

Attempts have been made to force Saturday to correspond to Loki, but these have been largely unsuccessful. A closer similarity lying between Saturn and Nerthus might be suggested, as both are chthonic deities with power over agriculture and keepers of the dead, but there is no historical reason to maintain this correspondence in the days of the week. The strongest influence in scheduling your rituals will probably be the phase of the Moon.

The New Moon is good for beginnings and the increase of growth; the Full Moon is the night when magical power is at its strongest flow in the open; the waning Moon is good for bindings and putting magics into concealment; and the dark of the moon is the night of the greatest hidden magical power. Most magic is traditionally done at either the new or full Moon. The most important times of the year are the solstices, the equinoxes, and the full moons immediately following these peaks of power. In tradition, at least, the mightiest time of magic is the twelve nights of the Yule feast, beginning at the night of the Winter Solstice. At this time, the Wild Hunt rides and the other worlds are closest to the earth.

12: OTHER MAGICAL SYMBOLS

Along with the runes, the Teutonic people used a rich array of other symbols which were mighty emblems of both religion and magic. Most of these are older than the runes, having been used during the Bronze Age (in Scandinavia, roughly 1600A50 B.C.E.), but their use continued through the runic period.

AEGISHJALMAR: (Helm of Terror) This symbol appears carved beside the figures of warriors; a more complex form is still used in Icelandic magic. It is worn or traced between the brows to cause terror to your foes [1]. The dragon Fafnir wore it while guarding his hoard. [2]

SPIRAL: The spiral represents the coiling layers of that which-is, Serpents are often drawn coiled into spirals, and in the runic era it became fairly common to carve runes inside the outline of a wyrm.

THE SHIP: The ship is the emblem of passing between the worlds, usually at death. The sun-wheel has also been drawn in a ship, and it may be that the wagon shows its daily faring across the sky while the ship shows its passage beneath the earth at night. The ship is an emblem of fertility as well, as is the wagon.

FOOTPRINT: The bare footprint is a fertility symbol associated with the Vanic cult from the earliest times (see the chapter on Njord).

AETT-RING: The ring of the heavens divided by the eight winds; the eight worlds with Midgardhr in the center. Tilted so that the spaces mark direction, it is the Icelandic solarhringar (ring of the sun; see raidho). [3] Also appears as an eight-pointed star.

 CRESCENT: Symbol of the Moon, showing reason and measured change.

 TREFOT: The trefot shows whirling might like that of the swastika set into a threefold pattern, showing direction and thrust. It shows power spinning from and into the three realms Asgardhr/ Midgardhr Hel.

 VALKNUT: The proto-shape is three triangles set in a triangular pattern; the later valknut, or knot of the slain, is a sign of the Odhinnic cult. Wearing the valknut is a sign to Odhinn that one is ready to be taken into the ranks of his chosen warriors at any time he chooses. In this symbol you may see the interwoven workings of Urdhr-verdhandi-skuld, or of Odhinn in his many tripartite forms. Meditation upon this image is well worthwhile.

 HAMMER: The hammer of Thorr is the greatest of Teutonic symbols of warding. It can be carved, painted, or magically traced anywhere that guarding is needed (over doors, windows, etc.). The hammer sign is traced over food and drink before eating. A hammer symbol is worn both for warding and to show that one has taken up one's ancestral faith. Wearing this sign was the heathen answer to the Christian cross.

 BEASTS: The images of beasts were often used as religious and/or magical symbols (for specific uses, see Beasts).

13 HERB LORE

Herbs are a great part of Teutonic magical practice. They are often worked into charms or hung with red thread over the windows and doors of a house to ward it. Herbs were also used in brewing and in aid of other forms of magic, both galdr and seidhr. A great deal of the deeper herb lore of the Germanic peoples has been stamped out by Christianity, but echoes of it have remained in the folk names and traditions concerning some plants, and the keen eye which knows what to look for may find the traces that lead back to the workings of our ancestors.

ACONITE: Called Tyr's Helm or Wolfs bane, this plant is so poisonous that it should not be touched even barehanded. It is associated with the harsher justice-dealing sides of tiwaz. Another name, Auld Wife's Hood, suggests a possible tie with the Norns and perthro.

AGRIMONY: Traditionally laid under the head to cause a deathlike sleep, which was supposed to last until the plant was removed. Still used to aid sleep and quiet distracting thoughts. Agrimony works well with isa.

ANGELICA: Angelica is traditionally an herb of warding and cleansing. It is thought to guard against and even cure the plague. The plant was once prominent in Lettish paganism. Its harvesting in the early summertime was marked by a ritual song which has, unfortunately, be- come either so antiquated or corrupt as to become unintelligible, but which is still learned in childhood and sung today.[1] Christianity associated this plant with the Archangel Michael. It was fairly common for Christianity to substitute the term angel for "valkyrja,' "fylgja," or "dis." The mention of Michael may show that this plant was originally tied to Heimdallr, the fairest of the Aesir. All of the Angelica's parts are considered effective against woe-working magic of any sort. Angelica is used in touching the highest realms of Yggdrasil being associated with elhaz and the cleansing fire of Bifrost.

APPLE: Apple trees which are good bearers are wassailed at Yule, and their fruits are eaten at that time of blessing. It is the Apples of Idunn which give the gods their endless youth and strength. The Apple is a tree of fruitfulness, healing, and joy. It works well with jera.

ASH: The Ash is a very holy tree. Yggdrasil is said by some to be an Ash; Askr and Embla, the first humans, were made from an Ash and an Elm by Odhinn, Hoenir, and Lodurr. Ash wood is good for the gandr and for the vitki's harrow. It is associated with ansuz and hagalaz.
BEECH: The Beech tree was connected with the casting of lots in early Germanic times. Its name in some Germanic dialects means "book," hinting that its wood was used for runic writings. It is associated with perthro.

BISTORT: Also called Twice-Writhen, Adder-Wort, Snake weed, and Dragon-Wort. The root is known for its twice-turned shape which writhes back upon itself. It is fitting to use with nauthiz.

BLACKBERRY: The Blackberry is frequently used in the cure of various forms of swelling, the sufferer being passed through a natural loop in the hedge. It is particularly useful in turning back runes of woe. The Blackberry is good to use with kenaz.

CHAMOMILE: Called Baldur's Brow (a name shared with several small white flowers in the North), this plant makes a calming tea and brings joy and peace on all levels. Chamomile works well with wunjo.

COWSLIP: The Cowslip is also called Key Flower. It is thought to open the door into Freyja's hall or mound. It is closely tied to kenaz.

ELDER: Also called Hylde-Moer, this tree is closely tied to the female Vanic powers. The name Elder comes from the Anglo-Saxon aeld, "fire," being a reference to the use of the hollow branches in blowing up fires. The Elder tree is still held in great respect in England and the Northern countries. Her wood is not burned for ordinary purposes and is only cut after one has asked permission with the formula, "Lady Ellhorn, give me some of thy wood and I will give thee some of mine when it grows in the forest." It is thought that if a cradle is made of Elder wood, Hylde-Moer will come and strangle the child laid in it. The Elder tree is associated with second sight. In Denmark it is thought that standing under her on Midsummer's Eve will enable one to see "the king of Fairyland" and all his men come riding by. It is also written that the pith of the branches can be cut into rounds, soaked in oil, lighted, and floated on a pan of water to show one all the witches and sorcerers around one. [2] The Vanic might can be seen in all of these workings; Hylde-Moer is a form of Holda or Hel; as Freyja, she rules the doings of "witches" and the visionary power of seidh-magic. The Elder tree is associated with fehu and, to a lesser degree, with berkano.

ELECAMFANE: Called Elf-dock or Elf-wort by the Anglo-Saxons, Elecamfane was used largely to work against the ills done by elves-to stab the plant's root with an iron knife was to break the elvish magic. Elecamfane may be used to gain the favor of the Alfar as well. A gift for them may be left by the roots of a wild patch. If the root is being used in recels, a drink, or a taufr, it should be dug before sunrise without the use of iron and covered, and the digger should speak no word from the time she/he leaves the house to the time he/she returns with the root. It should be kept hidden, preferably under the harrow.

GARLIC: This plant's name means "spear-leek." It is also called Gruserich ("king of the grasses"). [3] Sigurdhr's wife Gudhrun likens him to "the garlic grown the grass above," [4] a reference to this plant's quick-springing might. Garlic is a great strengthener, both magically and physically. It is associated with both laukaz and tiwaz.

HAZEL: The Hazel tree was used for hedging in courts of law in earlier Germanic times. "Wishing rods" were made of peeled Hazel boughs, and Egill Skallagrimsson used a Hazel stave in making his nidhing-pole pole against Eirik Bloodaxe and Queen Gunnhild. It is said that oak and Hazel cannot be planted or used together. The Hazel is fitting to use with raidho.

HOUSE LEEK: Also called Thorr's Beard. This herb is traditionally planted on the roofs of houses to ward off the danger of lightning or fire, and was thought to be a protection against sorcery as well. It is fitting to use with thurisaz.

LEEK: The leek is very like the garlic in its springing, shining might. Its name, laukaz, is an alternate name for the rune laguz and a powerful formula for runic talismans.

LOOSE STRIFE, YELLOW: In folklore, yellow loose strife is thought to quiet savage beasts and ease the struggling of oxen at the plow and restless horses. It is good to use with ehwaz.

MANDRAKE: The European Mandrake (Atropa mandragora), which should not be confused with the American Mandrake or May-Apple (Podophyllurn peltatum), is called by the name Alruna and thought to be one of the most powerful of herbs. Alruna is also the name of a wise-woman, and the Mandrake is often spoken of in the feminine. It is associated with eihwaz. Certain customs connected with the transfer of the family's root from father to son or brother to brother [5] also may tie it to the kinfylgja. The Mandrake is highly poisonous—it should not be eaten, rubbed on the body, or used in recels.

MISTLETOE: Mistletoe is one of the most highly magical plants known to the Teutonic peoples. It was the arrow which slew Baldr. It has power over both life and death. It should not be allowed to touch the ground, as a great deal of its might comes from its heavenly birth and growth. It is fitting to use with sowilo.

MUG WORT: The Mug wort is a great aid to faring forth from the Lich and to all forms of visionary magic. It is used as a stuffing for pillows which open the vision of dreams. Mug wort can be made into amulets to aid travelers. It guards one from woe-working beings on both bodily and spiritual journeys.

The Nine Herbs Charm mentions it as a protection against poison, serpents, and "the loathsome foe roving through the land" (probably an ill-wishing seidh-farer). [6] It is gathered on Midsummer's for greatest magical effect. Mug wort is associated with the rune raidho and with Sol (the sun) and her two horses Arvakr and Alsvith.

NETTLE: The name nettle is derived from the passive form of an Indo-European root meaning "to spin or sew." [7] It is sometimes used in undoing curses. It is fitting to use with nauthiz.

OAK: The Oak is unquestionably the holiest of trees in all Indo-European societies. It is the tree of the Sky-Father in his original form. In Teutonic tradition it is associated with Thorr and Tyr (but not Odhinn!). The hlaut-teinn (twigs for sprinkling the blood of the sacrifice) were usually oak, as probably the Irminsul and the main pillars of the temple would have been. The mightiest mistletoe grows on oak trees. Oak is the preferred wood for the harrow of the godhi (Teutonic priest). It is a warder against all workings of woe. Oak increases strength and male fertility. A common kenning for a warrior is "oak of battle." The runes with which the oak works best are thurisaz, jera, tiwaz, and othala.

PERIWINKLE: Also called Sorcerer's Violet. Used in love potions and for making garlands; called an "herb of immortality" in Germany. This plant works well with gebo.

PENNY ROYAL: Also called Dog Whistle (Dwarf's pestle). Thought to be a cleanser of water and corrupt blood, and used against the ill-workings of all watery wights. Penny royal is fitting to use with uruz.

ROSEMARY: The herb Rosemary is said to strengthen the memory and the powers of thought in general. It was used in incenses for cleansing, and it was also among the plants used for Yule decorations. It works well with mannaz and jera.

ROWAN: The Rowan tree or mountain ash is one of the best-known trees of warding, particularly in regard to protecting one's home and lands from ill-wishing wights of uncanny nature. It is said that Thorr clung to it to keep from being swept away in a torrent caused by a giant maiden; hence there is a proverb, "the Rowan is the salvation of Thorr," It traditionally protects against fire, lightning, and storms. Rowan is fitting to use with thurisaz.

ROYAL FERN: This herb is also called Osmund the Waterman, a name which relates it to the rune ansuz (os in Anglo-Saxon) and to Odhinn, whose name was also changed to St. Oswald by nominally Christianized Germans. Odhinn often appears as a ferryman carrying away the dead - another side of ansuz's being.

RUE: Rue is traditionally an herb of warding and cleansing. It is fiery and intense in being, and has been worn for gaining second sight. It is fitting to use with elhaz.

SOW THISTLE: Also called Carline Thistle (Carlina vulgaris) and Boar's Throat. According to Teutonic tradition, this herb can be used to steal the vitality of another for oneself. It was also said that if this herb were tied to one of a married couple without being noticed, the other partner would waste away and die.[8] It works well with ingwaz.

SUNNAS WORT (St. John's Wort, renamed for heathen use): This plant is best plucked on Midsummer's or Ostara. It is used in the holy fires at Midsummers and hung over the door or window to ward off ill. It is also used for invincibility and strengthening the will. Sunnaswort is good to use with sowilo.

TANSY: The new leaves of this herb are traditionally mixed with eggs and made into cakes to be eaten at "Easter," the spring festival of Ostara. Tansy is fitting to use with dagaz.

VALERIAN: Called Velandsurt (Wayland's Wort), this herb is fitting to use with kenaz.

WILLOW: The Willow is a tree of water, life, and swift-springing force. It has also been associated with funeral rites. It is fitting to use with laguz.

YARROW: The Yarrow is traditionally used to bring prophetic visions and dreams. It is thought of as a witches' herb and may be used in visionary works of seidh-magic. It is fitting to use with fehu.

YEW: The mysteries of the Yew tree are discussed under eihwaz. It is fitting to use with hagalaz, eihwaz, and elhaz. Remember, yew is very poisonous and should not be used in recels.

14: SPAE AND SEIDHR: NORTHERN SOUL-WORKINGS

-UPDATED IN 2018-

Heidhr she hight who to houses came,
Völva spae-wise wand-craft she knew
Worked seidhr where she could seidhr playing with souls
To baleful women beloved
(Völuspa 22)

"Óðinn knew that accomplishment...which is called seiðr, and from
that he could know the ørlög of men and things that had not
happened, and also thus cause the deaths or loss of hamingjur or loss
of luck of men, and also thus take from one man wit or life-force and
give it to others." (Ynglinga saga, ch. 7)

The first edition of this book was written thirty years ago. At the time, the magical
art the Norse called "seidhr" was believed, by some of the best scholars in the
academic field, to be a form of Shamanism. Everyone was all excited at the time
about Dag Strömbäck's monograph Sejd, which was about the similarities between
some of the seidhr-techniques and Saami Shamanism, and I followed the teachings
of those who knew far more than I without questioning them as closely as I should
have. Since then, I achieved my own doctorate in Norse studies (The Cult of
Odhinn: God of Death?), which included a closer look at the matter of whether
Odhinn could be called a shaman, or whether, indeed, the Norse practiced
Shamanism at all; and used my academic resources to investigate the question of
what our forebears were actually doing when they said they were practicing seidhr
or spá (the Norse word translated into Scots dialect as "spae").

The answers weren't what I, or a lot of my esteemed predecessors in the field of
Northern studies, had thought—though it is true that many of the techniques of all
three arts are closely related. Since the publication of Teutonic Magic, one group in
California, Hrafnar, has been working on recreating the soul-skills of the North,
using elements from all three, plus Michael Harner's modern attempt to coalesce
techniques from genuine shamanic cultures. Unfortunately, they chose to use the
term "seidhr", which has led to many gross historical misunderstandings (to which
I regret to say that I contributed in the first edition of this book).

But since there are no actual Heathen-Age Norse around to be appalled, burn
their houses down, and throw them off cliffs with sealskin bags over their heads,
they will probably continue to live quite happily while being known in public as
practitioners of "seidhr". Which, being ethical people, they don't actually do;
Hrafnar "seidhr" is an effective form of foretelling, answering spiritual questions
(spae), and occasionally speaking with god/esses, wights, and ghosts (the seeress in
Eiríks saga required a song "that was needed to practice seidhr", but she was lucky
to find anyone who knew it; others managed to speak with all manner of beings
without such a song).

For a long time, it was the general practice, among academics and Heathens alike, to divide Germanic magic into "galdr" (specifically the magic of words and rune staves) and "seidhr" (unfortunately used in modern times by many as a generic for "soul-working magics"). This ignores the frequent overlap between the two, and, more than that, leaves out the widest and most-practiced class of Northern magic. There is no specific term for that class, but it may best be described as the magic of amulets, stones, and herbs. Galdr is strongly attributed to Odhinn, Freyja to seidhr; the third class was too common, ancient, and widespread to be named or attributed, but because the bulk of it tended to fall into the woman's sphere of the home, I think of it as closest to Frigg. There is also the sub-division of textile magic...spinning and weaving...which most certainly does belong to Frigg.

Techniques from each of these classes were constantly used to strengthen each other. In this chapter:, however, I am dealing only with the magics of soul-working in the North. Seidhr, as the quotes at the beginning of this chapter show, is a form of active magic which works mainly on the mind and soul of someone else, though it is quite possible to kill with it. One of the oldest definitive surviving uses of the word is the line in a poem of Kormákr's (tenth century), "Odhinn seidhr til Rind"...Odhinn practiced seidhr on Rindr...referring to the fathering of Vídharr.

As Saxo Grammaticus describes it, the god used magic to drive Rindr, who had refused to sleep with him, insane; disguised himself as an old woman on the pretext of curing her; warned Rindr's father that the medicine might cause a violent reaction and got him to tie her to the bed; then raped her in order to father Váli, Baldr's avenger (Gesta Danorum, Book III). The word "seidhr" only even begins to be conflated with "spae" as the sagas become more romanticized and fantastic. The family sagas, however, continue to stress that seidhr was a magic of ill-working.

It was used to cause nightmares (Gísla saga Súrsonar, ch. 18); to inflict mental and emotional disorders (Egils saga, ch. 59 –Queen Gunnhildr uses seidhr upon Egill so that he will never rest comfortably in Iceland until she sees him, causing restlessness and near-suicidal depression); to put the members of a household to sleep for ill purposes (Laxdaela saga, ch. 36 – and when the twelve year-old son of the household does wake up and steps outside, he immediately falls dead); and to doom men to drown (Laxdaela saga ch. 35). Seidhr could occasionally be used for purposes that, though unquestionably doing ill to the victim, were intended to work weal or justice for others. Landnámabók describes how Thurídhr Sound-Filler, in a time of hunger, used "seidhr" to bring a shoal of herring into the nearby sound to feed the folk (ch. 114).

Ill to the herring, but weal to the hungry Icelanders – and truly, it would take a very over-scrupulous modern person to be worried about the ethical implications of non-consensual mind-magic worked on the tiny brains of herring. Interestingly, Thurídhr was from Hálogaland, which is the Saami area of northern Norway. It is quite possible that she had learned how to do this from Saami shamans, who also used such magic in the coastal areas; but the Norse had no word other than seidhr for it. Thurídhr does not otherwise function as a shaman: she does not guide fishers to where the fish will be shoaling, bring back messages from the wights of the land or their forebears to the settlers, or serve as the chief rede-giver for the settlement.

In Gunnars saga keldugnúpfifls, Thórdís, who has no one to bring a suit for her at the Thing uses seidhr to inflict mental and emotional disorders on Gunnarr (so that he could not sit comfortably at home or away, causing a state of desperation and despair to fall upon him – similar to the seidhr worked upon Egill Skalla-Grímsson by Queen Gunnhildr) until he finally does the right thing and pays the weregild due her for his killing of her brother. This is clearly no worse than gathering a few friends and going after the killer to force him to pay up with sword and ax...though it does tell us that even when seidhr is used in a fitting manner, it's meant to hurt someone. There are various statements that it was "unmanly" to work seidhr, for reasons unclear.

It has often been suggested that, as seen in some shamanic cultures, folk who are outside the standard gender roles of their own society are better able and/or more likely to develop visionary and Otherworldly abilities. Hrafnar had a trope that women and gay men made the best seers; but plenty of straight men have showed themselves to be first-rate seers. Cross-dressing may have been one of the elements used: Odhinn is known to have cross-dressed at least twice in a context of seidhr – once with Rindr; and Loki accuses him of going about in a witch's likeness in Locasenna. It is also a point that while women who took up the manly role were admired, men who forsook the manly role were thought rather less well of; and the manly role definitely meant smacking your enemy with a big weapon rather than harming his mind by magic. Spae is a general term for "prophecy", and could be done either in a ritual context or when the spae-person was inspired or could not ignore their sight.

There are accounts of spae-folk seeing fylgjur under everyday circumstances, or suddenly speaking up with a warning or advice without needing any ritual warm-up. It should be noted that almost everyone has a touch of this gift, especially in times such as approaching death, just as everyone has a fylgja which may sometimes go out and do things even without the human knowledge. What makes a spae-person is (1) being able to do it reasonably often and consistently; (2) probably being able to use at least some of the common techniques of the Northern soul-worker; and (3) the respect - rather than the fear, hatred, and contempt - of your neighbors. Shamanism did not exist in Norse Scandinavia after the end of the Hunting Stone Age.

Shamanism is not a magical "technique" or "pathway"; it is a complex of techniques (all of which are variously common to everyone from St. Francis to Aleister Crowley and Israel Regardie) in the context of a crucial and well-defined social role, in a type of society that makes that social role not only possible but necessary. Shamanism is seen among hunter-gatherers and herders (the Saami, the pastoralist Mongols); it disappears when agriculture arrives, for one simple reason. A hunter or pastoralist can leave the land when the spirits say it's time to move on; a farmer can't. To survive, hunters and pastoralists need someone in the tribe who can tell them where the game or good grass is, and when to stop moving and buckle down because there's an angry storm on the way. A farmer has to build as best as possible, and then trust, pray, and make offerings to the gods, because a farmer can't leave their land.

Individual shamanic techniques, individually indistinguishable from basic techniques to be found in any other given magical way, undoubtedly survived through the Heathen era and right into the modern age. The Saami most certainly were and are to some degree still a shamanic people, and Norse folk such as Queen Gunnhildr even went to them to learn magic; but Gunnhildr was not a shaman. One simply cannot talk about a Germanic or Norse Shamanism after agriculture got there, except that it nearly happened once. In Greenland, the Norse settlers were being thrown increasingly back on hunting as a way of life. The seeress of Eiríks saga raudha (ch. 4) is well on her way to functioning as a shaman, including the fact that her method is to please the "nátturur" ("natures" – frustratingly not a native word, so we'll never know who she was calling; may just have meant "the author of Eiríks saga didn't know who she was talking to either") and ask them the questions that are put to her.

This account tells us a great deal about the overlap in technique between spae and seidhr: the song used is called a seidhr-song, and clearly isn't part of the seeress' usual way of working, since she has to find a member of the settlement who chances to know the song she needs to lure the nátturur. She, however, is clearly a highly respected spae-woman, bearing the honorable by-name of litilvölva ("Little Seeress"). Even when using a seidhr-song to get more knowledge, she is working as a seeress - but looking chiefly at the things crucial to the settlers' survival: the harvest, the weather, and only occasionally a special person's ørlög. But for the conversion, her grand-daughters would most likely have been telling hunting parties when and where to seek the walrus and the narwhal every year, and her great-granddaughters asking the spirits of those animals to please offer themselves for the life of the village.

Perhaps as telling are the peculiar burials of rows of highly decorated walrus skulls in the actual churchyard at Gardar cathedral. It might be that, had it not been for the conversion which moved the Greenlanders to identify strongly with greater Europe, the next wave of Europeans would have gotten there to find a people who looked like a blend of Norse and native Greenlander, spoke a language with words from both, and practiced a full shamanism calling on the god/esses and wights of the North.Another example of the incipient reversion-forwards to Shamanism on the Greenlanders is the tale from Eiríks saga describing how, in a time of starvation, Thórhallr veidhimadhr ("Huntsman") goes off by himself and is seen on a cliff, making peculiar faces and chanting to Thórr.

A whale beaches shortly thereafter, which Thórhallr considers a response to his bidding. This is not full Shamanism – Thórhallr is praying, not taking part in two-way speech, although he may be using other techniques to help his bidding along - and he is more of an outcast than a central figure in the group; but it is easy to see how such practices could have evolved back into Shamanism in a culture thrown back on the hunting-gathering ways of their forebears. The Germanic folks hadn't been shamanic for thousands of years, but some of the techniques survived (or were re-learned from the Saami by some), and when time, weather, and lifestyle changed, they had the tools to become a shamanic culture again.

My rede is to look very strangely at anyone who uses the phrase "Germanic/ Northern/Norse Shamanism" unless they are either talking about the early Stone Age or the Greenlanders. The only reason the academic community is no longer laughing at Stephen Glosecki for his Anglo-Saxon Shamanism is that, hilarious as it was at the time, the joke wasn't funny enough to justify remembering the book longer than a year or two.

Tools

The Stave: One of the chief magical tools of the seidhmadhr (seidhr-person) or spámadhr (spae-person) was certainly the stave, which was often made out of iron and decorated with a ring or knob on top, or even more elaborate ornamentation. The stave of Thórbjörg litilvölva is described as having a knob on top and being made of brass, with stones set in the knob. We have found many such items in graves; but it is nearly impossible for archaeologists to tell the difference between a distaff and a seidhstafr (seidhr-staff). There may not have been a meaningful difference in any case, given the key position of textile arts in women's magic – and the convenience, especially if one were a woman bent on working seidhr, of being able to carry around a seidhstafr without making others wary.

Both staves and distaffs came in many sizes, from arm-length to the height of a standing person. In Icelandic folklore, the stave, or gandr, was used as a device for flight in much the same manner as the witch's broom of later European folklore. To make it work apparently required the magical belt and gloves that went with it. The word used for this practice was gandreidh ("wand-ride"), a term also applying to the riding out of the álfar, which was the closest equivalent to the Wod-Host ("Fury-Host") or Wild Hunt of Northern Europe.

Gloves and Belt: Gloves and belts were also of great meaning to the Northern soul-worker, particularly together with the stave. In later Icelandic folklore as mentioned above, belt, gloves, and stave were the chief tools of the witch going on her gandreidh (wand-ride). These were also the gifts Gridhr gave Thórr when he fared to Jotunheimr without his Hammer (there is a good deal more to Thórr than most folk ever realize. We don't see him flying on the stave...but Thórr likes his feet braced on his mother's strength, thank you, and seems none too excited about even riding a horse. Or too heavy for it). The Eiríks saga description famously mentions the seeress' gloves being made of cat skin, which they probably were, given that what were obviously cat fur farms have been found in Viking York and Viking Cork, and the probable link between cats and Freyja.

We still don't know if Snorri, the only reference to it, got the "wain drawn by cats" from an older source or made it up to match the other descriptions in the stanzas he does quote about Baldr's death; but the cat-ornamentation all over the Oseberg sledges, and the practice of burying lynx-skins with women vs. burying bear-skins with men, suggest that if Snorri did invent the cat-drawn wain, at least he didn't pull it out of his cap.

Happily, cat skin is not required...though if you have access to fur from a long-haired cat and know someone with spinning capabilities, cat-fur gloves or mittens would make a very fine substitute. The seeress' belt is described as made of "touch-wood", an uncertain term, but clearly it was something more meaningful than simple cloth or leather. A leather belt may be tooled with runes; a tablet-woven belt may be woven with a pattern of might (fylfots, however, are to be avoided if anyone but you is ever going to see it, in order to avoid causing huge amounts of unnecessary and fully-justified distress); both may have amber (wards, stores might) or other amulets of your choice sewn onto them.

The Cloak and Hood: At the time when the issue of conversion was tearing Iceland apart, Thórgeirr the Lawspeaker went "under the cloak" to speak with the gods. The answer he brought back – a compromise by which Iceland officially converted to keep the peace, but Heathen practices were still permitted in private (Íslendingabók, ch. 7) – not only made it possible for the colony to survive, but to preserve almost everything we know from Norse texts, which allow us to have at least a chance of understanding our forebears' iconography and archaeological leavings.

The hooded cloak: like the stave, was a clear marker for a soul-worker: the dead seeress in Laxdæla saga is seen for what she is at once because she is carrying a seidhstafr (found with her bones later) and "was in a costly woven mantle and hidden in a hood"(ch 76). The black cat skin-lined hood of Thórbjörg litilvölva (Eiríks saga, ch. 4) was not only a working part of her ritual gear and a sign of her role, but may have been meant to give her the Otherworldly sight of a cat. When the colour of these cloaks is spoken of, they are either as black (svartr) or, like Thórbjörg's mantle, blue (blár...but the "blue"-word, to the Norse, could be used to describe anything from the color of the sky to the color of a raven's wing, so it is often translated "blue-black" – one may compare Snorri's description of Hel as half-sallow and half-blár).

There are several examples of a seidhr- or spae-worker covering their own eyes in order to either see something beyond the light of ordinary day or cause a magical darkness (Thorsteins þáttr uxafóts, Flateyjarbók I, pp. 252 ff; Sturlunga saga, ch. II, vol. I; Brennu-Njáls saga, ch. XII; Harðar saga, ch. 25). By blinding oneself to Midhgardhr, it becomes easier to look into the other worlds and to work upon them. When Thorgrímr Dýrason sends his fylgja out to spy on the farm of his foe, he "slept and spread his cloak over his head" (Hávarðar saga Ísfirðings, ch. 29). There is also at least one saga suggesting that the power of the worker could be stored in the cloak and lent out.

Thórdís spákona (and note that, while the magic is the mind-working of seidhr, everyone politely calls her spákona!) has a wand (stafsproti) which she can lend out to others for use: when Thorkell hires her to help him in an upcoming law-case, she tells him to "fare you now in my black (svartr) hooded cloak (kufl) and take the stafsproti which is called Högnuðr ...Now you shall go to Guðmundr and strike him three times on the left cheek", which causes Guðmundr to briefly lose his memory so that the case can be settled peacefully. When that is done, Thórdís has Thorkel strike Guðmundr on the right cheek with the stave, and he regains his memory" (Vatnsdoela saga, ch. 44). The stave by itself is not enough - or perhaps will not obey someone who isn't literally cloaked in its mistress' might; the cloak also seems to serve to render Thorkell invisible.

The High Seat: A special "high seat" or otherwise working from a high place such as the top of a grave mound (best) or a hill (all right) is a significant part of Norse soul-workings. We see this even among the gods, with Odhinn's Hlidhsjkálfr from which he (and sometimes Frigg; and once, unauthorized, Freyr) looks out over the worlds. When Gríma is hiding Thormóðr Kolbrúnarskáld from his pursuers (who include a woman who is also able to go on the gandreidh), she has him sit in a large chair carved with the images of the gods. Meanwhile her husband seethes seal-meat in a cauldron and casts the sweepings on the fire to make a great steam and smoke, which seems to bring about a magical darkness; while Gríma spins and speaks or chants to receive the unwelcome visitors.

They look straight at the chair, and she has to do some quick talking to imitate at least a nominal Christian (Fostbræðra saga, ch. 23). The "empty chair" amulet appears occasionally in Norse burials, notably that of the "Fyrkat witch", and may symbolize either Odhinn's seat, or the high seat of the seer. Perhaps it could even have served as an amuletic replacement for the Fyrkat witch's own when she was traveling. If one hasn't got the ability to set up a high seat at home or to find a suitable high place outdoors, one might enchant and don such an amulet in order to make an ordinary chair temporarily into a high seat.

The Cauldron: The cauldron was also a great tool of the Northern soul-worker. To my some embarrassment, I recently looked into this and found that most of the elements associated with the late Renaissance/early modern witch folklore all the way up to the modern Broom-Hilda witch caricature may well actually be survivals of real Northern magical practice. When the neighbors of the seidhkarl (seidhr-man) Thórólfr Sledge got tired of his ill magics and came in a mob to get him, they found that his home was defended by eighteen large and ferocious black cats, sufficient to deter a pack of full-grown Norsemen with armor and swords. The cats bought him time to seethe mysterious substances in his cauldron, creating a reek of steam and smoke that allowed him to disappear invisibly.

Seething a spell of invisibility in a cauldron was also, as described below, done by a woman named Gríma in order to hide a fugitive from the eyes of both his ordinary pursuers and another soul-worker, with spinning and sitting on a special chair also a part of the spell (Fóstbræðra saga, ch. 23). Certainly the "flying ointment" of the late Middle Ages onwards mixed in a cauldron (and given the things that went into it, that cauldron better not have been used for food preparation afterwards!) was ultimately of Northern origins. Salves were the most common way of applying medication among both the Norse and the better-documented Anglo-Saxons, and the Vikings absolutely were using at least henbane for magico-medicinal purposes.

A number of the seeds were found in a bag in the Viking Age Danish grave that has been dubbed the "Fyrkat Witch", due to the many interesting things with which she was buried, including one of those stave/distaff items. Deadly nightshade was well-known to the Norse; mandrake probably was, since it was well-known in England from the Southern medical lore (and yes, it will grow all the way through southern Scandinavia; the best specimen I ever saw was in Krusemynta Herb Gardens in Gotland). Only the broom is lacking – and the stave replaces it in Northern lore. Please remember that henbane, deadly nightshade, and mandrake are extremely poisonous, and other herbs attributed to the flying ointment such as hemlock are even worse. Don't try making a traditional flying ointment at home – you could well find that your ticket to the Otherworld was only a one-way.

Herbs in Soul-Working: Herbs were often used in Northern magic. Direct combustion was less common, though may have been done on occasion; usually they were applied to a person in ointment form, or seethed, perhaps with other things, in a cauldron to raise might in the steam (as in the examples above). For the modern apartment-dweller, a fair equivalent would be essential oil in a water/candle diffuser. Be careful: mug wort, one of the best herbs in whole form for this purpose, is quite toxic as an essential oil due to the high thujone concentration.

No more than one drop in the diffuser; do not apply to the skin, even heavily diluted; do not use in any way whatsoever if you might be pregnant and want to stay that way until your baby is born. If you don't know an essential oil, look its safety profile up: it is not usually identical to that of the natural herb. Cleansing was also done at least in later Norway by steeping a few juniper branches or berries in water, and sprinkling the water around the house or washing the floor with it outright. A few of the other herbs which are useful for enhancing soul-work include:

Birch—used for cleansing, notably in the sauna (common throughout Scandinavia, not just Finland). Linked, obviously, to the rune stave Berkano; see the chapter on that stave. Caraway seeds are used in Scandinavian folklore for magical insulation; both caraway and flax seeds are used for warding. If undertaking something that could be particularly risky, pouring either of these in a circle around yourself might be a good idea.

Flax is the better choice if you want to send might outwards, since the object of keeping a thing of might in a casket of caraway seeds is not only to avoid contamination, but to keep its might from leaking.

Elder (Sambuca nigra)– Linked particularly to Freyja and/or Frigg, and also possibly to soul-sight, as per the Danish belief that if one sits under one on Midsummer's Eve, one can see the King of the Elves (Freyr, ruler of Álfheimr) and his host riding by. A cup of elderflower or elderberry tea before beginning a working may help to enhance awareness, and also discourage incipient respiratory viruses.

Holy grass (Hierochloe odorata, Anthoxanthum nitens)– same plant, two Linnean names. Also known as musk grass in Swedish trolldom traditions or sweet-grass in the Americas. A sweet-smelling cleanser in all the circumpolar areas and southwards in both Europe and America. We used it in the same manner as rushes on the floor in the Middle Ages and for scenting clothes; in Swedish trolldom, it plays a special role in love spells, and might be particularly suited to Frigg and Freyja – both goddesses notably linked to the soul-working magics.

Juniper– the most common cleansing and protective herb of Scandinavia.

Mugwort–is the traveler's herb; there is nothing better to aid the far-faring of the soul.

Rowan– is well known as a warding tree, in the Otherworld as well as this. Snorri quotes the saying, "The Rowan is the rescue of Thórr" regarding Thórr's Hammer-less visit to the jotunn Geirrodhr.

Yew– spoken of at length under the rune stave Eihwaz. A stave or gandr of yew (or ash, if you prefer that for "Ódhinn's horse" Yggdrasill) could serve well for riding to the Otherworld with gloves and belt in the manner of an Icelandic witch, particularly if you can tie a strand of horsehair about it. Remember that both yew and ash are trees of death (ash being the favorite as a hanging-tree for executions long after the conversion); your "horse" may tend to turn its head to dark places if not kept under firm control. In the first edition of this work, there was no point in discussing the possible use of entheogenic herbs in Norse magic. Most of the ones used or probably used are simply too dangerous to try at home.

At the time, hemp was illegal everywhere in the Western world except maybe Holland, and there was little hope that it would ever be made legal; its uses as an anti-nauseant and appetite stimulant were recognized due to the benefits reported by cancer and AIDS patients, and the synthetic THC Marinol had already been approved by the FDA...but that was as far as it went. Now that the tide has decisively turned, especially given the bag of hemp seeds worn by the younger Oseberg woman, it is time to consider.

Shortly speaking: the Norse probably were aware of the psychoactive effects of hemp. Their own fiber hemp was lower in THC and CBD than the varieties grown in the Southlands, but they would have been familiar with those through their interactions with the Arabic world; and Scandinavian hemp would have been higher in THC than the varieties used for industrial purposes now, which are carefully bred to be effectively THC-less (they would not have bothered bringing back "indica" seeds from their Arabic friends, because the whole point of hemp grown for fiber is that it needs to be tall, and the then-more-powerful indicas were characteristically short). Did one or both of the Oseberg women use hemp flowers for soul-workings?

We can't tell; seeds of flax, the other fiber, are also amuletic in Northern folklore; so the Oseberg woman's bag could have been related to the entheogenic uses, the fiber uses, or, considering how crucial textile work was to Northern women's magic, both. Entheogenic use, if any, would probably have been through steeping it in butter or fat as a mild salve, or brewing ale or mead with it. In practical terms, the word from modern experimenters is that hemp aids sensitivity, but diminishes control; where it is legal (I do not advise breaking the law where you are!), it might be an adjunct to spae-work, but is unadvised in the context of active workings.

Other psychoactive which the Norse might have known: those who most interacted with the Saami would have been familiar with fly agaric (amanita muscaria). This mushroom was not used to initiate berserkergang – not only do all our accounts suggest that this was usually a spontaneous and sometimes an unwanted state, but the effects are in no way congruent with the berserk experience. It may have been used to initially help strengthen the ties between a warrior and a wolf- or bear-fylgja to allow easier possession...but we'll probably never know. Also, it's dangerous to use. I wouldn't. The Norse were probably also familiar with the native psilocybin [psychedelic prodrug], the "Liberty Cap" (psilocybe semilanceolata), which grows all through northern Europe, even up to north Sweden. Did they actually use it? If so, how, and for what? Until we find a vessel with enough well-preserved mushroom residue in it to identify the species, this, too, remains a mystery.

The "flying ointment" of the late Middle Ages onwards, like the black cats, the cauldron, and the flying stave (later broomstick), was certainly of Northern origins. Salves were the most common way of applying medication among both the Norse and the better-documented Anglo-Saxons, and the Vikings absolutely were using at least henbane for magico-medicinal purposes. A number of the seeds were found in a bag in the Viking Age Danish grave that has been dubbed the "Fyrkat Witch", due to the many interesting things with which she was buried, including one of those stave/distaff items. Deadly nightshade was well-known to the Norse; mandrake probably was, since it was well-known in England from the Southern medical lore (and yes, it will grow all the way through southern Scandinavia; the best specimen I ever saw was in Krusemynta Herb Gardens in Gotland).

Only the broom is lacking – and the stave replaces it in Northern lore. Please remember that henbane, deadly nightshade, and mandrake are extremely poisonous, and other herbs attributed to the flying ointment such as hemlock are even worse. Don't try making a traditional flying ointment at home – you could well find that your ticket to the Otherworld was only a one-way. In any case, it is far better practice to develop the skills of soul-working first before attempting to intensify what you are doing with an entheogen: starting with the entheogen may impair your ability to work without an herbal crutch, or it may dump you into a situation which you don't have the knowledge or ability to escape.

This is enough of a risk for the soul-worker who doesn't have an experienced teacher guiding them anyway. In the immortal words of a friend of mine, "Never trance without a buddy...always trance towards shore". The Thórr's Hammer is the best warding-amulet you can have for doing soul-work, especially for faring into the Otherworld. A great many of these amulets from the Viking Age seem to have been crafted specifically as burial amulets, often with one or several made from iron and hung on an iron ring, though silver was also used both for the burial-amulet type and the showier (and later) answer to the Christian practice of wearing a cross.

Amber is also very well suited for this purpose. Amber was sometimes placed in the mouths of the Norse dead, as seen in the rich weapons grave 54 at Simris (southern Sweden); and several amber Hammers and miniature ax-heads were found in the Viking Age workshops at Hedeby. If you have your stave, gloves, belt, dark hooded cloak, and cauldron, and a high place to sit, with perhaps a pouch of herbs, you may consider yourself a well-equipped Northern soul-worker, whom any historical Norse Heathen or later Icelander would know at once.

TECHNIQUES

Singing and Chanting: We know that seidhr (and shamanism, and probably spae-work when done ritually) was strongly associated with singing/chanting, and probably drumming (Locasenna). The function of these is various. As seen with the seeress in Eiríks saga, the songs may sometimes have been used to lure and please wights of the Otherworld in order to ask them questions and possibly make requests. They probably served to aid the participant(s – often practitioners of both seidhr and spae worked in groups) in achieving the trance state and keeping their awareness on their goals once they were there. It is likely that they were also at times meant to directly shape and send the might raised in the same manner as any other incantation.

However, if you lack skill in poetry, a very simple repeated chant will serve most of your purposes here. If you can manage it, a simple alliterative rhythm such as that seen in Beowulf with a break (hearty drum-thump or string-strum) between half-lines. Half-lines alliterating, is good. End-rhyme was not used anywhere in the Heathen Germanic world (except once, as an added technique to perfectly-formatted Norse poetry: and Egill was doing it to show off, because he had to produce something spectacular enough to save his head from an angry Eiríkr Blood-Axe).

It did, however, make its way up from the South and into Scandinavian folk culture at an early enough date, so is not likely to be a problem if you just can't make Heathen-era Northern poetry work for you. If you have musical skill, it is worth being aware that Norwegian folk music preserved two quarter-tones; the one between F and F sharp, and the one between B and B flat.

Many Scandinavian folk songs include alternating accidentals, which seem to be a Western ear's way of trying to capture these quarter-tones. If working in a group, the Icelandic tvísöngur folk harmony (singing in parallel fifths) will certainly not only be fitting, but, having a particularly eerie tonality, will aid in trance and concentration. The style is believed to be slightly post-Heathen, but is indisputably Icelandic now.

Drumming: The drum is known worldwide as an aid for entering altered states of awareness – for magic; for religious community unity; for going into battle. Saami shamans place a high worth on the drum as the vehicle of their soul-farings, and it is quite likely that the Norse used the same technique, as suggested in Locasenna 24, where Loki says to Odhinn:
> "And seidhr you worked in Samsey once,
> And beat on a drum like a völva.
> In witch's likeness you went around folk…"

Saami drums are carefully painted with symbols showing various beings of might (or danger), fitting to the directions, and so forth. They are always oval. The beater or "drum hammer" has a curious shape, a cross between a Y and a T. It is used both to beat the drum for trancing, and for divination, when a "pointer" (a small cup-shaped piece of bone, antler, or brass) is laid with the bottom of the "cup" upwards on top of the drum. As the drum is beaten, the movements of the pointer in relationship to the symbols show the shaman their answer. We do not know if the Norse ever picked up that method of divination, but they did drum for magical purposes.

Saami drumming is described as starting slowly and then speeding up (there are also recordings of it available), and seems a reasonable model for Northern Germanic usage in the absence of any recordings from the Viking Age. The Gaze of Might: Both the Heathen Norse and their Scandinavian descendants recognized the eyes as a great means of directing might. Thórr's fiery eyes are described in Thrymskvidha, and the wide staring eyes of all probable Thórr-images bear this out. The gaze of the undead Glámr does not quite overcome Grettir the Strong in the end, but wounds his soul deeply enough that ever after he, the strongest man in Iceland, was afraid of the dark (Grettis saga Ásmundarson).

In ch. 26 of Vatnsdœla saga, the witch Ljót says that she would have been able to overcome the sons of Ingimundr "if you had not seen me before I saw you", with the result, typical of seidhr, that they would have "all become frenzied with terror and become boars (yrðið at gjalti – a common phrase describing a state of mental frenzy, not a bodily hide-shifting!) Afterwards on the outer ways with wild beasts". Her words are echoed in later Scandinavian folklore where the importance of who gazes upon whom first is key in dealing with ill-willing magic workers, as in the Norwegian account of the trial of Ingerid Eirik's Daughter Kaaljørju (burned in 1661).

A man named Per had brought suit against her for casting the spell that caused his wife to drown herself. He went to her stepdaughter to ask advice; she told him that if he managed to look at Ingerid first when she came into the courtroom, he would win the case, but if she saw him first, she would go free.

He drilled a hole through the ceiling so that he could lie above unseen and watch people enter. When Ingerid came in and he saw her, she started and gave an ugly scream, for she knew Per had seen her first and she had no hope. The end of one of the Oseberg sledges carries a repeated design of a cat-woman either dancing with, or fighting, a sort of reptilian creature; she is drawing her hand away from her eyes, as if to reveal them to the other being. The constant use of the huge-eyed mask as both a decoration and a warding symbol is also likely related to this understanding, as was bagging the heads of both seidhr-workers and the holy horse Freyfaxi before they could be killed, most probably to keep their mighty gaze from striking the killer.

Faring Forth: Traveling out either in one's own form or fylgja, or sending the fylgja to find something out or do something, was a common practice for Norse soul-workers. A working for this is given below.

Reading Dreams: Telling the meaning of a dream was one of the chief jobs of the Norse soul-worker. It is common in the sagas for the dead and wights to come to folk in their dreams. Dreams also have their own meanings. The problem is to read them right. In Laxdaela saga, Gudhrún's fourth husband Thórkell Eyjólfsson dreams that he "had a beard so great that it spread over the whole of Breiðafjörðr." He thinks that means he will become such a great man that his might will spread over the whole area, but Gudhrún warns him that she thinks it may mean that he may drip his beard in Breiðafjörðr. (Ch. 74)

Thórkell drowns in Breiðafjörðr two chapters later. Occasionally a man's wife may dream his wyrd for him: Atlamál in grœnlenzku (10-29) describes the dark dreams of the wives of Högni and Gunnarr (Hagen and Gunther) before the men go to the slaughter in Atli's (Attila's) hall which marks the end of the Burgundian realm in Germany. In this passage, as in Laxdaela saga, the men come up with their own, much cheerier, readings of the imagery in their wives' dreams...until verse 29, when Gunnarr admits that he knows what is going to happen, but that it is already set. This may be linked to the overall Germanic thought that women were just a bit closer or more open to the Otherworld than men, hence slightly better able to get messages meant for their husbands.

PRACTICAL EXERCISES

OTHERWORLDLY SIGHT

This is one of the most useful skills a soul-worker can have. The better you are at it, the easier it will be to judge the amount and character of might in an object, place, or working (and sometimes to tell what you shouldn't touch before you actually touch it), and to see fylgjur, ghosts, and other wights. Start by closing your eyes to a fine slit, until your sight blurs. If you are nearsighted, you have a huge leg up here when you take off your glasses or contact lenses. With the tip of your right forefinger (left for left-handers; consider this said from now on whenever I mention hand preference) or your gandr, trace the shape of a rune stave in the air while softly chanting its name. Concentrate on seeing a trail of the color fitting to that stave from your finger, as if you were writing on the air with a colored pen; when you are done, concentrate on seeing the afterimage still glowing faintly there. You may find that one eye is better for this than the other.

This will help your Sight, and will also be useful in helping you to concentrate and direct your might in active workings. When you can do this reliably, move to objects. Take a thing of known might (such as one of your own magical or religious tools), hold it in your left hand, and look at it in the same way until you see what surrounds it. Most people see colored glows; some see movement and more elaborate images. Also pay attention to the way it feels in your hand. This gives you a sense of the feeling associated with what you are seeing; and some people are more sensitive to touch than to sight.

Likewise, pay attention to any sounds you may hear or other things you may perceive. Because you know what you are looking at/feeling/, this gives you a baseline on which to judge other items. When you feel comfortable with this, it is time to move to testing yourself on unknown objects. If you have a friend who is a practitioner (in any style), ask them if they have anything charged that they wouldn't mind you examining – explain why. You shouldn't be told what it is meant for or what they did to it until after you have described your own impressions. As your accuracy improves, you can then start working with unknown objects and places.

A WARNING: it is easiest to find, and to see things, in places where really bad things have happened. This is not a good idea for the new seer. It is not even always a great idea for the most experienced. Also, at this stage, try to avoid places that would psychologically creep you out even if you were as psychic as the average McDonald's Styrofoam hamburger box. It is very easy for your own preconceptions to interfere...and if you're strong enough and go somewhere like a graveyard at midnight (if that bothers you; if not, fill in your own here) in a creeped out state, you might even manage to give the horrors of your own mind a degree of reality.

Looking for fylgjur following others, again, starting with those whom you both know, then those that the other person knows but you don't, and finally those altogether unknown...is another excellent exercise, and if you find out that you are good at it, you will be very popular in all magico-religious circles. Hence to the next technique, if you haven't been able to see your own fylgja or want to find out what it is not.

DREAMING TRUE AND READING DREAMS

The greatest part of dreaming true is learning to understand your dreams. This is best achieved by keeping a dream diary, and writing your dreams down in detail the moment you wake in the morning (they tend to fade quickly from the waking mind). Mark also how meaningful they felt to you – as you work on this skill, you will start to find it easier to sense the difference between a dream of might and a dream of brain-fluff. As soon as you have the chance, consider at least two different possible readings of the dream and write those down too. Then pay attention to what is happening in your life and the world around you, in order to see which reading, if either, was right – or if there was another you didn't think of – or if the dream was, in fact, brain-fluff. The more you do this, the better you will get at it. If you can talk someone else into sharing their dreams with you and practicing the same skills on them, it will aid you in telling the difference between your symbolism and someone else's.

Books on "if you see this in your dream, it means this" are absolutely useless. To one person, at one time, a snake may be a sign of ill lurking in their path; to another, or the same person at a different time, it may be a sign of blessing and might. The context is important; the feeling is important, but not always definitive. That dream, to someone who is frightened of snakes, may mean that they are about to be in a position to face a fear of another type; or it may be that someone in the Otherworld is trying to bless them straight-out, and their own fear is keeping them from recognizing it. If reading for someone else, your deep feeling may actually be a truer guide than theirs, for the same reason that Tarot readers rarely do readings for themselves: your own thoughts and wishes get in the way, as Thórkell Eyjólfsson did. There are a few things that you can do to aid in true dreaming.

A leaf of mugwort laid under your pillow, ideally with a Hammer and/or bit of amber beside it to help keep you safe, can urge the dreamer to travel. If you know your fylgja, you can either think about shifting into it as you fall asleep, or concentrate on bidding it to go out and come back to you with news. If you want to speak to the land-wight of a certain place, make a small offering to it – a beer, a piece of bread and cheese or meat, or something of that sort – tell the wight that you would like to speak with them, and take a stone or a bit of earth in return (note: plastic is spiritually neutral, so keeping the earth in a plastic bag is fine) to put under your pillow. Land-wights may take on all sorts of shapes – human or human-like, various sorts of animals – so pay attention. It is also good to practice the art of controlled dreaming, both because that will help you to fare about in your dreams by choice, and so that you can get away if things start going bad. The first exercise is a classic one; I got it from the writings of Carlos Castaneda initially, but it works anyway.

As you're going to sleep, concentrate on the thought of looking at your hands. The moment you suspect you might be dreaming, deliberately look at your hands. Any action of your deliberate will and sight could be used, but looking at your hands is simple, easy, and not something you'd usually do without a reason in waking life. When you have done this, you can then start trying to make deliberate changes in your dream...flying, say; or walking towards the Rainbow Bridge. Often the dream will start shredding at this point at first, but if you keep at it, you can maintain a dream and then use a controlled dream as a staging point from which you can seek what you want to find, or to which you can call those with whom you wish to speak.

FINDING YOUR FYLGJA

The most common question I have been asked over the years is, "How do I find out what my fylgja is?" There are several ways to do this. Some folk have a strong affinity for the natural animal, or as close to it as they can get in everyday life. A closeness to dogs might suggest a hound, a wolf, a coyote, or even a Dire Wolf. A closeness to cats might suggest anything by way of the cat-kin, from a Black-Footed Cat (five cute pounds of the deadliest predator on Earth, apparently) to a saber-toothed tiger (just because it's extinct doesn't mean it can't be a fylgja...although if you go around telling people your fylgja is a T. Rex, expect to get laughed at a lot. It might actually be, but you'll still get laughed at). And so forth.

Others, especially in childhood, may have felt or even caught glimpses of an animal walking behind them, that vanished when they turned to look. Sometimes this is a frightening experience. As a child, I was occasionally unnerved to feel that I was being stalked by a large wolf. You can be "scared by your own shadow", and children often are, especially if there's no one to explain to them what they're actually perceiving. If you remain clueless, the next step is to look for yourself. In a quiet place where there is no risk of disturbance, clear your mind and rist a rune ring about yourself. If you wear glasses or contacts, remove them. Sit down in a comfortable position and murmur:

My eyes grow clear that I may see
The one who walks behind.
Fylgja faring with me, following might,
Show yourself to my sight,
Make yourself known to my mind,
Hail yourself to my heart.

Touch your eyes, the center of your forehead, and the middle of your breast-bone with the tip of the index finger of your left hand (or right, if you're left-handed). Speak the charm again. Close your eyes, bend your left arm, and lift it so that your elbow is at your forehead and your left hand is touching your right shoulder. Speak the charm once again and turn your head and upper body as much to the left as possible so that you are looking (more or less) over your left shoulder. Open your eyes, gazing through the arch of your crooked arm. How you perceive your fylgja may vary in many regards.

You may actually catch a visual glimpse of a being or its shadow. You may hear it; you may feel it brushing against you and you may simply get a sense of what it is without any sensory clues. If you feel your fylgja in any way, try to hold the feeling while returning slowly to a normal position. Say:

With me now and with me aye,
The one who walks behind.
Fylgja faring with me, following might,
Stay you aye in my sight
May you be aye in my mind,
Hold yourself in my heart.

Clear the rune-ring. To help secure the closer conscious tie, you may want to get some food of the sort that your fylgja would naturally eat and share it with them. In any case, it is always a good idea to eat something after a working. It is very effective, but requires two experienced people to help you, one of whom must either have a predatory fylgja or be able to shape-shift at will in the Otherworld, and one of whom is able to act as the guide. The guide will use the basic techniques that they are familiar with, but the gist of the ritual is: The guide brings the predator-fylgja assistant and the subject into a moderate trance (can still hear and reply, but most of the consciousness is elsewhere).

The subject is encouraged to merge with their (undefined as yet) fylgja and describe the landscape around them. Note: if the predator is a land creature and the subject is now underwater or high in the air, the ritual may have to do without them at this point. The guide is then responsible for creating and presenting suitable threat-stimuli: a shark or orca in the ocean, a large bird of prey in the air, etc. Assuming that the predator and the subject can exist in the same environment, the guide takes the subject through a brief walk (or swim, or flight), asking what they feel, how they are moving, and so forth, all of which provide clues. At this point, the predator emerges and menaces the subject.

The subject's instinctive reaction to this is not only the key point in terms of information, but may help jolt them into a generally clearer awareness of what they are. When sufficient information has been gained, the predator backs off and the guide returns both of the tranced parties to themselves. Debriefing should follow at once, before details fade; the predator may also have seen, or the guide perceived, something of which the subject was unaware. At worst, this may not identify species precisely, but at least you will have a good idea of what type of creature your fylgja is. At best, either the subject perceived exactly what their fylgja is in some way, or one of the other participants saw/perceived them clearly enough to, say, tell the difference between a red-tailed hawk and a golden eagle. One thing to keep in mind about fylgjur: everyone wants a big cool fylgja, and the high preference is for big cool predators. People with shark-fylgjur would usually rather be a Great White than a Bonnethead; people with canine fylgjur would rather be a wolf than a Chihuahua.

But it is more important to know what your fylgja actually is than to stroke your ego. If it's not as impressive as you hoped, that means that you need to learn more about the natural animal...its strengths, its weaknesses, its capabilities, its role in the Otherworld...which in turn will help you develop strengths and capabilities, and be aware of weaknesses in yourself, of which you might never have thought. Most people would be put off by finding their fylgja was a spider (and not even a cool venomous spider, but a simple little house-spider) – but the Navajo could tell you a lot about spiders and why that little brown house-spider is a fylgja of might. Plus, in the Norse, a spider- or even fly-fylgja (or fox, or coyote, or magpie) just might mean that Loki could be particularly well-disposed to you, which is a blessing not to belittle.

FARING FORTH

The first of these crafts, faring forth in the shape of an animal, is the most commonly written of among the seidh-skills. The Heimskringla mentions that "Odhinn could shift his appearance. When he did so his body would lie there as if he were asleep or dead; but he himself, in an instant, in the shape of a bird or animal, a fish or serpent, went to distant countries on his or other men's errands." [2] It is also described how another wizard went forth in the shape of a whale to scout out Iceland for an invasion, both judging the earthly lay of the land and testing the strength of the guardian spirits of the land (see the chapter on Landvaettir). This tale shows that one of the advantages of seidhr is that when one is faring forth, one is able to see all manner of things which are hidden from the eyes of the body.

This practice has survived long past the coming of Christianity in most Germanic areas. Tales of witches going forth in the hides of other creatures were not unusual as late as the sixteenth century, when the well-known witch Isobel Gowdie confessed to having gone into the skin of a hare or a cat. Faring forth in an animal hide should not be confused with the berserker gang, although both have been classed as forms of lycanthropy. When one fares forth, one keeps one's human mind and only the shape changes.

In the berserker fit, one is altogether overcome by the beast within, and dressing in the animals skin is merely an aid by which its spirit can take one over. The two workings are similar in many ways, but one is a magical means to a number of possible ends while the other is an end in itself and belongs properly to battle-magic and the mysteries of Odhinn. Also, the berserker gang, being limited to one type of animal, would seem to call upon the might of the fylgja, while one wight can take many forms through simple shape-changing. This is further discussed under Out-dwellers.

FARING FORTH: THE WORKING

Earthly Tools: Gandr, sax (held in the hands); if the circle is large enough, the staff should be used in place of the gandr.

Recels (by choice): Will vary according to the faring's goal, but should always contain a great deal of mugwort.

Garb: Seidh-robes, vitki's garb, or sky-clad. There is reference to Freyja using a cloak of falcon feathers to fly through the worlds, and using a mask or similar symbolic garment to take the spiritual shape of an animal is a frequent shamanic practice. Should it be wished, if one has a hide of the creature one is going to become - an item of clothing with a claw, tooth, feather, etc., or a mask - one can enspell [enchant] that item with the power of holding the animal's shape, so that simply by putting it on one's spirit can be shaped and freed.

The runes fehu (for the hamingja-force), ansuz (for the loosing of the soul and traveling on the wind-roads), and raidho (for the faring-forth and to ward one on the way) are good for this working; others may also suggest themselves to the aspiring seidhkona or -madhr. Runic aids should be worked before the first faring; the filling of the garment with the shape-power should be done at its end, in the same way that one charges an item with a magical persona.

The garment is, however, not necessary to this particular craft. It is wise and prudent to do all one's trance-workings from the inside of a warded circle. The empty lich is vulnerable to anything that might wander by, and if the soul should find a swift withdrawal necessary, it is much better to have a circle to come back into. Of course, one's working room should already be well warded, but the extra guarding is still good when one is leaving part of oneself open.

Time: At choice; however, this work may be easier at first if done at night.

Circle-Walking: Deosil, if faring to the elemental worlds or above Midgardhr; widdershins, if faring to Svartalfheim or Hel or if one will be calling upon the hidden powers in one's workings outside the lich.

Rite:
• Circle Rite (see Rites)
• Light the coals, chanting (if recels is used),
    Fire from Muspellheimr free recels' might
    Forth fare the flame-clouds ready my road.
    Wafting, shall ward me in my wide wanderings.
    Walk the circle thrice, bearing the recels.
    Facing northward, raise head and hands and chant:
    Heidh, I hail thee hide-wise in faring
    Woman of seidhr's secret soul ways.
    Fearless, I fare forth hide and hugr flying
    To see and shape things hidden to see and shape my will!

- Lie down on your back, sax in right hand and gandr or staff in left, making very sure all body parts, hair, etc are within the circle and out of danger from the recels burner. Close eyes and breathe deeply, setting up a regular rhythm. Feel your hide within your lich, the two shaped the same, the hamingja-force pulsing through both with breath and blood-but different-the one finer, freer, bound only to the other with a silver cord connecting the navel. Now picture in your mind the shape of the animal you want to take.
- Breathe it into yourself { feeling your arms become wings or hands narrowing to paws, feathers or fur sprouting or skin hardening to scales, face jutting forward into a beak or muzzle. When you have fully changed, you should be aware of the separation between your animal hide and your human lich. Open the eyes of your hide and breathe in with it, lifting or turning away from your body. Stand or hover, raising your head, and look about your room, clearly seeing both the earthly room in full detail and whatever magic has been worked upon it or lingers within. When this sight has become clear, you may fly or run forth from your room. It is best at first to fare to close and well- known spots on the surface of Midgardhr. When you have become skilled in this, you may try to go higher to Alfheim or below Midgardhr's skin to Svartalfheim.
- For faring forth to the elemental worlds, you should see yourself in beast-shape standing at the beginning of a road or root which arches through the mist in the direction of the world you seek. Do NOT STEP OFF THIS ROAD.
- Should you be threatened by another wight on it, you should either make the sign of the Hammer or trace and send an elhaz-rune at it, which will ward away unhallowed wights. You should also be able to shield with your staff. Asking questions of these beings is good and can be a source of much wisdom, but you should be wary of giving your own name; rather, like Odhinn, you should have a number of use-names for the road. Remember that it is unwise to trust strange wights, no matter how fair they may seem. The roads between the worlds are dangerous, and it is not uncommon for a wound received in this faring to appear in the earthly body, or for mages to die of a seeming heart attack while traveling. When in doubt, return to your body at once.
- To return in your body, see yourself merging into your empty lich. Feel every detail of your shape changing back into that of a human. Now aware of the human-shaped spirit within the body, let the two breathe deeply together three times, melding until they no longer feel separate. Even if you seem to have had little or no success in faring forth, this step MUST BE DONE EVERY TIME, or else the hamingja may be lost, which can cause illness or worse. Separating hugr (thought) and minni (memory) from the lich can be hard for some people; the only cure for that is frequent practice. You may, at first, find yourself going forth in your sleep without having planned to.
- In this case draw a circle about your bed or attach a copper wire to your sax and string it around the legs of your bed to form a closed circle of warding, and always be sure to do a full and mindful returning to your body.

With more experience in faring forth, one will probably find, as in runic workings, that one has less need for the trappings of ritual. The purpose of the rife is both to concentrate one's faculties to use one's full power effectively and to train one so that the essence of the working becomes ever more accessible at need. Faring forth with the aid of one's fylgja may be done in the same manner as written above, except that rather than changing one's hamr, one remains in human shape and rides on the back of the fylgja, which should be easy to see with the eyes of one's soul. When one has established an aware relationship with the fylgja, one may send it forth to gather information or fill it with added hamingja-power and have it act for one.

SPAE-CRAFT

The craft of fore-seeing has not been worked with much in modem times, but it has been thoroughly written of. The practice of this form of visionary magic was looked on with more favor than were the forms typically described as seidhr, as it was almost always used for weal and its practitioners were wise and holy people. Spakonur often went about from place to place prophesying, and a thorough description of one is given in the Saga of Eirlk the Red. The woman wore a blue cloak with fastenings of straps, and it was set with stones around the border down to the hem. She wore glass beads around her neck and a black lambskin hood lined with white cat skin. She carried a brass-mounted staff the head of which was inlaid with stones. She was girded with a young bearskin belt and to this hung a large pouch in which she kept her instruments of magic.

On her feet she wore shaggy calfskin shoes with long, heavy thongs, on the ends of which were large brass buttons. She had cat skin gloves upon her hands, the white fur of which was turned inward. The food given this woman to honor her was prepared from the hearts of every kind of animal that there was in the neighborhood. To enter her trance, she sat upon the witch's seat (seidh-hjallr). The women formed a circle about her and a young girl sang the ritual song called Vardhlokur (Watch-guard) which had been taught to her by her foster-mother.[3] Another saga tells of an Icelandic Vala who traveled accompanied by fifteen boys and fifteen girls, who would presumably form the circle and sing the song.

The greatest tools of spae-craft seem to have been the staff and hooded cloak. The staff was a symbol of the spae-worker's authority and may have been used in typical shamanic fashion for the journey between worlds. The hood was placed over the head during the working. It would seem to have cut off the spae-worker from the seen world and made her/him able to receive wisdom from the hidden realms. This was done for both fore-seeing and to deal with problems that could not be solved by ordinary means, as when the Icelandic law speaker Thorgeirr, faced with the problem of reconciling pagans and Christians under one law, contemplated the issue in silence "under the cloak" for a day and a night before he called the folk to the law-rock.[4]

SECTION III: GODS AND WIGHTS

The religion of the Teutonic peoples held within itself every possible level of spiritual consciousness and earthly practicality. All weal-working wights were honored at the proper times, from the spirits of rock, stream, and tree on up to All-Father Odhinn. This honor however, even when paid to the highest of the gods, never took the form of the mindless submission that some sects of Christianity have been so quick to promote. The Teutonic belief is that humans are siblings to the gods; we are literally "Heimdallr's children."[1] Thus we honor them as the parents and elders of our house who have brought us forth, who teach us, and who give us the wisdom and strength to follow the paths of might that they themselves walk. We are sisters and brothers to the wights of the land, with whom we meet and work on equal terms. Teutonic worship is for those who are proud and strong-not sheep led by a shepherd but humans who can act on their own, though able to listen to redes of wisdom and glad of the gifts that make us more like to the gods.

Only a fool would scorn their help at need, but to gain that help you must be strong and worthy of it, depending first of all on yourself. The main act of worship was the blot, or blessing. The greatest blessings, and those most widely practiced among the Germanic peoples, were the four seasonal blessings of Yule, Ostara, Midsummer's, and Winternights. With the exception of Midsummer's, which was celebrated on the Summer Solstice, the dates for these blessings would vary within roughly a month after the marking point of the solar year.

The Winternights blessing was called Winter-fyllith (Winter Full-Moon) among the Anglo-Saxons. This may show that one way of choosing the exact time for the blot was by the Full Moon following the equinoxes. The Yule feast began on the Winter Solstice and continued until January 1 or January 6. Winternights will usually be held in the month following the Fall Equinox. This blessing is also called Alfablot, Disablot and Freyblot. At it the ancestral wights and the Vanic powers are honored. It was generally, though not always, the custom for a woman to carry out this rite. The most characteristic runes for this festival are berkano, ingwaz, and jera. All the gods and goddesses can be honored at Yule, thought it is particularly associated with Odhinn (one of whose many names was Jol), Freyr, and perhaps Ullr. The sacrifice was a white boar which was led around the benches.

The folk would put their hands on this animal and swear oaths for the coming year before it was slain. The oath-ring was also passed at the Yule festival. It was, and is, traditional to decorate the hall or home with holly, ivy, pine, and mistletoe at this time of year. The "Christmas tree" is also a pagan custom: gifts of food and drink were left for the alfar and land-wights beneath trees in the wood, and when hanging real animals and men on trees as sacrifices had been discouraged, the folk turned to bread images and then to decoration in general. The burning of the Yule log is also traditional, and the last of one log should be saved to light the next year's fire. Appropriate runes are jera, eihwaz, and sowilo.

Ostara is associated with the goddess Ostara, of whom little is known otherwise. It usually falls in the month following the Spring Equinox, possibly on the Full Moon of that month. Processions were made through the fields at this time to bless them. The giving of colored eggs was also a part of this ritual and still is, Bonfires were lit at this time, and it is said that maidens in white (perhaps Ljosalfar) were visible in the hills and wild places on Easter morning. Good runes are dagaz and berkano. Tyr, and perhaps Forseti, would have been especially honored at Midsummer's, as it was near to this time that the Thing took place. The lighting of the need-fire is traditional; it should, if possible, be built of nine kinds of wood and have nine kinds of holy herbs burnt in it. Fitting runes are raidho, tiwaz, and sowilo. The central act of the blessing was the sacrifice of one or more animals. The blood was spilled upon the altar and sprinkled over the folk; the flesh was seethed in a cauldron and eaten at the feast.

Evidence shows, however, that sacrifice was performed less for its own sake than as a hallowing of the slaughter, which was a practical necessity. The month of slaughtering was called Blotmonath (month of blessing) in heathen England, and it is likely that each animal was hallowed before it was slain. For this reason, unless one owns a farm at which animals are slaughtered regularly, it is not needful or even desired to revive the custom of animal sacrifice (it is also illegal, and leads to bad press). Pouring an offering of mead or ale over the harrow or onto the earth is all that is needed. Alternatively, one can make animals out of bread (charging them strongly with life-energy) and ritually slaughter and eat them, sprinkling mead or ale from the blessing bowl.

The gift of loaves shaped like animals was used in Germany for several centuries after the Christianization of that land, and even today in Sweden the Yule boar survives as a pig- shaped cake. It is further customary to drink several minne horns (horns of memory) at these feasts, according to the gods being honored. The best-documented toasts are those of Yule, where the first horn was drunk to Odhinn for victory, the second to Njord for fair winds and good sailing, and the third to Freyr for peace and prosperity. It is also written that some drank to Odhinn for victory in battle, but those who trusted more to their own strength called upon Thorr. If you feel particularly drawn to one of the gods or goddesses more than the others, you should of course drink that toast. Likewise, it is fitting to drink the minne of heroes, dead ancestors, and absent friends.

Blessings can be offered at any tie of great need. You should, however, remember that the giving of a gift creates an obligation and that if you do this too often it begins to become annoying-to the gods as well as to humans. The practice of Teutonic religion is not necessary to the practice of Teutonic magic, but it is helpful both in that it strengthens your relationship with the gods-all of whom can aid in different aspects of magic-and in that it brings you to a greater awareness of the godly forces expressed in the runes, as well as of the Teutonic mindset as it grows to encompass the twentieth century. Performance of the blessings is also good for strengthening your sensitivity to the seasonal flows of power, just as the rite "Hail to Sunna" raises your ability to feel and use the greatest points of power in the course of the day.

In magical work with the gods, it is best to spend some time reading about them and performing meditations before you start performing rituals that involve them. Kevin Crossley-Holland's The Norse Myths is a good beginning source; the Eddas are, of course, invaluable. Meditations on the gods themselves can be performed from the descriptions here as searches. For guided meditations, one possibility is to use the meditation for the appropriate rune and instead of following it all the way through, stopping the reading at the point where you meet the god or goddess and allowing that being to speak directly to you, bringing yourself back to your own body and the earth after a space of time (no more than two to five minutes for a beginner). For this you will do best to tape yourself reading it. Stephen McNallen's tape "Pathways to the Gods" is an excellent source of truly beautiful guided meditations.

AESIR

The Aesir are largely gods of spiritual awareness, intellect, and war. The masculine Aesir are generally characterized by air and/or fire; the feminine (Asynjur), by earth and/or water, often overlapping with the Vanic goddesses.

ODHINN

The greatest god of the runes is, of course, Odhinn. Saying this, you must keep in mind that the word "rune" speaks not only of the runic alphabet, but also means "secret." Odhinn is the lord of hidden wisdom and of the roots of power. The name Odhinn means "fury" or "inspiration." It is derived from the Indo-European Wodanaz, "Master of fury/inspiration"[1] and related to the modern German wuetend and archaic English wood, both of which carry a meaning of "furious," "mad," and "wild." His name has been suggested to be roughly cognate to that of Vata, Lord of the Winds, in the Rig Veda. Odhinn's first form was probably that of a wind-god known by his furious rushing through the sky.

He is the leader of the dead, as seen in that most enduring survival of Teutonic lore, the Wild Hunt. The Wild Hunt is thoroughly documented in every country where Germanic people have settled. It has even been suggested that the song "Ghost Riders in the Sky" is a contemporary version of the same.[2] This first naming of Odhinn as the lord of fury and death is one of the keys to his being: considering that fury is also inspiration and death the pathway to the greatest knowledge, one can see the pattern forming behind the seemingly capricious and sinister being of the greatest of the gods.

Odhinn's late usurpation of Tyr's position as All-Father brings into focus an interesting anomaly of Teutonic belief: in no other Indo-European religious system is the god of writing (and/or conductor of the dead) set in the highest place. The Roman invaders of Germany identified Odhinn with Mercury-both are psychopomps; both are associated with intelligence, swift movement changeability, and deception; and both encompass aspects of the archetypal Trickster - characteristics that are not normally associated with rulership in the Indo-European mind.

While it has been suggested that Odhinn is analogous to Varuna as the king-magician of Dumezil's tripartite Indo-European system, Tyr being the king-judge, the problem with this is that the cult of Odhinn All-Father is a fairly late development, found and spreading at a time when the tripartite system might naturally be expected to be breaking down as a consequence of migration and changing circumstance, rather than shifting back into the exact pattern of the Rig Veda. Indeed, the tripartite system is not supportable within Germanic social or religious history. Part of Odhinn's change in status is undoubtedly due to his association with war: from leader of the dead he became chooser of the dead and Valfather (father of the slain), hence finally the chooser of victory in battle.

However, the primary source of Odhinn's cultic might is the source of his own power: Odhinn's rise to the All-Father's seat corresponds closely with the rise of runic magic among humans, both in time and in space. This is borne out by the great importance given to runic wisdom among the Teutonic peoples and the respect in which those who knew it well were held, as contrasted to the less complimentary view of the Vanic seidh-magic the magic of a cult which, though never displaced by the Aesir and more beloved by the folk than the cult of Odhinn, was nevertheless overshadowed by AllFather, especially among the skalds, of whom Odhinn was the patron.

As the lord of runes and incantation, Odhinn also became the lord of poetry. The story of his theft of Odhroerir, the mead of poetry, offers great insight into his nature. Here Odhinn is seen as shape changer, trickster, betrayer, rescuer of the hallowed mead, and giver of poetry's power to other wights. He mingles the holy inspiration which is the height of Teutonic spirituality with oath-breaking, the act most despicable to the Teutonic mind, because both are part of his purpose; he becomes serpent and eagle at need. Thus, by the mystery and paradox of Odhinn's nature, he holds all things within himself.

He builds the walls to ward Midgardhr and Asgardhr, but wanders outside at will. He is a lord of oaths and of betrayal, of making and unmaking. As a god of war he makes his heroes invincible till he himself comes to take them in battle. It is said, and rightly, that Odhinn enjoys stirring up strife: only through struggle can one be tested and grow, and only by the clash of opposites can synthesis be achieved. Every step of the Odian path is a battle of some sort, whether external or internal. He is not a comfortable patron and was seldom loved by the folk as a whole.

The worship of Odhinn was usually left to princes (who had often been personally chosen by the god), berserker, rune-masters, and skalds, that is, to the initiated to those whom Odhinn himself had already touched from birth or before. He was most worshiped by the Saxons, the Danes, and the Norwegian aristocracy. It is worth noting that the Norwegian settlers in Iceland, being mostly peasants who wanted nothing to do with aristocracy or ceaseless warring, built no temples of statues to Odhinn, although his touch was still prominent in families such as that of Egill Skallagrimson. Odhinn follows an endless quest for wisdom. He is master of both galdr and seidh-magic, the latter of which he learned from Freyja. A great deal of his knowledge comes from the dead and the realms of death. He is often spoken of as calling forth the dead to learn from them; in the Harbardzljodh, he says the source of his knowledge is "the howes-of-the-home,"[3] that is, barrows.

On the Continent, Odhinn was also honored as a god of fertility and the harvest. The last sheaf in the field was left standing for his horse, and certain harvest-rites were performed to him.[4] Truly a god of all things! A large part of the mystery of Odhinn is hidden in his many hypostases (aspects of a god which are well-defined enough to act on their own). The most obvious of these are Odhinn's "brothers": Vili (Will) and Ve (Holiness) with whom he slays Ymir and shapes the worlds; and Hoenir and Lodurr, with whom he creates the human race from trees. In Odhinn/Hoenir/Lodurr we see the three active elements of air, water, and fire which also form Bifrost: Odhinn supplies ond, the breath of life; Hoenir gives the óð gaf, which is usually shown as a drink; and Lodurr supplies the spark of life and hamingja force, which is expressed as color and hair growth.

Lodurr, fire, is further divided into Loki and Heimdallr, ungoverned fire and hallowed fire (they will be discussed individually). Hoenir appears later, twinned with Mimir in circumstances which would identify them as anthropomorphic counterparts of Huginn and Muninn, thought and memory. He is spoken of for the last time after Ragnarok, when he will "handle the blood-twigs"[5] as Odhinn returned and made whole. The animals associated with Odhinn are the wolf, the raven, the horse, the eagle, and the wyrmbeasts of battle, death, and spiritual wisdom.

Names by which Odhinn may be called upon in incantations for various purposes include Grimnir (hooded one), Gangleri (Way-weary), Vegtamr (Way-tame), Hejan (War-god); Hjalmberi (Helmbearer), Thekk (Welcome), Har (One-Eyed; High One - homonyms)1 Sath (Truthful), Svipal (Changeable), Sanngetal (Truth-finder), Bolverk (Bale-Worker), Fjolnir (Concealer), Hroptr (Hidden or Maligned), Sigfadhir (Victory-father), Valfadhir (father of the Slain or Chosen), Alfadhir (All-Father), Galdrfadhir (Father of Magical Songs), Jalk (Gelding), Gondlir (Wand-bearer), Svithur/Svitlrrir (the Wise), Harbardhr (Graybeard), Vafuth (Wayfarer), Offlir (the Entangler) and Svafnir (Luller to Sleep or Dreams)-both names of serpents at the roots of Yggdrasil, Mimir' [5] Friend, Gagnrath (Giving Good Counsel), Drauga Drottin (Lord of Ghosts), Hangatyr (God of the Hanged), Karl af berge (the Man of the Mountain), Hnikar (Thruster), Frigg's Husband, and others. Odhinn is generally seen as a tall gray-bearded man in a dark blue cloak, one eye being covered by a broad hat or with the cloak's hood. He is master of all disguise, however, and appears in many forms both animal and human, even disguising himself as a woman at need. He rides the gray eight-legged horse Sleipnir; his weapon is the spear Gungnir. He is followed by the ravens Huginn and Muninn, who fly out every day to gather wisdom and tell him what has happened in the Nine Worlds, and by the wolves Freki and Geri.

LOKI

Loki was never worshiped; blessings were not made to him and his minne was not drunk. As the most destructive and counter- social side of Odhinn's being, he was viewed with little favor. In the myths he was sometimes helpful and sometimes unhelpful. It is possible that the influence of Christianity may have diabolized him somewhat, creating the wholly baleful being of the later parts of the Norse cycle. At his best, Loki shows the more fallible and humorous sides of the Trickster; at his worst, he is betrayal and raw chaos.

In secret lore, he brings forth those sides of Odhinn's being which were seen as unfitting for the All-Father: his sexual ambiguity and the externalization of "Loki's children," the Fenris-Wolf and Midgardhr's Wyrm, both acknowledged as antitheses to the weal-working powers of the gods, and both being beasts associated with the cult of Odhinn and necessary for the transformation of Ragnarok. Loki is a fire-spirit. He is never counted among the gods by anyone, but he is the blood-brother of Odhinn, a part of Odhinn, as all the beings identified as his "brothers" are, who carries out his will in ways that may either be clear to see or hidden behind the veil of poetic drama.

HEIMDALLR

Heimdallr's origin is shrouded in much vagueness, due to the loss of the poem which is supposed to have told of his history and legends, the Heimdalisgaldr. It is written that he is the son of nine mothers, who are also nine sisters; these have been identified with nine waves and/or giantesses. He is called brightest and highest- minded of the gods, and the white god. Although seemingly one of the Aesir, he shares the Vanic wisdom of foresight. He has been slain at least once, with a man's head. It is suggested that the "nine mothers" motif may show that he was killed and reborn nine times. He is the guardian of Bifrost, keeper of the Gjallarhorn which he will blow at the beginning of Ragnarok. Heimdallr can hear everything that happens throughout the Nine Worlds. His hearing, like Odhinn's eye, is kept in the Well of Mimir.

One might easily suspect that both references indicate the identical awareness of "that-which-is" as well as "that-which-is-becoming." Branston suggests a similarity between Heimdallr and Agni of the Rig Veda: both are sons of the waters, both are described as white with teeth of gold, both are sons of multiple mothers, guardians, and fathers of the social classes of humanity. The association with Agni, who is clearly identified as sacred fire, and his role as guardian of the fiery bridge Bifrost, as well as his ceaseless struggle with Loki (the spirit of uncontrolled fire) would seem to show Heimdallr as the embodiment of the sacred flame.[6]

He is also called Vindler (Turner or Borer), which might associate him with the need-fire. Alternatively, the Odhinn/ Heimdallr/Loki triad may be seen as a precise reflection of the Odhinn (air)/Hoenir (water)/Lodurr (fire) triad, with Heimdallr distinctly watery and virtually Vanic in nature. The animal associated with Heimdallr is the ram; he also turned himself into a seal to fight with Loki once. As a side of Odhinn's being, he embodies the omnipresent and uplifting Odian consciousness-that which strives ever after the highest.

TYR

As mentioned in the description of the rune tiwaz, Tyr (also called Tiwaz, Zio), cognate to Zeus, was the original Germanic sky father god, although only a few stories about him have survived, most notably that of the binding of the Fenris Wolf. Tyr is the chief god of the Thing. He gives justice, honor, courage, and wisdom in battle. He is associated with the sword as well as the spear. The sword-dance was part of his worship among the Swabians, and several scholars have identified him with the sword-god Saxnot. Though largely left out or displaced in myth, he remained one of the great figures in the religious life of the folk, particularly on the Continent.

ULLR

This god, whose name means "glory," was not known on the Continent; he appears to be a native Scandinavian sky-god, possibly Finnish, whose place was taken by Odhinn. He is particularly singled out, even by Odhinn, as among the highest of the gods. It has been suggested that he is the "all-powerful god" by whom, along with Freyr and Njord, vows on one oath-ring were sworn; he is associated with the oath ring in other places as well. His worship was fairly widespread in Scandinavia, although he is seldom mentioned in the myths.

It is written in one source, the severely Christianized and euphemistic Saxo, that Ulir took Odhinn's place and bore his name for a time; and there are also references to the alternating worship pf Ullr in the winter and Freyr in the summer, which would show that the worship of this god was confined to the winter months, at which time it equaled or superseded that of the others. The name "Ulir" may be etymologically connected with Yule; it has also been suggested to be a reference to the lights of the aurora borealis in the winter sky.

Ullr is the son of Sif and an unknown father, supposed by Ingvisson and others to have been a rime-thurse. He is the stepson of Thorr. He is also associated with Skadhi, of whom he is considered to be the male counterpart. He is said to be fair of face and a great warrior. Ullr is the god of snowshoes, of the shield, and of archery. He is called upon in duels and has knowledge of the runes. The tree holy to Ullr is the yew. The attribution of Ullr to the Aesir is solely a matter of conjecture, as there is equal reason to number him among the Vanir.

THORR

The god Thorr was, along with Freyr, the most generally worshiped of the Teutonic gods. In the great temple at Uppsala, his statue was set in the highest place between and above those of Odhinn and Freyr. Thorr was generally seen as a faithful warder and provider, a god who would keep faith with his worshipers, as contrasted with Odhinn. In myth, Thorr is usually shown as the common man writ large: A tireless eater, drinker, and fighter (though none too bright). The Eddic lay Harbardzljodh gives an interesting picture of the differences between Thorr and Odhinn. The two gods meet. Odhinn being disguised as a ferryman, and they engage in a contest of boasting. Thorr's list of triumphs deals with his slaying of giants and berserkers; Odhinn's with seduction, betrayal and stirring up war. Odhinn then insults Thorr, who can only reply with the threat of force, and refuses to ferry him over the river, forcing him to walk around the long way.

It is interesting to note that Thorr, who fights against the giants, is very like them in strength, size, great appetite, and seemingly uncomplicated character. This is why he is so effective as a warder, being able to beat them at their own game, as it were. Thorr is the foe of the Midgardhr's Wyrm; this side of his being is spoken of further in Chapter: 20. Thorr is the warder of Midgardhr; he is also the warder and hallower of all things holy. The hammer is swung over something to hallow it. It is put in the lap of the new bride both as a fertility symbol and as a consecration; it is also used to hallow the funeral pyre. The uses of the hammer symbol have already been described. A flash of lightning at the beginning of any undertaking was thought of as a very good omen. In this side of his being, Thorr is sometimes called upon in runic inscriptions to hallow the runes or that upon which they are carved. He is also called Veun-Hallower or Holy Warder-and Vingthorr, "Thorr the Hallower."

Like Odhinn, Thorr seems to have usurped certain aspects of the Sky-Father's position. He is often compared to Jupiter, as the benevolent sky-god who can also hurl thunder and lightning and who is the greatest of gods. Thorr's aid was called upon in bringing ships safely out of storms. He is also the god of the pillars which support the roof of a house or temple. His image was sometimes carved into these, and some of the early settlers in Iceland called upon his aid in finding their steads by throwing their house pillars overboard and building where the god sent them. As the god ruling thunder, lightning, and rain, Thorr is something of a fertility god. The hammer is, of course, a phallic symbol, and the success of a harvest is as dependent on the sky as it is on the earth. He was thus invoked for prosperity and for a good harvest.

Thorr can always be seen to embody the powers of order, protection, and holiness. He, rather than Odhinn, was the defender of Norse heathenism against Christianity; the battle of the faiths was the struggle between Red Thorr and the White Christ. The most beloved of the Teutonic heroes were those such as Beowulf who, like Thorr, fought only against the woe-working chaos embodied by the out-dwellers. If one should be unable to restrain a need to call upon Loki, or if that wight's presence should seem to be making itself known in one's life, one should at once call upon Thor~ "whose strength keeps Loki in line" (Ingvar Solve Ingvisson, conversation).

Thorr is always shown as large, burly, and red-bearded; flame flashes from his eyes. He walks or rides in a chariot drawn by the two he-goats Tanngnjost (Tooth-gnasher) and Tanngrisnir (Tooth- gritter). It is interesting that in parts of Germany, Santa Claus also rides in a chariot drawn by the two goats Donner and Blitzen (Thunder and Lightning). Thorr can slay and eat his goats, and when he hallows their hides and bones with his hammer Mjollnir they come to life again. This hammer, which always returns to his hand after it has been thrown, is the lightning he wields. His name, Thorr, Thunar (AS) or Donar (German), means "Thunderer." He wears a girdle of strength, and iron gloves, as Mjollnir's handle is a little short. He is the son of Jordr (earth) and father of a daughter named Thrudhr (might), and two sons named Magni (the Strong) and Modhi (the Courageous). The holy animal of Thorr is the goat.

BALDR

Baldr, whose name means "prince" or "lord," is the god of joy and light. The tale of his death is well documented in a number of sources, and traces of his worship appear in several Scandinavian place names, although there are no reliable mentions of a cult of Baldr. His wife is named Nanna; he is the father of Forseti, god of righteousness. He is desired by Skadhi and welcomed gladly by Hel.

FORSETI

Forseti is the god of justice, who is said to reconcile legal strife between men. He was mainly worshiped by the Frisians. The greatest seat of his cult was the temple on the island Helgoland, near a sacred spring which the god brought forth when he gave the Frisians their code of laws. He hears oaths and keeps the peace between men, his justice being fair and reasonable to all.

BRAGI

Bragi was the god of poets and the skald of Valhalla, welcoming the honored dead into the hall. He is the husband of Idunn, and runes are said to be carved on his tongue. According to myth, Odhinn got Bragi on Gunnlodh when he stole the mead of poetry. The minne-cup is also called bragar-full when drunk to dead heroes or to seal an oath. Folk etymology connects it with Bragi, but it is actually derived from bragr, meaning the "foremost" or "the best."[7] Bragi is called upon for poetic skill and eloquence; the harp is traditionally associated with him. He is shown as old and long-bearded, in spite of the fact that his wife keeps the apples of youth.

VIDARR and VALI

These two gods are sons of Odhinn, both begotten for the purpose of revenge. Vali was fathered on the maiden or goddess Rind by trickery for the purpose of avenging Baldr's death on the blind Hodr. Vidarr is the son of the giantess Grid, and he rips the jaws of the Fenris-Wolf apart after the Wolf has swallowed Odhinn. He is called "the silent god" and is associated with the depths of the forest. These two gods together "will ward the gods' fanes/fates" after Ragnarok.

FRIGG

Frigg, whose name means "beloved" or "wife," is the best known of the Asynjur. A great many of the other goddesses listed are clearly hypostases of her, or else names by which she was known locally. She is the wife of Odhinn, and shares his high seat with him. Though she keeps her wisdom silent she knows what is and what shall be. In this side of her being, she is called Saga, "she who sees and knows all things."9 Like Freyja, she has a coat of hawk's feathers; she is a mistress of the highest aspects of seidhmagic. Odhinn comes to her for redes, though he does not always follow them. At times she deceives Odhinn into protecting her favorites or, when their chosen mortals are in contention, betraying his own. Above all, Frigg is the goddess of marriage and childbirth.

Among her handmaidens (hypostases?) are Lofn, who brings together those who have had difficulty in getting married; Vjofn, who inclines people to love and keeps peace between husband and wife; Hlin (Protector), who guards Frigg's favorites; Gna, who rides the horse Hofvarpnir (Hoof-tosser) through air and sea to tend to Frigg's works; Var1 who hears all vows made between men and women and punishes those who break them; Eir, goddess of healing; Snotra, goddess of prudence; and Syn, goddess of denial, who shuts out those who should not enter and aids in lawsuits. Fulla, a maiden with loose hair and a headband of gold who is said to be Frigg's messenger, her sister, and a giver of her gifts, is also probably a hypostasis of Frigg.

It is fitting to call upon her by the aspect which is most appropriate to one's working. Frigg is associated with, though not identical to, the various goddesses of spinning such as Holda and Bertha on the Continent. Frigg is a goddess of earth, though she also has a watery side, as seen by her dwelling in Fensalir (Ocean Halls). As Saga, her dwelling is spoken of thus: "Cold waves crash around the fourth I which is called Sokkvabekk. I Ódhinn and Saga drink there gladly I all their days from golden vessels."[10] Even though she is a goddess of the Aesir, her character is closely related to that of the Vanir, who are also gods of earth, water, and hidden wisdom. Frigg's symbols are the spindle and the distaff; she is mistress of all crafts of the home.

IDUNN

Idunn is the keeper of the apples of youth, which renewed the strength and life of the gods. She and her apples are stolen by Thjazi, the father of Skadhi, but Loki manages to steal them back and contrive the death of the etin. One may compare this to the many tales in which giants attempt to claim Freyja as a bride. Both goddesses embody the vital force on which the Aesir are dependent.

17: THE VANIR

The Vanir are gods of earth and water whose power is called upon for peace and prosperity. They are said to be wise and to have the power of foresight. The practice of seidhr-magic is associated with the Vanir. The war between the Aesir and the Vanir is thought to be a mythological representation of an actual cult-war which ended in the fusion of the two. Vanic worship was greatest in Sweden, and the Swedish kings were thought to be descended from Yngvi or Freyr. As gods of fertility, they were also gods of death, with whom the practice of mound-burial was associated, cremation being more characteristic of the Aesic cult. They overlap in many ways with the disir and the three races of alfar.

NJORD/NERTHUS

The name "Njord" is a form of the name "Nerthus," although the one is male and the other female; both derive from the Proto-Germanic* Nerthuz, which might refer to either gender. The root word ner from which our "north" is also derived means "under," bringing out the hidden character of the Vanic powers. The procession of the goddess Nerthus, described by Tacitus, has been discussed under the runes berkano and ingwaz, the key elements being the procession of the goddess in the wagon accompanied by the human priest, the sacred island, and the completion of the ceremony with the human sacrifice, the victims being sunk in the lake. Tacitus calls Nerthus "Mother Earth";2 Njord, on the other hand, is clearly a god of wave and wind.

The description of the holy island of Nerthus and the drowning of the victims may indicate an original union of earth and water in this figure, which was later divided. It is mentioned in the Eddas that Njord got Freyr and Freyja on a nameless sister; one may suppose that at one time or in different places Njord and Nerthus may have been, like Freyr and Freyja, seen as twins. The bog-cult of the early Germanic people is probably related to this cult also. Large staves minimally carved to make them either clearly female or male have been found in bogs, as have the bodies of men who were sacrificed either by being strangled or having their throats cut. In the Yngling saga, Snorri Sturluson mentions a golden necklace which was the bridal gift of the daughter of Audhi the Wealthy (possibly identical with the chthonic Audh, son of Night) and which a later Ynglinga queen, Skjalf, used to strangle her husband with.

It is possible that this story is based on the Nerthus sacrifice, being one of a long line of mysterious deaths of the kings of the Ynglings, which have been associated with the royal sacrifice.3 Certainly the necklace is one of the oldest symbols of this earth-goddess. Nerthus can be seen as embodying the earth, Njord as the fertile force of the ocean and its weal working aspects. Like all the Vanir, he is a god of wealth, which in this case are the treasures hidden beneath the water's surface and the wealth of food therein. He is called upon for fair weather, favorable winds, good fishing, and the riches cast up by the sea. Njord is also associated with the passage between life and death, and with the rune laguz in its fertile and mysterious aspects. His emblems are the ship, which in some places was drawn over the land in place of a wagon or plough, and the bare foot a symbol of fertility. Oaths are often sworn "by Freyr and Njord".

FREYR

This god's name is actually a title, meaning "Lord"; it is likely that he is identical to the early Yngvi or mg, consort of the goddess Nerthus. Several kings who are thought to be euphemistic representations of this god are named Frodhi (Fruitful), and Turville Petre suggests that his full name and title could be given as Yngvi-Freyr, "Lord Yngvi the Fruitful."4 Along with Odhinn and Thorr, Freyr was one of the most widely worshiped of the gods. Like Nerthus, Freyr makes processions in a chariot accompanied by a human votary of the opposite gender. Like Njord, he is associated with the ship, being the owner of a magical ship called Skidbladnir, which can sail over both sea and land, the realms of the Vanir.

Such concept of the holy kingship as the Norse had was wholly associated with the cult of Freyr, the proto-king whose rule was one of peace and plenty and who continued to make the land fruitful even after his death and burial in a mound, at which he received sacrifice. This may be tied to the veneration of the Dokkalfar or mound elves (discussed later). Freyr was also said to be bra of AIfheim and hence ruler over the Ljosalfar; like them, he is associated with the fructifying air and light of the sun.

According to Saxo, there were a number of kings named Frodhi, which may show that this was a title indicating the embodiment of the god in each mortal king.5 Freyr is called upon for fruitfulness and prosperity, but he is also associated with strength in war. The kenning "sport of Freyr" means battle. He carried a magical sword which he gave away to win the love of the maiden Gerdhr (symbolic gelding; see ingwaz, pp.147-50). He is called "protector of the gods" and "ruler of the hosts of the gods." One of his holy animals, the boar, was frequently used on helmets to strengthen and guard the wearer. Freyr is also called "God of the World." He is addressed magically when the earthly working of godly power is wished, especially in matters concerning peace, happiness, and riches, or courage and protection in battle. He is particularly honored at Yule and/or at Winternights.

The worship of Freyr is prone to running in families, and it is not uncommon for those of Swedish descent to feel a special fondness for this god. It is written that Freyr has a messenger named Skirnir (the Bright), who is often thought to be another form of the god himself. He also has two other servitors, Bviggir ("barley") and his wife Beyla (bee),[6] the personifications of both nourishment and drink. Statues of Freyr are usually phallic, and those who worshiped him often carried small images of him about. The animals holy to Freyr are boar, horse, bull or ox, and stag. His own horse is called Blodhughofi [1] (bloody-hoofed), and he also rides on the boar Gullinbursti (Golden-bristled), which is said to be able to run through the air and over the sea faster than a horse.[7] He wields a hart's horn in place of his sword, and it is said that he killed the giant Beli with this weapon. The stag's antlers put up at the corners of the hall Heorot [8] were probably a sign of dedication to Freyr, the more likely so as Scyld Scefing, the father of Hrothgar's line, has been identified with several Vanic figures.

FREYJA

The goddess Freyja was probably the most widely worshiped of the Norse goddesses. If she had a known true name other than her title of "Lady," she would likely be identified with Nerthus. As Odhinn is the most magical of the gods, Freyja is most magical of the goddesses. She is a wanderer in search of her husband Odhr, who is of course Odhinn himself as lord of mystical inspiration.[9] As Odhinn seeks out the hidden wisdom in the Vanic realm of the dead, so Freyja seeks the active power and wisdom of the Aesir, the ultimate mingling of these mights being found in the formula of Odhroerir. She is the mistress of seidh-magic, which she teaches to Odhinn, presumably receiving his knowledge of runic magic in turn. She has the feathers of a falcon, which she can put on to fly forth through the worlds; at one point she lends them to Loki.

The goddess Freyja goes by many names: Guilvcig, Heidh the witch, Heithrun (a she-goat), Vanadis (goddess of the Vanir), Horn (flax), Mardoll (sea-light?), Gefn (giver) and Syr (sow),[10] among others. Most of these names are probably forms by which the goddess was known in different locations, even as Frigg was known by a number of names and forms; she is said to have gone by several different names in her search for Odhr. The goddess Gefjun may also be one of her hypostases. Although Gefjun is said to be a virgin in the Prose Edda, Loki accuses her of selling herself for a necklace[11] and Odhinn speaks of her foresight[2]

There is also a tale in which this goddess has four oxen-sons by a giant for the purpose of ploughing out a chunk of Sweden to make the island Zealand.[13] Freyja is a goddess of fertility and sexual pleasure above all else. She is said to have slept with all the Aesir and all the alfs and to have lain with her brother Freyr as well,[14] an incestuous union like that of Nerthus and Njord1 which is furthermore the formula for the birth of a hero (cf. Sinfjotli, Hrolf Kraki). (The story of her giving her body to four dwarves for the necklace Brisingamen has been discussed under kenaz, p. 65.)

She also takes mortal men for her lovers, and it may be that the role of her consort was expected of her priests, as the priestess of Freyr was described as his wife. Like Idunn, she is the object of giants' attempts at theft. This is not only due to her beauty but also to the fact that she is the embodiment of the basic life- force which is necessary to the gods. In the same manner as Freyr, Freyja is as mighty in battle as in love. Her hall is called Folkvangn and she claims one half of the slain in every battle, Odhinn taking the other half. (She also receives the souls of unmarried women.) She rides to the battlefield in a chariot drawn by two cats; also upon a boar called Hildisvini (Battle-swine).

Freyja is particularly called upon today by women who wish to regain the strength which Christian culture has denied them for so long. In the mighty figure of this goddess you may find proof that the Teutonic path is neither patriarchal nor oppressive to women, but rather that it brings out the female power both as the source of life and as the woman's warrior- might. Animals sacred to Freyja are the sow, the cat, the falcon, the swallow, and the cuckoo. In magic Freyja is often called upon in matters having to do with love, prosperity, and women's mysteries, especially seidhr-magic. Different aspects of her power are discussed further under the runes fehu, kenaz, and berkano.

SKADHI

Although Skadhi is not herself one of the Vanir, she is classed among them because of her marriage to Njord. She is the daughter of the jotun Thjazi. It has been considered that like Ullr, she was one of the original gods of Scandinavia, possibly Finnish in origin, and Branston even claims that she was the eponymous founder of Scandinavia: Skadinauja. Her name may mean "Shadow" or "Scathe"; she is the goddess of snowshoes and a great huntress with the bow. She rules the high mountain regions and the farthest pathways. Skadhi came armed to the Aesir seeking weregild for her father Thjazi, whom they had slain. She set two conditions: The first was that the gods should make her laugh, the second that she might choose one of them as her husband.

To fulfill the first condition, Loki tied one end of a rope to his testicles and the other to a goat and the grotesque antics performed by the two of them until the rope broke and Loki tumbled into her lap finally made her laugh. Here one may see the formula of ingwaz again: the mock castration and the surrender of the fiery masculine to fertilize the frozen feminine. The husband Skadhi wished was Baldr [a solar figure] but she had to choose her husband by his feet alone, and it so happened that the handsomest pair of feet belonged to Njord. This is, obviously, part of the ancient fertility ritual symbolized by the bare footprint. They married and lived comfortably for a while, but since Skadhi could not bear to live by the sea and Njord could not bear the howling of the wolves and wind in her mountain home Thrymheim1 the two finally separated. In the tale of Njord and Skadhi one can see the relationship between isa and laguz, ice and water.

The two are closely connected (the rivers of Hvergelmir flow out of Nifiheim, the realm of primal ice) but not compatible: the nature of the yeasty waters is to seethe and bring forth life; though ice holds all that water is within it its nature is to still and May. They are wedded, but must remain separate. It is fiery Loki who must make Skadhi able to accept Njord, and indeed he claims later to have slept with her;[16] her desire is to the bright Baldr. It is also claimed that she had sons with Odhinn,[17] and it is fitting that the goddess of winter should mate with the god who is known by the wild winter winds. When Loki is bound by the guts of his son(as suggested by Skadhi), it is she who hangs a snake to drip venom onto his face as a torment, perhaps in revenge for the role he claimed in the death of her father.

She is not only huntress but a just, if harsh, avenger. Perhaps surprisingly, she was worshiped in a number of places in eastern Sweden;[8] she speaks of her "ve's (holy enclosures) and fields"[19] Skadhi may be called upon, together with Ullr, to hallow a hunt, and extreme cases, to wreak a righteous, if cruel, revenge. Ingvar Solve lngvisson suggests that on occasions when a criminal is being justly executed, a blessing be offered to Skadhi (or else Vali) in order to hallow the awe-full act of lifetaking.[20] Despite her dark and woe-working character, she is fair and a trustworthy ally. Besides the Aesir and the Vanir, there were a few other gods who were recognized by the Teutonic peoples, and who might be prayed and sacrificed to even though thcy were not generally the objects of cult like worship.

AEGIR; RAN

Aegir (the Terrifying), also called Æger (the Shelterer) and Gymir (the Concealing), is a god of the sea. He is probably older than Njord and is described several times as a giant. As Le~he is one of the three sons of the giant Fornjot, the other two being Kari (wind) and Loge (fire), who embody the Odhinn/Hoenir/Lodurr air/water/fire triad on the level of elemental forces. Njord rules the bounty of the sea; Aegir personifies the sea itself. He is less well- wishing than Njord, though not as cruel and greedy as his wife Ran (robber).

Aegir and Ran take those who die in shipwrecks, and it was customary for sailors to hide a little bit of gold about them during storms so that Ran might welcome them well if they were drowned. Aegir's hall is lit with shining gold, and thus gold is called Aegir's Fire. He is the brewer of ale for the Aesir and is associated with the rune laguz. The daughters of Aegir and Ran are the nine waves, who may also be the mothers of Heimdallr. Ran carries a net with which to catch the drowned. Aegir is associated with the great cauldron in which he brews ale, which may be related to the cauldrons of plenty in Irish legend.

SOL; MANI

Sol (Anglo-Saxon Sunna) and Mani are the personifications of the Sun and the Moon. It should be remembered that in all Germanic languages and cultures, the Sun itself is feminine, while the Moon is masculine. Although it is not uncommon for some neo-pagans to identify this or that Teutonic goddess with a moon goddess (Paul Schroeder), it is thoroughly incorrect. There are no moon goddesses in the Teutonic pantheon; the concept is linguistically and culturally impossible. Sol is called "the shining goddess" from whose fires the earth is protected by the shield Svalin, "Cooler." She is drawn in a wain by two horses, Arvakr (Early-Awake) and Alsvith (Very Swift),~ and pursued by the wolf Skoll.

Mani is said to measure the time of the Moon's waxing and waning. In Teutonic thought, the Moon is not associated with emotion and the subconscious but with measurement regulation, and reason. He is attended by the two water-bearing children Hjuki and Bil, who are thought to be Jack and Jill of the folk rhyme. Mani is pursued by the wolf Hati Hrodhvitnisson (son of Fenris), also called Managarm, "Moon's Dog."[22]

18: WIGHTS OF HELP

The term disir means "goddesses"; it is applied to goddesses of a Vanic character, as distinct from the Asynjur who are the Aesic goddesses (though Freyja is sometimes classed among these). These goddesses are generally tied to a family. They rule the fertility of the land and the prosperity and success of individual houses. They often seem to be the spirits of particularly powerful female ancestors who, rather than going to their appointed halls, have chosen to stay among the beings of the earth and continue to either work weal towards their descendants or call them to death when their wyrds are done. They are, as it were, handmaidens of Nerthus who hold the powers of fertility, prosperity, and death. The disir are not only ancestral spirits, however; Freyja is called "Vanadis," dis of the Vanir, and Hel is referred to as "jodis", dis of the horse-that animal being of course used in funeral rites a great deal.

It may be that the female ancestral spirits become blended with the Vanic goddesses in the same way that some male spirits blend with the Alfar. They are also associated with the Norns that come to every child that is born in order to shape its life. It is said that the good Norns that come from good stock shape good lives, but those that meet with misfortune owe it to the evil Norns.[1] These Norns are associated with the Vanic powers of the elves and dwarves, or Alfar and Svartalfar, to which the disir are closely related. There was an active cult of the disir: they were especially worshiped at the Winternights festival. Their worship was mostly presided over by women, although men also made sacrifices to them.

Sometimes a disarsalar (hall of the dis) was built for this purpose, but the worship of the disir was usually carried out in the individual home, since they were the goddesses of the family. In later pagan times the sacrifice was that of a bull or ox, and mead or ale are currently used; however, in earlier times, they may have received human sacrifice. The Ynglinga Saga states that during one disablot, Adhils, king of the Swedes was thrown and killed while riding his horse around the hall of the goddess. The horse's stumble was blamed on a witch,2 but there is no way to tell whether this was arranged as a royal sacrifice or whether the attendant dis took her sacrifice by force.

There is a later story in which the eldest son Thidhrandi heard a knock at the door on the Winternights festival and went out, although everyone had been warned to stay inside. He was set upon and mortally wounded by nine black-clad women on horses, while nine dressed in white stood by. The prophet (spamadhr) who was present at the feast told the family that the women were the disk of the family, the black being those who clung to the old religion and were not willing to be defrauded of their sacrifice in years to come, and the white, those who awaited the new religion.[3]

The Christian influence in the tale of Thidhrandi is obvious; however, the disir are characteristically divided into those who aid in life and those who call one to the grave, the former being dressed in shining garments and the latter in black. If the disir are provoked to turn against members of their household, the result is death. The disir are closely associated with the kinfylgja and at times confused with her, as is the hamingja. The difference is that the kinfylgja is a single being who usually is attached to one member of the household for the duration of his (always male; women are more directly connected to the disir-power) life, while the disir are plural and look over the welfare of the entire family. The kinfylgja is sometimes called the hamingja, but she is the collective hamingjia-power of the ancestors embodied in a self-aware form, rather than the "luck" or mana of the individual hamingja.

The disir often appear as women in dreams; they are also called draumkonur (dream-women). They are more likely to appear to a man's wife than to the man himself. They prophesy victory or death, and among the Germanic tribes they were also said to aid in battle in the same manner as valkyrja, strengthening their charges and laying fetters on their enemies. The disir Thorgerd Horgabrudhr ("bride of the altar") and Yrp, ancestral spirits of the Haleygir, were called forth by sacrifice made by the Jarl Haakon Sigurdsson during a battle and appeared in a raging hailstorm from the north, arrows flying from their fingertips. [4] The disir may be called upon for wisdom or help at need, although the same cautions should be observed in their case as when making sacrifice to the gods. The Rite of Disir-Redes may be found in the chapter on Rites.

ALFAR

The Alfar are divided into three races: Ljosalfar, Dokkalfar, and Svartalfar, or Light Elves, Dark Elves, and Black Elves, the last being also called dwarves. The word Alf may be derived from a root meaning "shining" or "white," being related to the Latin albus and Sanskrit rhbu. Ingvisson suggests here that a connection may also exist between the original Celtic name for Scotland, Alba, and the Alfar-folk. It is also possible, however, that "alf" is derived from the Indo-European *lbh-/ *lehb-/*lobh-, which means "to cheat" or "to be cunning."[5] At different times and in different forms the Alfar fit both of these descriptions. They are commonly thought to be the cause of sickness; their arrows (elf-shot) cause stroke and paralysis, and the Anglo-Saxons had a number of charms which were meant to heal the ills given by elves. All the Alfar are wise magicians. They will frequently take an interest in individual humans, as shown by such names as Aelfrede (Elf-counsel), Aelfgifu (Elf-gift), and so forth. The Alfar are also unpredictable, taking pleasure or offense at the slightest things; your manners and bearing are exceedingly important in dealing with these wights.

The first distinction made between the races of the Alfar must be between the Ljosalfar and Svartalfar, who are created independently of humankind, and the Dokkalfar, the mound-elves, who have much in common with the disir, being thought to be in some aspects the masculine counterparts of these beings. The clearest account of a human becoming numbered among the mound-elves is the story of Olaf Gudrudsson, a minor king who, after his death, was called the Elf of Geirstadhir and to whom sacrifice was made for good harvests.

Other accounts, however, show that the mound-elves were not wholly masculine nor wholly human in origin, and it is likely that what occurs in cases such as Olaf's is similar to what occurs with the disir: when a human has become altogether identified with the land and its fruitfulness in life, that person, if buried in a mound, may remain with the Vanic spirits who dwell there and rule over those things, becoming one of the Dokkalfar. It is these elves to whom blessings are made for healing and good harvest, and probably these elves to whom the autumn alfablot (held, like the disablot, at Winternights) was given. The Dokkalfar dwell in mounds, hillocks, and rocks.

They are great magicians and teachers of magic, and it may have been to their abodes that Odhinn refers when he says that he learned his wisdom from the "men, very old men, / who dwell in the wood of the home."[6] Blessings may be made to the Dokkalfar in one's own home, or one may seek out a place where they dwell if one wishes to ask a favor from them. The best time to approach them is at sunset for they are not fond of daylight. They appear as very beautiful, though pale, human-like wights in noble clothes (the term "Dark Alfar" refers to their abodes, not their appearance or moral character, despite the attempts of modern fantasy writers to attach it to one or the other of the latter characteristics).

They may be seen at their dwellings or in dreams after one has made a sacrifice to them, The Dokkalfar at times need the help of humans, and they always repay such help richly. The Ljosalfar are wights of light, air, and thought who dwell in Ljosalfheimr, the upper reaches of Midgardhr's atmosphere, which is ruled by Freyr. It is these Alfar who are often spoken of together with the Aesir, whose spiritual dwelling borders on Asgardhr. Unlike the Dokkalfar and Svartalfar, they love the brightness of the Sun, and they are sometimes seen at the festival of Ostara as white- clad women in the far reaches of the hills. They are often, though not always, personified as feminine, in contrast to the Svartalfar, who are almost always masculine.

The Ljosalfar are the keepers and teachers of wisdom, and they are the source of earthly inspiration, as the Svartalfar are the source of earthly manifestation. It is probably from these wights that the Anglo-Saxon adjective aelfsciene, "bright as an elf," was first derived. The Ljosalfar communicate with humans in dreams and sudden bursts of inspiration. They may appear as shining4air humans or as flashes of light-colored brightness. Of the Svartalfar or Dvergar, there has been more written than about their kin. They were created by the gods out of the maggots that had crawled through the flesh of the slain Ymir. They are very clever smiths, who forged Freyja's necklace, Thor's hammer, Sifs hair, Freyr's ship, and a hoard of other treasures of the gods.

Their dwelling, Svartalfheim, is beneath Midgardhr's surface, and it is there that they hoard their gold and jewels. The dwarves are the earthly craft and power which give shape and being to the inspiration of the Ljosalfar. It was Svartalfar who slew Kvasir and made the mead Odhroerir from his blood (kenaz), transforming the raw material of wisdom into the craft and art of poetry from which any who could might drink. The kobolds of the German mines maybe classed as Svartalfar, as may all of the knocking spirits heard in subterranean works. The Svartalfar are said to be miserly and grudging, as well as more ill-tempered than the other races of Alfar.

The word dwarf is etymologically connected with the idea of harming, oppressing, or maliciously deceiving.[7] Like the Dokkalfar, they are skilled in magic, having learned the runes through the dwarf Dvalin, and they know magical songs; unlike them, they almost never willingly teach their magical knowledge, though at times they may teach the art of smithing to a mortal. The name "Gandalf" meaning Wand-Elf or Sorcerer-Elf, was originally the name of a Norse dwarf![8] It is not uncommon for the Svartalfar to curse things that they are forced to make, such as the sword Tyrfing, or that are stolen from them, such as Andvari's hoard. They are also said to steal human women and children, perhaps because there are few dwarvish women.

Yet although they are often untrustworthy, viciously vengeful, and malicious, they can be surprisingly loyal and friendly to humans who treat them well. Sacrifice is seldom made to Svartalfar, except in rituals where all the Alfar are honored together, such as the Alfablot in [5] Book of Troth. In matters of craft it is best to call upon the Ljosalfar and the Svartalfar together, as the two are complementary forces. The Svartalfar are said to be dark of complexion, ugly, perhaps twisted; they often appear as short but very powerful men with long gray beards.

LAND VAETTIR

The name laud Vaettir means "wights of the land." In this group can be classed all the beings who guard certain places, those who are bound to rocks, streams or trees, and the lesser nature spirits in general. They are very clearly distinguished from the ancestral wights: Indeed, the land Vaettir seem to have been most powerful in Iceland, where humans had just arrived. It was written in the pagan law of Iceland (roughly 930 C.E.) that the dragon heads of ships had to be removed before the ships came into sight of land, so as not to frighten the land Vaettir. At one point King Harald Gormsson hired a wizard who went to Iceland in the form of a whale to spy out the land, and who saw that all the mountains and hills were full of land-wights, both large and small. At every place where the wizard attempted to come to land he was attacked—by a dragon heading a herd of poisonous beasts; by a huge bird and an army of birds; by a mountain giant and an army of giants.[9]

These were the native landvaettir of Iceland, who were thus seen to be so strong that it would be useless to attack the country. Land Vaettir have been known to befriend particular humans, helping all things to go well for them in their daily lives. One example of this was the Icelander Beorn, who dream that a giant came to him and asked him to be his partner.

He agreed, and was thus befriended by the Vaettir, who followed him and his brothers about and could easily be seen by those with second sight. Bloody sacrifice was not offered to these wights, but it was very common to leave a bit of food or pour out ale in front of those places which they were especially known to frequent, or else go to these places, hallow the food to them, and eat it oneself. Rocks, trees, waterfalls and sometimes streams or wells are the commonest dwelling places of the Land Vaettir. It was thought that they would not stay in a place where someone had been slain, whether from anger or from fear is uncertain.

In modern times they are not likely to dwell too near major highways or where there is a great deal of pollution or disturbance; however they do not shun human company and do not object to houses, roads and such as long as their holy places are not destroyed so that these may be built. The Land Vaettir are visible to the sensitive and to those faring forth from their bodies. They also appear in dreams. They do not change shape, but an individual landvaettir may appear as almost anything.

VALKYRJA

The concept of the valkyrja is one of the most complicated in Teutonic thought. The name means "chooser of the slain" and the most widely accepted description of the valkyrja is that she (or they; valkyrja often ride in troops of nine or three times nine) rides on horseback over the battlefield, taking those whom Odhinn wishes for his own to Valhalla. Valkyrja can be seen by those who are sighted in the realms of the spirit; they usually appear in times of strife and storm. Like Odhinn, they first appear as furious and warlike, characteristics which never entirely vanish from them.

The names of the valkyrja in the Grimnismal include Skogul (the Raging One), Hlokk (the Shrieker), and Hild (battle). Before the Battle of Clontarf twelve valkyrja are seen weaving a web of human entrails, the reels and shuttles of which are arrows and a sword, the spindles spears, and the warp weighted with men's heads. As they weave they sing a song of prophecy about the battle to come, and finish by tearing the cloth in two - six carrying one half to the North and six to the south.[10] As weavers and choosers of men's deaths, they are associated with the Norns, and Skuld is the name of a Norn and a valkyrja alike.

Only with the aid of the valkyrja can a mortal human cross Bifrost as has been mentioned earlier. Within Valhalla, they bear drink to Odhinn and the einherjar (his chosen warriors). The valkyrja hover invisibly over the heads of their chosen warriors and shield them both in battle and from magic. They are often said to wear swan dresses when flying out to battle. The valkyrja Sigrdrifa teaches magical wisdom to Sigurdhr. In the cycle of the Helgi lays and the story of Sigurdhr, one sees these magical maidens in mortal bodies from which they fare forth to shield the hero who is destined for them. The hero and his valkyrja are reborn, meet again, and live out their lives together several times, though his is always shortened by violence either as a direct or an indirect result of his mating with her.

The valkyrja is best understood as a guardian spirit and personification of that in the soul which is closest to Odhinn, as both her furor and her mystical wisdom show. Like the fylgja, with whom she has much in common, she is a semi-independent being who is capable of going forth on her own. She often acts in ways of which the ordinary person is altogether unaware, except as symbolically shown by the tales of these battle-maids. One of the greatest goals of the male vitki is to be "wed" to his valkyrja to be consciously reach her, learn from her, and be led upward by her; the goal of the female vitki is to become consciously one with her valkyrja to be a valkyrja in the sense that the title is given to mortal women. Those with a subtle understanding of this will know that these purposes are not necessary different; but the human mind is normally so constructed that they call for different forms of symbolic expression. When the valkyrja is seen, she usually appears as a shiningly fair woman dressed in armor and carrying weapons. If the weapons are bloody, it foretells a battle.

19: OUT DWELLERS

The concept of the innangardhs and the utangardhs has been somewhat discussed under Nine Worlds of Yggdrasil (see Chapter 1). The innangardhs is the realm of ordered space, social structure, the human, and the known; the utangardhs is the realm of disorder, the inhuman, the uncanny, and the unknown. It is the wild world of the forest and the outlaw. It is also the realm into which you fare to gain wisdom and magical power as does Odhinn. Magic is, indeed, by nature characteristic of the utangardhs, as ordered religion is of the innangardhs. Those wights which are specifically characterized as "out-dwellers" are those whose beings are strongly contradictory to the ordered nature of the innangardhs.

However, you should never forget that not only are parts of the vitki's own being - such as the fylgja and even the valkyrja in some aspect closely akin to the outer world, but the most powerful mediator between the realms is the vitki her/himself. Hastrup further points out that only one who is him/herself a part of the utangardhs can effectively deal with its uncanny wights, as seen in the Grettis Saga in which Grettir is the only human who can deal with the malicious trolls and ghosts troubling more ordered folk, precisely because he is an outlaw and thus sib to these beings.[2] Likewise, a number of the greatest Teutonic heroes bear markings or come from families which tie them to the powers of the utangardhs, and it is precisely from this that they derive their uncanny might, even as the gods must often turn to the jotuns for mates.

THE VARGR

Perhaps the most characteristic inhabitant of the utangardhs was the wight called the vargr. This term means wolf," though it. Has a more brutal connotation than the standard ulfr; it was also used colloquially to mean "outlaw," which may have been its original sense. Etymologically it is connected to u-argr, "restless,"[3] which should at once lead the mind back to Odhinn. The heaviest form of outlawry was called skoggangr ("forest-going"); one who had been outlawed was a forest-man or an outlying man, the latter term being used for any wight who lived outside the bounds of society, whether as outlaw, robber, or uncanny being.

The term utilegja ("lying out") is also related to the sitting-out of seidh-magic[4] (see Chapter: 14). The outlaw, being outside of the gardhr had ceased to be human; he is "wod-freka werewolf"-the fury-greedy werewolf- in the laws of Canute wulf-heafod (wolf's head) among the Anglo Saxons. It is obvious that the vargr (outlaw) is closely related to and frequently the same as the vargr (ravening wolf). He is, in fact, often a skin-changer or a berserker. (The vargr is almost always a he in the stories-although women often have wolf-fylgur, they ordinarily ride on their backs rather than putting on their skins, and only one vague poetic reference to a female berserker exists.)[5]

The Volsunga Saga describes how Sigmundr and Sinfjotli become outlaws for a time, when Sigmundr wishes to test the strength of his son, and how the two of them find a house in which other outlaws are sleeping with wolf skins hung over their heads. The Volsungs steal the skins and put them on, turning into wolves, and go forth from there to kill some more travelers. By putting on the skin of an animal in company with the proper ritual, one can either fare forth in its shape or draw the fylgja-mind into oneself to become a berserker. Those who do this are called eigi einhamir, "not of one skin."

This is a trait which is passed down through family lines, so that one sees genealogies such as Bjorn, son of Ulfhedhinr (Wolf-skin-coat, another name for a berserker) son of Ulfhamr (Wolffiide/shape) son of Ulf (Wolf) son of Ulfhamr who could change forms.[6] Unfortunately, those who received this heavy gift of Odhinn's in the latter generations were (and are) usually untrained and unable to control it; the ability to control it usually came through initiation into the secret cults of the Germanic warrior-band. The berserker is not always an outlaw, but he is always outside the bonds of society, and the rules of the innangardhs do not bind him as they bind other people.

It was not uncommon for berserkers to roam through the land, challenging peaceful farmers to holmgang (ritual single combat), which the victim could only escape by forfeiting all he had to the challenger. The berserker was a fearsome opponent: he characteristically gnawed at the edge of his shield, frothing at the mouth In his battle-trance he had the mind of the creature which was his fylgja, usually a wolf or a bear. His strength was several times greater than normal, he did not feel blows, and those berserkers who were especially skilled in trance and battle-magic entered a state in which weapons would not bite on him. When combat was over he became exhausted and frequently passed out for a time. The berserker fury is one of the oldest aspects of the cult of Odhinn.

The Heruli, who were also the first rune masters and possibly the greatest spreaders of Odhinn-worship, cultivated the practice of fighting with only shield and cloak as protection. The best latter-day example of the tie between the berserkergang, runic magic, and Odhinn's other gift of poetry can be found in the family line of Egill Skallagrimson. Egill's grandfather, named Ulfr, was said to be cheerful and active during the day but given to fits of uncontrollable savagery and drowsiness as evening approached. Because of this, "people said that he was much given to changing form (hamrammr), so he was called Kveldulfr (Evening Wolf)."[7]

This would refer to Kveldulfr faring forth in the form of a wolf; later in the saga it is described that he became a berserker in battle, although he was an old man and the strain killed him shortly after. Kveldulfr had two sons, one of whom, Skallagrimr, took after him in both appearance and temperament, and who was prone to berserkergang not only in battle but also in games. Egill Skallagrimson was dark and ugly, like his father and grandfather but unlike his brother and uncle. He is not described as a berserker in his saga, but he was possibly the greatest of Old Norse poets and certainly of rune masters within written history.

In modern times, the path of the berserker is not to be followed by anyone who has not been subject to great physical discipline (such as intensive martial arts training) in conjunction with the magical and spiritual disciplines of Odhinn. Even in the wilder times of the Germanic tribes and Vikings, berserkers were viewed with mistrust and often horror; one can imagine how someone like Skallagrimr, who became too excited in a game and began to kill people, would be treated now. For almost everyone now, knowledge of the berserkergang is only useful inasmuch as it throws light on the process of shape changing and faring forth in the fylgja or another hide (hamr).

THE LIVING DEAD

Among the Teutonic undead are ghosts, which are souls without bodies, and draugar, which are dead bodies animated by part of the human soul. The ghost would seem to be the hamr or hide, sometimes together with the mind and sometimes lingering as a sort of spiritual memory of a person's death. The Eyrbygga Saga describes men drowned to sea who came, dripping wet, to drink the Yule ale and were welcomed by their relatives. The Faereyinga Saga tells of how a Faroese magician summoned the ghosts of three missing men to see how they had died; two were dripping wet, but the third was bloody and held his head in his hand, showing that he had swum to shore and been slain there.

These ghosts do not seem to hear or speak, and if they are motivated it is in the vaguest sort of way. Spirits also appear without hamr(form) but as fiery shapes, like will-o-the-wisps.[8] These would be the hamingjur of the dead which have no thought, and barely feeling. Although they have no lich or hamr to sustain their forces, they may try to steal hamingja-power from whatever is around them. This being the case, it accounts for the cold felt in the presence of some dead, which are themselves felt as warm spots; it is a sort of low keyed and semi-sentient vampirism. The dead are often thought of as living inside their barrows.

In a lay of Helgi Hundingsbana, the dead man's wife Sigrun goes into his barrow. He stays there with her at night, but he and his followers ride up to Valhalla to fight in the daytime. Barrows are sometimes seen open, with lights burning within. In these cases those who dwell inside are written of as feasting and joyous. These, however, do not fall into the realm of out-dwellers but are rather a continuance of social order: one is with one's ancestors or in on&s home. These dead stay where they are and do not trouble the living, though they may give their descendants gifts or good advice; they often overlap with the Dokkalfar. Only when the barriers are broken-when the living enter the barrow uninvited or to steal from the dead-do the dwellers within the howe become ill-wishing.

The most terrifying sort of Teutonic undead is the draugr, the living corpse. The body of this wight did not decay, although it might show signs of death such as swelling or changing color. The draugr is inhumanly strong and often hungry for living flesh and blood-the vehicles of the hamingja force. Like the loose hamingja, its touch is cold, stealing life and courage. It is also said to be ringed with fire, the hamingja-force that enlivens it. Sometimes it is held to its barrow; often it walks and kills whatever it can find outside, banging on the roofs and doors of houses and trying to break in.

With some exceptions, this being can be described as the lich (body) enlivened by hamingja-force and possibly hamr, but without any of the conscious aspects of the soul. The true draugr does not recognize people who were known to it in life, nor, with only a few exceptions, can it speak. The Egill's Saga tells how Skallagrimr's corpse was taken out through the broken wall, apparently so that if he should walk after death, he would come to the wall and not the door-the blind movement of the undeads instinct. Although no overt connection appears between the berserker or skin-changer and the undead in Germanic myth, as in Slavic countries where it is thought that a werewolf will become a vampire after death, precautions are frequently taken to prevent anyone with uncanny powers from walking: the corpses of witches are often staked down with rune-carved sticks, heads cut off, and so forth.

The Grettis Saga describes Grettir's fights with two wights who are said to be draugar, although they differ from the usual walking dead in their level of awareness and mental activity. The first is Karr the Old, who has characteristics of both draugr and Dokkalf. Although he is clearly described and seems to act as an undead, his hauntings are carried out for the sole purpose of increasing his son's holdings, and his son's wish is enough to act as a warding for others. Grettir slays this wight by cutting his head off and clapping it alongside the draugr's thigh, a traditional means of laying these beings[9]

The second, Clam, is the mighty and vicious draugr of a mighty and vicious man who was slain by an unnatural being on the first night of Yule. His body was found, blue and swollen, but so heavy that it could not be moved, which is one of the usual traits of draugar. Glam walked for two years, more in the autumn and winter and less in the bright seasons, slaying men and destroying farms, and finally Grettir came to grapple with him. Grettir eventually overcame Glam by wrestling, but when their eyes met by moonlight he was horribly dismayed (compare with the eyes of the sorcerer).

The saga says that there was more fiendish craft in Glam than in most other ghosts, giving him the ability to speak to Grettir. Glam cursed Grettir so that he should never grow in strength, that he should always be an outlaw and alone, and that he should always see Glam's eyes before his own, which left him with a hideous terror of being alone in the dark.10 Glam is an exceptional draugr, as he seems to have become undead by his own will and strength, thus retaining something of a mind and the power to curse. In most cases the draugr is mindless, seeming to be accidentally created when the hamingja for some reason or other remains with the body. Otherwise, the lich is sometimes animated by a sorcerer for the purpose of working woe, and the hamingja filling it might be that of the sorcerer or of a sacrifice.

This is not to be confused with Odhinn's practice of carving runes to make the dead speak, or of summoning up ghosts; those works are concerned with the actual mind of the dead person, and any other parts, body or soul, are incidentals which make communication between the living and the dead easier. When the consciousness of the dead person is willingly present, it is usually in the setting of disir, Dokkalfar, or other well-wishing barrow wights. However, disturbing the dead or angering them is very dangerous, and even a magical circle is not always warding enough when you have called an unwilling ghost up to Midgardhr. In workings with the undead, runic magic was more often called upon to prevent their workings or to keep them from doing harm than to create them.

JOTUNS

The term jotun is used in English as a general description of the descendants of Ymir. These beings embody the proto-forces of the universe before it was divided into utangardhs and innangardhs. They are thus chaotic by nature and belong to the world of the utangardhs now. In general, it can be said that they embody the raw forces of wild nature. The jotuns are loosely divided into three separate races, although these frequently blurred, especially under the demands of the Norse poetic form. Nevertheless the functions and nature of these beings can be clearly seen, even though the terminology has broken down. In Rune-lore, Thorsson classifies them as etins (ON jotunn, jotnar), which he writes forth as ageless, non-evolving beings of great power, wisdom, and magic; rises, the characteristic "giants" of legend; and thurses, the unintelligent antagonists of consciousness and order, which are further divided into rime-thurses and fire-thurses.

Risir commonly dwell in mountains and cliffs, rime-thurses among the rocks in cold, icy places. Risir sometimes mate with humans, and the hero Starkadh was the grandson of such a pairing. The gods frequently mate with etins and risir, and none of the Aesir are without some trace of the blood of the jotun kindred. The nature of etins and risir varies as drastically as the nature of any other highly conscious class of being. Some, like Aegir and the wise etin Mimir, are helpful to the gods; others, like Utgardsloki and Surtr, are their foes. The thurses, on the other hand, are always foe to the innangardhs.

Loki is of the race of etins, and he may be taken as in many ways characteristic of that kind, although his light and humorous side is not generally seen as a part of etinish nature. With individual exceptions such as Mimir, there is no reason to make blessings to any of the jotunish kindred; their types and names may, however, be used as specifics in banishing (etins Thrym's kin, and so on), and it was also the custom in cursing to threaten one's foes with mating a particularly loathsome thurse such as Hrim grimmnir12 or Lothi, "the Hairy."[3] Also, it should be remembered that humans as well as Aesir partake of the jotunish heritage through our godly ancestry. It is thus our part to seek (as Odhinn does) after the wisdom and might held by the etins and risir, as well as that of the gods.

GRENDEL, GRENDEL'S DAM

The first two monsters with whom Beowulf fights are beautifully typical of the out-dweller. They are numbered among the "children of Cain," a Christianization of the out-dweller concept which nevertheless carries the sense of the original thought of outcast/outlaw well, encompassing "giants, elves, etins, orcs, rocs" 4 as well as the monstrous Grendel himself. Grendel is called variously etin and thurs; like a berserker, he and his mother are both invulnerable to ordinary weapons. They are dwellers in a stagnant mere, the abode of the worst Teutonic water-wights (see laguz).

These two are particularly terrible because they are not kept out by the walls of the innangardhs, but must rather be slain by its guardian, Beowulf, who has certain characteristics in common with Grettir, although he is a far more socialized and reasonable figure. Like Grettir, he was said to have been a lazy child; he had superhuman strength which made him a fit bodily match for monsters. Beowulf prowess is greatest in the water, in which he is initiated in shamanic fashion; 15 this is his heritage from the utangardhs, and because of it he can vanquish the water-monsters, only being slain at last by a wyrm of flame and earth.

TROLLS

The Troll is a Scandinavian breed of wight which is in many ways similar to the jotun kindred, though usually smaller and less fearsome. "Troll" is also a term used to describe most things uncanny-a witch or someone else's dis will be called a troll-wife, while bad weather is still "trowie weather" in the Shetlands.[16] Again, the name of troll is sometimes used interchangeably with that of etin, ris, or thurs. The trolls are able to possess people, as well as drag them off and kill them. Like the berserker gang, this possession was supposed to be extinguished by baptism; and it may be that the two were related, as it was possible for a person to have a troll as fylgja.

"Trolls take you!" is a common curse, but there is no way to tell whether it means mental possession or simply murder. Trolls range from small and rather comical creatures to large and ferocious wights which have much in common with their cousins the thurses. They are often ugly and misshapen, though not always; like all the races of Ymir's children, the troll kindred has a few among it who are both beautiful and wise. They dwell inside of mountains, hills, and hillocks. The sun turns them to stone. Trolls can do favors for mortals and sometimes breed with them: troll-women seduce human men, and troll men often capture human women. There are several people called Half-Troll in the sagas. Grettir himself was sheltered for a while in the valley of the half-troll Thorir.

HULDRU–FOLK

The Huldru-folk (hidden people) or Elle (alder)-folk are halfway in nature between trolls and landvaettir, They are peoples of the mound and forest, not slain by sunlight, but who often try to capture mortals by tricks and magic. These peoples are beautiful but usually deformed by animal parts or hollow backs. The Wood-folk of the German forests are similar to their Scandinavian cousins in both character and nature. All of these beings can be both helpful and harmful to humans, depending on their whims and how they are treated. Food is sometimes left for them. They are keepers of magical wisdom, generally that related to the lore of plants and healing, though they also cause sickness at times.

20: BEASTS

In Teutonic tradition, as among most people who live closely in tune with their own world, animals of various kinds are known to have special elements to their beings which make them particularly appropriate to the cults of certain gods, in certain magical workings, or as tutelary spirits. By knowing the greatest beasts of the Teutonic world and the thoughts which our ancestors associated with them, you can enhance your workings and your own understanding. Often animals will be seen in visions or dreams, and these beings must be understood if you are to receive the wisdom being given you.

BEAR: The Teutonic people thought of the bear as the greatest of the beasts. It is frequently the fylgja of someone who is exceedingly strong, both in body and in mind. Along with the wolf, it is a common favorite of shape-changers and berserkers; one often finds Bjorn (bear) as a personal name. The bear is thought of as being similar to a human in intelligence, aware of honor and fairness. Although it is a beast of the utangardhs, it is not one of uncontrolled fury and destruction such as the wolf, but rather more good humored and moderate. The name "Beowulf" literally means "beewolf" which is a kenning for bear, and Beowulf is typical of bear-heroes in his strength and in that his strength is directed against monsters rather than men. Bjorn was also a side-name Thorr, although the bear was never specifically made holy to him.

BIRDS: The smaller, lesser birds, such as cuckoo, swallow, and titmouse, have the Vanic gifts of foresight and wisdom. Sigurdh is told by the wood fowl where the sleeping Sigrdrifa lies and that Reginn plans to murder him.[2] Folk beliefs still hold that the cries of the cuckoo can tell you the length of your life remaining and whether good or ill will befall you.[3] The robin is hallowed to Thorr; if you disturb its nest your house will be struck by lightning.[4] Shape-changers often take the forms of swallows. The flight and actions of birds of all sorts can be omens. The greater birds are more important to Teutonic magic and are spoken of individually.

BOAR: The boar is the greatest of the Vanic beasts, holy to Freyja and Freyr. According to legend, he taught humans to plow by rooting up the earth with his tusks. He is also a fearsome warrior. The boar's head was used on helmets, especially on those worn by the followers of the Vanic cult, to protect themselves in battle and frighten their foes. One of these was named Hildisvini (Battle-swine), the name of Freyja's own boar, and Davidson suggests that the story of Freyja disguising her lover Ottar as her mount really refers to the use of a boar-mask in Vanic ritual.5 Served at table, a boar's head cannot be carved by someone who is not of clean reputation and tried bravery.

CAT: The cat is sacred to Freyja. The cats who drew her chariot have been mentioned earlier. Treating these creatures well will bring the goddess' blessing on one's love and marriage. The cat is frequently the fylgja of women and strongly tied to seidhr-magic. For this reason, it has been thought of as the familiar of witches down to this day. Although the cat and its place in magic are usually feminine, there was one wizard, the Icelander Thorolf Skeggi, who had twenty black cats that guarded him bravely when he was attacked. The cat is also seen as a sort of helpful home-sprite, servant and family luck in one.[6]

CATTLE: The bull and the ox were frequently sacrificed to Freyr, Thon, and the disir or alfar. Like other animals of great strength, these are very powerful fylgjur. War-chariots were drawn by oxen; the cow was also honored, and the hallowed cow Sibilja was even led into battle.[7] The cow would seem to be associated with Freyja, as Nerthus' wagon was drawn by kine. Milk is, obviously, a source of strength and vital power (see uruz). The horns of cows were decorated and adorned with gold and are still decked with flowers and ribbons today in Germanic areas. Tame cattle are spoken of further under fehu, the aurochs under uruz.

DEER: The stag is the fylgja of a noble man or king. Helgi Hundingsbana is compared to the stag towering above all the other forest animals.[8]. Stag's antlers are put up, as at Heorot, to hallow a place to him and call upon h is protection. After the loss of his sword, Freyr fought with the horn of a hart. According to one version of the Sigurdhr story, the hero was nursed by a hind in the woods. To the dying Fafflir, he names himself "Stag" (or "noble animal"). [9] He also appears as a stag in a dream, it being his animal fetch. Four harts gnaw at the bark of the World-Tree; these embody the entropic forces of earthly nature. The stag often leads the one who follows it to a magical place or to a vision, and it is not uncommon for otherworldly beings to take the shapes of deer in order to lure a hunter onward.

EAGLE: The eagle is the greatest of birds. An eagle sits at the top of the World-Tree. The eye of the eagle is the far-sighted, piercing, wise eye of the Teutonic hero, and the eagles scream at the hero's birth.11 In the hidden lore of the Teutonic people, the eagle is the bird embodying the noble one, the one who has fulfilled her/his spiritual potential. It is associated with jera,12 being in fact this rune in its highest form. As the transformation of that which is hidden in earth to that which flies forth into the heavens as their ruler-the noblest bird-jera is the upward spiral of the eagle's path.

This may be seen in the story of Odhroerir, in which Odhinn brings the mead forth from inside the mountain and carries it back to Valhalla as an eagle. The winds are often embodied as an eagle: Hraesvelg (Corpse-gulper), an etin in eagle's shape, sits at the end of the world and the beating of his wings Mows forth all the winds. [3] Shetlanders are said to call forth the storm wind as a great eagle.

The eagle is a bird of Odhinn, and his followers sometimes made sacrifices to him by the carving of the blood-eagle. The falcon shares many characteristics with the eagle, though it is usually feminine, whereas the eagle is most often shown as masculine.

HORSE: The horse is associated especially with the worship of Freyr and of Odhinn. The god may take up residence in the body of a horse, as is hinted at by the Freyfaxi (Frey-mane) of the Vatnsdaelasaga, which was worshiped by its owner, and that of Hrafnkell, which was hallowed to the god and which its slayers had to hood before pushing it over a cliff as a sorcerer would be hooded, in order to avoid the magic of his gaze. Horses were very often sacrificed, and the eating of horseflesh was the mark of a heathen, which is why people of northern Christian countries have been brainwashed to react to the thought of eating horse with revulsion. The phallus of the horse was especially holy. There is a story of one family which preserved this organ with onions and herbs, keeping it wrapped with a linen cloth in a chest and bringing it forth every evening to pass it around the people in the house.

It was affectionately called Volsi, and each person who held it spoke a verse ending with the refrain "May Mornir receive this sacrifice."[15] Mornir is thought to be the name of a giant-woman, comparable to Gerdhr or Skadhi; arguments to the contrary seem rather forced. The horse's head is put up on or carved on a stake to make a nidhing-pole (pole of insult), which is used for curses and political criticism. Horses' heads are carved on the gables of the roof in Lower Saxony or buried in a barn for the sake of warding.[16]

In its oldest form, the horse is a solar animal. Its mane seems like the rays of the sun, and it is the beast which draws the wain of the sun across the sky (see raidho). As the horse of Odhinn, it is the bearer of the dead, and misshapen horses or grays were often thought to be omens of death and disaster. The horse is also the vehicle of travel between the worlds: It may be that the stick of the gandreid was sometimes a sort of hobbyhorse, and a number of folk tales have survived in which a witch turns a stick or reed into a horse and rides it to "meet with the devil" the Christian term for the myrkreid (dark-ride) or kveldreid (night- ride) of the seidhr-worker. The use of the horse in divination and as the vehicle of godly wisdom is discussed under ehwaz.

RAVEN: The raven is the bird most associated with Odhinn. It is the bird of battle, and for one to be followed by ravens on the way to war is a good sign, because it means that one will feed them well. Ravens flying overhead or croaking is a sign that Odhinn has heard one's prayers or accepted one's sacrifice and will help one. The raven was often embroidered on magical banners-an Anglo-Saxon account says that the Norse flag was of plain white silk, but a raven appeared on it in wartime. When the army was to win the day, its beak was open and wings fluttering, but when they were to lose, it sat still and its feathers drooped. The Jarl Sigurdhr of the Orkney Islands had a raven banner which his mother had made.

This banner was so enchanted that whoever it was borne before would win the battle, but the standard-bearer was doomed to die. Sigurdhr won many fights with its aid, but at the Battle of Clontarf (1016), after two men had been killed under the banner, he was forced to take it up himself and so lost his own life and the battle. The raven is a bird of cunning, wisdom, and trickery as well as of war. Odhinn's ravens Huginn and Muninn have been spoken of often-they are the bearers of Odhinn's mind, who often fly before his chosen to show them their way. The deceptive nature of the raven appears often in later Germanic folklore, and Grimm says that the raven seems to combine within himself the folklore characteristics of wolf and of fox, melding the greed of one with the other's cunning.

WOLF: The nature of the wolf has been somewhat discussed under the chapter on the vargr. The wolf is the fylgja of a ferocious person, usually a warrior or a witch. Witches ride on the backs of their wolffylgjur, using serpents for reins. The wolf is the embodiment of fury and chaos, which is seen in all its forms in Odhinn. As a being of woe, the nature of the wolf is shown in the Fenris-Wolf, the epitome of brute wildness. Coupled with this, however, one should consider the fact that it was lucky to meet a wolf when setting out on any undertaking, just as it was lucky to meet a warrior. The wildness of the wolf is also its great strength.

WYRM: First printed as The Northern Dragon, Northways. The word wyrm is the original Germanic-based term for a serpent or dragon, draca being adopted from the Latin draco at a very early time. When the dragon appears in Teutonic legend, it is nearly always as a frightful menace which must be slain by the hero. Sigurdhr's victory over Fafnir is his deed of daring "which soar(s) highest the heavens beneath."[18] In the case of Beowulf and Wiglaf, the dragon is the only fitting end for the aged Beowulf, who is clearly too great a hero for any man's sword to cut down, while Wiglafs role in the right raises him to the position of Beowulf's heir (the king lacking any heir of his own body). The hero is raised up by his victory over the dragon, but these are heroes who are already exceptional in some way. Beowulf has already proved himself mighty against the out-dwellers, and indeed has a few traits of the out- dweller himself (see the chapter on, Grendel).

Sigurdhr is the son of a shape changer, lineage which gives him added strength in dealing with the dragon. The hero who holds this might, who stands at the border of the gardhr, is the one who is closest to the great workings of Wyrd. The rewards which the wyrm holds for the hero who slays it also write its own nature forth. The first of these is, of course, the gold which is the embodiment of the dragon's vast magical might (see fehu; note that the wyrm is said, when set upon a pile of gold, to grow to the exact size of the treasure), as is its power of breathing fire or fiery venom. The hoard is concealed within a mound, which in Beowulf is unquestionably a burial mound.

In the story of Fafflir, while no burial has taken place, the hoard is an inheritance, Sigurdhr's first plan being to win back that portion of Hreithmar's gold which Fafnir had kept from his brother Reginn. Not only is the power-hoard hidden, but it comes specifically from the "past"-the concealed layers of that-which-is, which lie dark until a further turning awakens them. As Bauschatz points out the dragon only flies forth when disturbed by some deed which brings into the play the greatest turnings of Wyrd, coiling and layering in secret for years and coming forth at the point in becoming when the entirety of that- which-is is to be shifted.[19]

This can be seen in the figure of Nidhoggr who lies at the very roots of the World-Tree, hidden in the deepest layers of that-which-is, and who does not take flight until the end of Ragnarok when all is reshaped (the tie between the burial mound and the Well of Wyrd can be seen in the rune perthro and its triad, kenaz-perthro-ingwaz). In both Beowulf and the Sigurdhr story, a great deal of thought is given to the act of bringing the hoard forth from its place of hiding, which is to say, bringing the power forth from darkness so that the living may make use of that inheritance which they have won from the deeper layers of that-which-is.

The corpse of the Beowulf dragon is then tossed off a cliff and into the sea, showing its return to the hidden layers, even as Nidhoggr must sink back after his moment of flight.[20] It will be noted that the dragon of Teutonic folklore is as often a creature of water as of earth; this is another means of showing the understanding of the dragon as the power dwelling beneath that which one can see. Water is, like the grave mound, the holder of the gold/power of those who have lived before; it is, further, an even clearer sign of the Well of Urdhr and its springing water which, through the layers of that-which-is, shapes that-which-is-becoming. The second reward which the dragon holds for the hero is the shaping of this inherited hoard in wisdom. Fafnir warns Sigurdhr of the weird which he will win if he takes the dragon's gold and answers questions about the workings of the worlds. By drinking Fafnir's blood and eating his heart, Sigurdhr gains the knowledge of things hidden, which is one of the greatest parts of the dragon's being.

Only when he has claimed this inherited wisdom can he learn the secret of the sleeping Sigrdrifa (see the chapter on, Valkyrja) and work the next great turning of his weird. As the embodiment of hidden might, the dragon is also present in the pathways of power which flow beneath the skin of the earth. Lore showing this side of the dragon's being is particularly rich in England and other parts of Britain where the patterns of power have been marked with such care, but the Norse certainly knew about this might and its use. The clearest showing-forth of the dragon or serpent as the great flow of earth-power is the Midgardhr's Wyrm which girdles the globe. Thorr's struggle with it in Hymiskvidha shines forth as the shape of the tales in which a heavenly wight binds the earth-dragon to its task of holding the world together either by pinning it down or by slaying it, As Thorr's power comes from the meeting of Odhinn's wind-might with the earth his mother, he is most well-matched with the Wyrm.

The dragon/serpent flow is a pathway for those who know how to use it; witness Odhinn's taking of snake-shape to enter Baugi's Farm and reach the Odhroerir-mead. These paths are, like the wyrms of the story, a source of power and wisdom for the strong and a danger for the weak and unwary, holding the roots of the world together or gnawing at them in the same buried darkness. The chief open uses of the dragon were on weapons, as the prow of the long-ship, or in intertwined ornamentation; the coiled, rune-etched wyrm is a well-known sight to the learner of Teutonic lore. The wyrm coiled on the hilt of the weapon to strengthen the wearer's hand, and ran up and down the blade so that it would be mighty and deadly in battle. As the ship's prow, the dragon worked in several ways: it showed the ship safely through the dark paths of the waters; it brought the force of the dragon's fiery strength and bravery into those warriors who used it as their battle-sign; and it aided in wreaking fear and woe in those it was used against.

It will be marked that the dragon's head had to be removed before coming into sight of land, and this was perhaps done in order not to frighten the landvaettir, but moreover because the dragon in the open was the sign and agent of a great upheaval in the land-a weird unwanted, when one hoped to return to a peaceful home. The use of the rune-carved wyrm on a memorial stone showed the power of the person remembered and of the deeds done which, though hidden in the layers of lives, would still work upon the worlds and be reachable to those who know how to draw forth might from hiding. The wyrm further hints that secrets are held in the actual writings which only those who know can read and learn, thus shielding the mystery and gaining the added might of concealment.

The wyrm has sides of being which make it sib to the workings of several gods. As the keeper of secret wisdom, it is a part of odhinn's mysteries-the god takes the form of a serpent and shares names with the wyrms at the roots of the World-Tree. The use of the wyrm in runic writings has been spoken of, and the understanding of the dragon-paths is needed by the vitki. The relationship between Thorr and the Midgardhr's Wyrm is well known: though foes, they are in a sense sib, Thorr's lighting (as sowilo) being the heavenly mirror of the earth's dragon might and the moment of greatest power being the meeting of the heavenly flow with that of the earth (thuriaz). However, most of the shapes of the dragon's being show it to be as much a Vanic wight as one of Aesic works. It is a dweller in the mound, the place of Vanic burial and the stead of a number of rites honoring Vanic beings.

As the keeper of earth-hidden treasures, it can be said to ward Freyja's wealth, just as the water dragon coils around the sunken riches of Njord. The foresight of the dragon seems nearer to the fore-sight and soul-deep knowing of the volva's seidhr-magic than to the rune-readings of galdr-power. The foresight of the Vanir is well known. Its concealment beneath earth or water makes the wyrm well fitted for a place among Vanic wights, as does its fiery wealth. Like Freyja and Freyr, it strengthens the warrior-it holds the Vanic wisdom of the mound-dead from whom even Odhinn can learn and to whom he comes for knowledge of what should become. The claiming of the ancestral might which is shown so strongly in the dragon's being is also as much of the Vanir as of the Aesir.

SECTION IV: APPENDICES

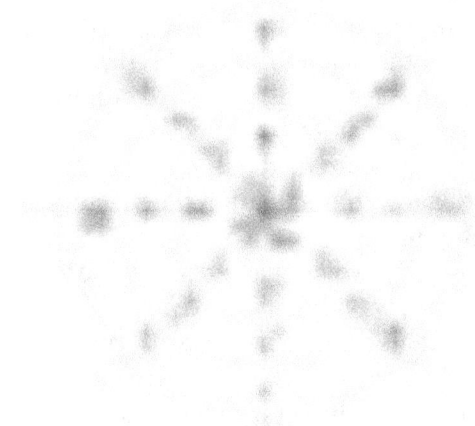

RITES

CIRCLE RITE

Purpose: To set up a holy enclosure of warding and power for the performance of a rite. Earthly Tools: Gandr or sax; otherwise, as needed for following ritual.

I. Facing north, with gandr or sax in your strong hand, begin meditative breathing until you have reached a state of semi-trance. Draw your earthly circle around you or trace over its lines, charging them with bright-burning power. Your arm stretched out fully, trace the rune fehu large in the north, singing its name three times as you write its shape in glowing red before you. Turn to the northeast, your arm still stretched out, tracing a band of red power with the point of the gandr or sax and do the same with uru, the east with thurisaz, etc. So that the last rune of the first turn is wunjo in the northwest. Complete the circle of light, which you should now see as a sphere around you merging with the borders of your earthly circle, and continue onward with the other two aettir in the same manner, till you have made three turns and finished with othala in the northwest. It should appear to you now that you stand in the middle of a threefold sphere glowing red with the eight runic triads ringed at the heavenly aettir.
Cry out,
"Wielder of mighty Mjollnir-hammer, Hail to Thorr Veurr!
Hammer ward my works without!"

Trace the sign of the Hammer at each of the heavenly aettir, seeing it flame huge and brilliant as red lightning outside of your circle before each runic triad.

"Hammer hallow my works within!"

Trace a deosil swastika, or, if you prefer, a Hammer in brilliant white light above your head. It should seem to be whirling, spinning, and shining might forth into your sphere of power until your body tingles with it. Stand in the stadha of elhaz, head up and hands raised, and spread your legs as well so that you are solidly rooted on the ground. Sing,

"Above me Asgardhr's awesome might!"

Feel a stream of rainbow-sparkling golden power flow down into your up-stretched arms and around you, adding its light to the threefold sphere around you.

"Roots below in Hel's black hall!"

Feel a stream of dark might flowing up through your feet and into you, strengthening and solidifying the sparkling red-gold spheres. Bring your feet together and stretch your arms out to either sides in the stadha of hagalaz.

"The middle is Midgardhr's might!"

Feel all the streams of power, from above, below, and the aettir about you meeting in the center of your body. Breathe deeply from your center three times and begin your rite. When the rite is completed, either draw the energy of your spheres into yourself with several deep breaths or dissipate it back into the universe. Retrace the earthly circle in the opposite direction, drawing up the power in it with your gandr or sax. This might may be kept in the tool or dissipated.

RITE OF CARVING

Purpose: To carve a rune tine for poetic inspiration and skill In the writing of rituals.

Earthly Tools: Wood for tine (ash is best), gandr, sax, black cloth, thong, dark blue or red candle, horn or cup filled with ale, fire pot.
Recels: Juniper berries, mullein, ash bark, periwinkle, willow bark, clary, angelica, eye bright, and mug wort.

Time: Sunset, midnight, or sunrise on the nights of the New or Full Moon.
I. Perform Circle rite.
Light fire pot and sprinkle reels on chanting:

Flame-night from Muspellheimr free in the fire
Recels-smoke rising to hallow this hall Well it is wafting
My will it shall wreak.

Light candle from fire pot and set it on the harrow or at the north of your circle, chanting:

> Candle, kindled harrow's holy fire
> Brightness beam well to my work
> Burning bright weal to my work.

Raise hands and head to the north and cry out:

> Hear me, high ones Ye Aesir and Asynjur
> And hallowed, enfolding earth!
> My words through the worlds ring roaring run & might
> Ring in the Welt of Wyrd.
> Flail to Odhinn Odhroerir's lord
> Flail, Galdrgod great
> Who runes doth rede and songs send forth
> Hail to the Allfather high!

If pigment is used for coloring, chant the name of each rune while grinding. Repeat this three times, then intone:

> Skalds-galdrar aaa aaa.
> Rune-might is blended in bright blood of power
> Hallowed with shining stave.

Carve magical name in runes into tine and color, singing the names of the staves. Sing:

> I, (name), have written these runes. Power and poetry flow into me; I scribe the staves of my weird," Intone the names of each rune over the tine three times, signing the shape with each repetition.

Carve each rune in while singing its name, prolonging the initial sound. You must see and feel the shining power as it flows from the Nine Worlds through you and into the shapes you carve. Your voice should vibrate through the tine, your words resonate through all the realms of being. When the runes are carved, draw a straight line across the bottom to connect them, letting the kenaz rune float free. Inlay the runes with the blood of their life. As you color each on feel the intensity of its force flowing into the rune-tine. And guide its working by singing its line of the galdr:

> Sowilo —shining shield of will, Spin in me wheels of song
> Kenaz —flame-craft word hoard's gold Ansuz — awaken word-lore
> wit/un Laguz — bring dark depths to light
> Dagaz — be bright day of my mind
> Sowilo — spin the song-wheels shining
> Gebo — grant to me Odhinn's gift, that Odhroerir's good I may give forth
> Ansuz — awaken odhr and ond in me
> Laguz — bring life from my mind's dark waters
> Dagaz — be the day of word-wisdom

Raido — drive my word-road aright
Ansuz — awaken in me skald's ableness
Elhaz — call wisdom down to my words

Repeat for each of the ansuttrefots:
    Ansuz, awaken word-lore within me
    Ansuz, awaken odhr and ond in me
    Ansuz, awaken in me skald's ableness

Wrap the tine in the black cloth and bind it nine times with the thong. Sing,
    Wrapped in the womb of earth's darkness deep
    Nine nights in blackness be thy silent slumber
    Hidden in holiest home of dark Holda

Lay the tint down and walk the circle deosil around it nine times, your body turning widdershins, feeling the might that spirals in from heavens and earth as the sun wheels its way with you, from light to darkness to light again for nine nights. You sing the full formula, "skaldsgaldrar aaa aaa" with each walking of the circle. Unbind the thong and open the cloth.

Sing:
    Hail to Aesir, Asynjur and Alfar
    Hail the brightness of day!
    Born from the blackness
    Ripe is thy rune-might
    Written to work my will

Sprinkle the tine with ale from the horn, singing "llllll" into it as you do so, until you can feel it vibrating with the sound of your voice. Feel the strengthening, yeasty, watery quality of the life-force flowing from you into it. Pass it over the fire-pot, singing, ffffff into it. This time it should feel a great rush of quickening, hot hamingja-force into the tine. Facing north again, sing "aaaaa" Into it, feeling the rush of your breath awaken the life and might of your taufr. Hold the tine up and sing:
    My words are written in Well of Wyrd
    Staves stained with shining might,
    From thee the power of poetry flows into me,
    The skill of the skald.
    Into me, the magic-songs' might
    I wit the work of word-wisom by thee
    Awakened are odhr and ond,
    Bright in each breath
    In every song shining
    Written, the rune-might shall roar.

By Odhinn, Vili and Ve I have wrought it
By Urdhr, Verdhandi, Skuld have written it
Through Asgardr, Midgardhr
Hel I have worked it I(name), the vitki!
My word is the World-tree's mightiest wind
My will is the shining, ceaseless sun wheel
My works are all written in Yggdrasil's wood.
As I have written so shall it be!

As you chant the last words, see the tine enclosed in a sphere of shining might which guards and strengthens it and through which its power flows. Say quietly, but with utter confidence, "The work is wrought. It cannot be broken." Break th circle and return its energy to the world.

RITE OF DISIR–REDE

Purpose: To gain the help of the dlsir of one's family.

Earthly Tools: Horn/cup, ale, hlaut-teinn (twigs for sprinkling) harrow, ox made of bread or cookie dough sax, hammer. Time: sunset.

Go to the harrow at sunset, facing northward, Make the sign of the Hammer over the ox's head and the ale or hallow them by swinging them. Say, "I give thee to my disir" and cut its throat with the sax, pouring the ale into the horn.
Sprinkle the ale about over the harrow. Raise your head and hands and call:
Disir, I call you kinswomen kind
Coming with holy help
Sig disir shining show me my way
Speak to me wisdom and weal.
Grant to me good redes spoken aright
Give you a grim fate forth to my foes
Be in all battles by my side ever
I hail you, disir of help!

Eat a piece of the ox in silence, concentrating on the shining disir-spirits of your family. When you feel that you have done this long enough, pour the remainder of the ale out in front of the harrow (if outdoors) or onto the earth outside. The disir should appear in your dreams or visions.

HAIL TO SUNNA

This rite should be performed at sunrise, midday, sunset, and midnight, or as close to those times as one can manage. If possible, one should stand with head and hands raised, facing east at sunrise, south at midday, west at sunset, and north at midnight.

(SUNRISE) Sing:
>"Hail to Sunna shining in rising Hail the burning bringer of day.
>Dawn-breaking light is life of the earth.
>Whirls the sun-wheel ever onwards Hail to thee in the dawn!"

(MIDDAY) Sing:
>"Hail to Sunna shining in brightness
>Hail in holy heavens of day
>Mid-day light shining is life of the earth.
>Whirls the sun-wheel ever onwards
>Hail to thee in the day!"

(SUNSET) Sing:
>"Hail to Sunna shining in setting
>Hail in darkening death of the day
>Evening's red light blood and fire of life.
>Whirls the sun-wheel ever onwards Hail to thee in the evening!"

(MIDNIGHT) Sing:
>"Hail to Sunna shining in darkness
>Hail to thee in night's blackest hour
>Shroud of dark water and earth hides thy shining.
>Whirls the sun-wheel ever onwards,
>Hail to thee in the night!"

RITE OF MIMIR

Time: Ideally done at midnight, preferably done at night before going to sleep.

Circle Rite

Light the coal and sprinkle the recels on, chanting,
>"Flame-might from Muspellheimr free in the fire
>Recels-smoke rising to hallow this hail
>Well it is wafting my will it shall wreak."

Light the candle and chant,
    "Candle, kindled Harrow's holy fire
    Through World-Tree's darkness
    To Well show the way.
    Well do I ken
    Where Ygg's eye is hidden
    In the wondrous Well of Mimir
    Where the Nine Worlds'
    Wisdom is written
    From Midgardhr I wend my way to the well."

Strike the edge of the cup or horn with the gandr or sax and vibrate:
    "Asgardhr!"

Wait until the last resonance has died down and repeat the action, vibrating,
    "Hel! Midgardhr! Alfheim! Svartalfheim! Muspellheimr! Vanaheimr!
    Niflheimr! Jotunheimr!" Pause for a moment of absolute silence, then
    strike the cup again, crying, "Mimir!"

Staring into the waters of the cup or horn, chant so that your breath stirs the
surface of the water;
    "Hail, Mimir, wisest of the etin-kind, Hail to thee,
    Bolthorn's famous son, Hail, warder of wisdom's dark well.
    I have come to thee in the hidden hour
    Beneath the root of Ygg's rune-ridden tree
    Where Odhinn bought his draught with an eye.
    Mimir, warder of memory's might
    My ancestors' draught I come to drain,
    The waters of wisdom I come to drink."

Meditate on the cup or horn until you can see that its rim is the rim of a stone
well, with a great evergreen rising from it, its roots concealed in the well depths. As
you slowly drain the contents of the cup in one draught, see the world of what is
around you: all that has gone to makeup that-which-is alive and stretching outward
into becoming, as the needles of the tree stretch outward, nourished by the water
flowing up from the hidden roots and through all the layers of wood to shape them.
Chant:
    "Mimir I thank, with hallowed draught homeward Fare I, all filled
    with memory's might."

Draw the energy of the circle in or return it to the universe; if you used a physical
circle, erase or counter-trace it before stepping out. Extinguish the candle with a
brief galdr such as "Candle-flame kindled now curl back to hiding," and the coals
with, perhaps, "Fire-might back to Muspellheim fare."

RITE OF TREE–GIFT

Purpose: To get wood for a taufr (talisman), gandr (wand), stave, ritual fire, or any other magical or religious purpose.

Earthly Tools: Sax or hallowed axe, horn/cup, mead or ale, small loaf of bread, gandr.

Time: Sunset or sunrise

This rite may be done either in two parts or as a whole. Generally it is best to find the tree when one has plenty of time and can concentrate on one's magical sense of which tree is right, rather than feeling hurried by the movement of the sun. Also, trees process knowledge more slowly than humans, so it is kinder to give your wooded brothers and sisters a little time to prepare for being cut, as well as working the first might you put into the tree more thoroughly into the wood. This is not, however, absolutely needful. Go silently out to a wooded place and sit down on the ground, facing north with your palms on the earth.

Breathe deeply and regularly, concentrating on the earth beneath you: fruitful mother, keeper of seeds, womb and tomb of all that lives. Do this until you feel her might thrumming through your hands and body, until you feel that you are touching the deep, hidden, and silent wisdom of Mother Nerthus. Whisper softly,
"Hail, holy earth who giveth to all,
All sib, who spring Sons and daughters, from thee."

Tell her your goal, singing the names of each of the runes softly, and ask for her help. Wait until you feel some sort of answer. It may be as clear as a voice in your mind; it may be a soft inner tugging or urging in this direction or that, or any of a number of other things. Follow your sense of where to go until you reach a tree past which you feel you should not walk any further. Sit before it, facing north. With your palms on its trunk, breathe deeply and clear your mind until you feel that you are touching the indwelling wight. Sing,
"Hail to thee, tree-sib! A gift for a gift
Give I at need that this work be wrought."
Whisper your purpose and need to the tree,
Singing the runes into it.
Hail, warder of wisdom's dark well.
I have come to thee in the hidden hour
Beneath the root of Ygg's rune-ridden tree
Where Odhinn bought his draught with an eye.
Mimir, warder of memory's might
My ancestors' draught I come to drain,
The waters of wisdom I come to drink."

Meditate on the cup or horn until you can see that its rim is the rim of a stone well, with a great evergreen rising from it, its roots concealed in the well's depths. As you slowly drain the contents of the cup in one draught, see the world of what is around you: all that has gone to make up that-which-is alive and stretching outward into becoming, as the needles of the tree stretch outward, nourished by the water flowing up from the hidden roots and through all the layers of wood to shape them. Chant:

"Mimir I thank, with hallowed draught homeward
Fare I, all filled with memory's might."

Draw the energy of the circle in or return it to the universe; if you used a physical circle, erase or counter-trace it before stepping out. Extinguish the candle with a brief galdr such as "Candle-flame kindled now curl back to hiding," and the coals with, perhaps, "Fire-might back to Muspellheim fare." Pour the mead or ale into your hallowed vessel and make the sign of the Hammer or widdershins swastika over it and the bread. Say,

"Hallowed the holy drink I give, Hallowed be this bread
Weal it work with glad heart given Given, a gift for a gift."

Set the bread down and pour the drink out at the tree's roots.

Find the branch that seems best-fitted for your use. If possible, this should be one whose pruning will only help the growth of the tree. Trace the runes you wish to use over it with your gandr, singing their names and a galdr telling the goal of your working. If you are doing this rite in two parts, tell the tree when you are going to return to cut it, continuing with step Vat sunrise or sunset. Do not speak to anyone while leaving or coming back. Meditate on the might of Nerthus flowing up through the tree and on the power of the tree itself flowing into your branch, shaped by the shining runes you sang. Aware of this power, you are also aware of the pain you are about to cause to your tree-brother or -sister. Put that energy into tree and branch as well.

If a tear falls, touch it to the place where you are about to cut. Cut the branch with one swift stroke if possible (this is why a hallowed ax may be needed),crying out sharply as a bright burst of might runs from your center down your weapon and into the tree, cutting through its limb. The wood should not be allowed to touch the ground, if possible. Hold it in both hands, concentrating on sealing the bright life-force it still holds inside a shining sphere, then wrap it in black cloth and put it away. Touch the tree where you have cut it, pouring some of your own strength into it to help it heal. It is thought right by many to put a drop of your own blood on the wound in the tree. Say a short blessing of thanks to the tree, then put your hands on the earth again and thank Nerthus for her gift. Return home in utter silence.

RITE OF WHEELS

Purpose: To enliven the magical wheels of the body through runic meditation.

The term "wheels of the body" is used in Teutonic magic for the whirling points of power along the spine which the Hindus call "Chakras" and the Celts "cauldrons." These wheels are gateways bringing might from the various forms of the soul into the earthly body and from the hidden worlds of power into the soul. Normally they are small and dim, moving sluggishly. For proper magical functioning, it is important to open and enliven each of them in turn, awakening the specific quality of power which dwells in every level of your being. This awakening will make both magical and psychic functioning easier, since in addition to allowing a greater passage of power through you it also increases your perceptions and aids in awakening your own hidden abilities. This exercise has been designed to strengthen and enliven the wheels of power from crown to feet and back again through the use of specific runes and colors.

Lie down or sit with back straight, knees and feet together, palms on thighs, eyes closed. Begin deep meditative breathing until you are completely relaxed and feel yourself in a state verging on trance. Slowly begin to vibrate the sound of sowilo, "sssss," seeing and feeling this rune whirling in wheels of white radiance at your crown, brow, throat, heart, solar plexus, groin/base of your spine, and feet. When you feel this strongly, throw your force up to the crown of your head, vibrating the rune elhaz and seeing a sphere of rainbow-sparkling white spinning there with a brilliant red elhaz at its hub. Do this until you can feel the crown of your head tingling with its radiant might. Breathe inward, seeing a white ray stretching downward to the center of your forehead. Vibrate the rune mannaz, seeing a deep violet sphere of glowing light whirling in the center of your forehead around a burning red mannaz while the wheel above your crown spins with none of its rainbow-white light lost.

Again, do this until you can feel the force of the wheel as a bodily sensation in the center of your brow. Breathe inward, sending a purple ray down to your throat. Vibrate the rune ansuz . The color of this wheel should be deep, shining blue, the rune, as all of the runes will be, red. Continue as before, sending a blue ray down to your heart, singing the rune wunjo and enlivening this sphere with gold. The wheel in your solar plexus should be a rich orange-red; vibrate jera. The wheel at your groin should be a deep green-blue with a glowing center of red-gold at the base of your spine; vibrate laguz.

At your feet, the wheel should be a shade of brown-green so dark it is almost black; vibrate berkano. Now aware of all the wheels spinning through your body, see the light they are giving off blend into a sphere of might around your body which glows darkly in the bottom third, bright red in the middle, and shades to shining gold at the top. This sphere is both might and shield around you. When you have become good at doing this, perform the rite as above. After vibrating berkano, breathe several times deeply while concentrating on all the wheels spinning together.

Then vibrate the rune sowilo, feeling an added power whirling into the lowest wheel. Sing eihwaz as you bring the might up from your root to the wheel at your groin in a brilliant stream of red-gold might, then sowilo as you strengthen that wheel. Repeat the eihwaz-sowilo process, letting the red-gold power flow up your spine and into each of the wheels to the top. Concentrate on the wheel at the crown of your head for a little while longer, then bring the might down to your roots again in the same manner. Stand with legs spread and arms and head upraised, vibrating, "Asgardhr-Midhgardhr-Hel!" Hold this peak for a few moments, then allow the fiery power to sink into darkness in your spine again. See the power of the wheels spinning out the dark-red-gold sphere of might and warding around you as at the previous completion.

TEUTONIC MAGIC COMPANION

GLOSSARY

- Aesir (eh-sir): Gods of air, war, and spiritual consciousness. Also, a term for gods in general.
- Aett (eht; pl. aettir): "Eight" or "family;" the runes are divided into three aettir. The term is also used to speak of the eight winds of the heavens (cardinal directions and points midway).
- Alf (pl. Alfar): Elf.
- Anglo-Saxon Futhark: The form of the runic alphabet used by the Anglo-Saxons, in which several runes were added to the 24-rune Elder Futhark for phonetic, rather than magical, reasons.
- Armanen (are-mahn-in): A modern German school of runic lore, using the 18-rune Armanen futhark developed by Guido von List.
- Asgardhr (ahs-gardhr): Dwelling of the gods; highest world on Yggdrasil.
- Asynjur (ahs-in-yur): Feminine of Aesir.
- Audhumbla (ow-dhumb-luh): Proto-bovine, created from the first mingling of fire and ice along with the proto-etin Ymir. Represents the primeval shaping force.
- B.C.E.: Before Common Era. The Common Era is a non-religious dating system which corresponds exactly with the traditional B.C./A.D., but which uses the Common Era of Roman supremacy as the starting point for general Western culture rather than relying on a Christian religious date. A Runic Era dating system, beginning from 250 B.C.E., also exists, but I do not use it here because it can be needlessly confusing.
- Berserker (bur-zurk-er): A fighter possessed by his animal fylgja, usually a bear or a wolf, who becomes inhumanly strong and fierce and does not feel wounds, losing his human awareness in battle-madness while the fit lasts.
- Fire pot: Brazier or burner for recels (incense).
- Fylgja (fflg-ya): "Follower"; the Old Norse term for fetch.
- Galdr (gahldr, pl. galdrar): Magical song, spoken or chanted part of a magical rite.
- Galdrabok (gald-ra-bowk): Magical diary, grimoire.
- Galdr-Magic: Runic magic, ritual magic (as contrasted with the shamanic seidhr-magic). Galdr-Sound: Mantra consisting of the actual sound associated with a rune.
- Gandr: Wand.
- Gardh, Gardhr: enclosure dividing the wild space outside(utangardhs) from the social space inside (innangardhs).
- Germanic: Either the cultures descended from the proto-Germanic tribe or the languages descended from Proto-Germanic. This is a linguistic and cultural term, NOT a racial term.

- Gingunnagap (gin-oon-guh-gap): The magically charged primal void between fire and ice at the beginning of all things.
- Godhi (go-dhih): Chieftain/priest.
- Hamingja (ha-mihng-ya): Personal power, mana, "luck."
- Hamr (hawmr): "Hide," shape (of soul); normally shaped like lich, but can be changed. Harrow: Altar.
- Holy: Filled with the might of the gods; hallowed (used for an earthly object or action).
- Horizontal Model: Worlds arranged into innangardhs/utangardhs: Asgardhr in the center, Midgardhr around it, elemental worlds separated by an ocean.
- Huginn (huhg-in): Thought; one of Odhinn's ravens. Hugr (huhgr): Thought; the rational; the left brain.
- Hvergelmir (hvair-gel-mihr): "Seething Cauldron"; the lowest level of the Well of Wyrd, from which the forces of primal water (holding yeast and venom flow.
- Hypostases: An aspect or attribute of a god which is sufficiently developed to act/be invoked on its own.
- Innangardhs (in-an-gardhs): Social, ordered space inside the enclosure of human culture.
- Jotun (yah-tun): General term for giantish beings (Ymir's kindred): etins, rises, and thurses.
- Jotunheimr: "World of Jotuns"; easternmost world, elemental air.
- Kinfylgja: Personification of inherited traits and might; usually dwells with the head of family, or else the most suitable member.
- Kona (koh-na; p1. konur): Old Norse inflection; designates female (seidhkona, spakona, draumkona, etc.) Krisjan: Old Norse spelling of Christian.
- Lich: Earthly body.
- Ljosalfar (lyos-al-far): Light elves.
- Madhr (madhr): Old Norse for ~ Used in this book as a suffix to denote gender (seidhmadhr, spamadhr, etc.).
- Mead: A favorite drink of the Northern European peoples, particularly for magical or religious purposes. Brewed from honey and water. It is seldom commercially available in America, but home-brewing shops generally carry books with mead recipes and the necessary items for making it.
- Midgardhr (mid-gardhr): The Middle Enclosure; the world of humankind; the middle point on Yggdrasil.
- Mimir (Mih-mir): The proto-etin who keeps Mimir's Well, holder of all that has ever existed; Odhinn's mother's brother.
- Mind: Consciousness; encompasses hugr (thought) and minni (memory, including ancestral memory and collective unconscious).
- Minni (mihn-ni): memory; right-brain, etc.; See Mind. Muspellheimr: World of primal fire.
- Need-Fire: Fire kindled directly from wood without flint by friction.

- Nidhing Pole: "Pole of insult." A pole with a horse's head or carving of the victim in an obscene posture, used for serious insult and damaging curses. One was put up by an Asatru group in Iceland during the summit conference in Rekjavik as a protest against nuclear arms.
- Norns: The embodiments of ørlög and causality. There are three Norns, Urdhr (that-which-is), Verdhandi (that-which-is-becoming), and Skuld (that-which-should-be) who shape the turnings of Wyrd through the worlds. Each person is also said to have his or her own norns who bring his or her personal weird. These may be related to or identical with the disir and Valkyrie, who also embody personal ørlög.
- Odhr (odhr): Inspiration, fury; given to humankind by Odhinn's brother Hoenir. Cognate to Modern German Wut and English wood (used archaically to mean madness).
- Odhroerir (odh-ruh-rir): The mead of poetry, stolen by Odhinn. Actually three cauldrons—Odhroerir, Son, and Bodhn.
- Oend: Breath of life, given to humankind by Odhinn.
- Ørlög (ahr-lahg): The primal layer of wyrd which determines what shall become and be. Out-dweller: Inhabitant of the utangardhs; uncanny wight.
- Recels (reh-kels): Incense.
- Sax: Ritual knife.
- Seidhr (saydhr): Witchcraft, shamanic traveling, speaking with spirits, visionary practices.
- Sleipnir (Slayp-near): Odhinn's gray eight-legged horse, child of Loki and a giant stallion, on which Odhinn rides through the worlds.
- Solarhringar: Ring of the sun; divided into aettir.
- Soul: All non-physical components of a being.
- Spakona, Spamadhr: Spae-wife, spae-man. A visionary seer.
- Stadhagaldr (stah-dha-galdr): The meditational practice of standing in a rune's shape and intoning its name. Developed by German Armanen magicians and presented in English by Edred Thorsson[3]. The stadha (p1. stodhur) is the physical position.
- Stave: A rune's letter shape; literally a staff or stick such as the runes were originally carved into. Also used generally to speak of runes themselves, as in "staves of healing," "mighty staves," etc.
- Structural Runic Relationships: Relationships between runes as determined by their place within the futhark order and/or aettir.
- Svartalfar: Black elves (dwarves).
- Taufr (tawfr): Talisman (with runes written on it).
- Teutonic: See Germanic.
- Thurse: Unintelligent personification of brute force.
- Troll: General term for ill-willing uncanny wight (though some are helpful to humans).
- Ur- (er): Mod. German; a prefix meaning proto- or original. Utangardhs (uht-an-gardhs): Wild/magical/unordered space; outside of human society.

[3] No longer viewed as a good source due to changes within the heathen community.

- Utgardhr (uht-gardhr): On the horizontal map, the ring of the elemental worlds outside Midgardhr.
- Valkyrja (Val-kir-ya, valkyrie): "Chooser of the slain"; the perfected self of a worshiper of Odhinn and the link between Odhinn and the individual soul.
- Vanir: Earth/water deities of fertility, death, and hidden wisdom.
- Vargr: Outlaw, wolf.
- Ve: Consecrated in the sense of being utterly separated from the mundane world; tabu.
- Vertical Model: Nine Worlds arranged according to energy level into Asgardhr (highest), Midgardhr and the elemental worlds (Jotunheimr, Muspellheimr, Vanheimr, and Niflheimr), and Hel (lowest). Vitki: Runic magician.
- Widdershins: Against the course of the sun; counterclockwise; used to draw up power from the earth and the worlds below.
- Wyrm: Serpent or dragon.
- Yggdrasil: "Ygg's (Odhinn's) steed"; the World-Tree, holding the three vertical realms of Asgardhr/Midgardhr/Hel and the Nine worlds together.
- Ymir (Uem-ir): "Roarer"; the proto-etin created by the first meeting of fire and ice in Gingunnagap, from whom all the jotun-kind (and most of the gods) descend. Odhimi and his brothers/hypostases Vili (will) and Ve (holiness) slew Ymir and made the sea from his blood, the earth from his body, and the vault of the sky from his skull.
- Younger Futhark: The sixteen-rune futhark of the Viking Age.

PRONUNCIATION GUIDE

RUNE–NAMES:

The rune—names given here are in Proto—Germanic. Pronunciation is relatively simple: there are only five vowel sounds, and the consonants, with the exceptions below, are as in Modern English.

- A — as in "father"
- E — ay, as in "day" i — ee, as in "speed" o — as in "home"
- U — oo, as in moon
- DH — a soft th, as in "leather"
- G — always hard, as in "give"
- H — may be heavily aspirated, almost as a ch j —always pronounced as y k — always a hard sound; no soft c exists r — trilled th — as in "thorn"
- Z — always buzzed, halfway between an r and a z

OLD NORSE

- A — as in "law" á — as in "father" e — as i in "gin" é — as ay in "day" i— as in "is" í — ee as in "speed" o — as in "omit" ó — as in "owe" ø, ö — as in "not"
- U — oo, as in soot" a — oo, as in "droop" y — u, as in French "tu" ý — u, as in German "Túr" ae — e as in "get" au — ou as in "house" ei — ay as in "day" ey — as ei dh — a soft th, as in "leather" f — pronounced as English f initially, as English v in medial and final positions.
- G —hard as in "give" j — always as English y ng —as in "sing" r — trilled; r on the end of the word is not given an extra syllable.
- S — always voiceless, as in "blast" th — as in "thorn" z — pronounced as ts (as in German)

CHAPTER NOTES

CHAPTER 1
1. Hastrup, Kirsten. Culture and History in Medieval Iceland (hereafter Has trup).
2. Grimnismal 21, 29.
3. Voluspa 47.
4. Rune-lore (hereafter Rune-lore).
5. Grimnismal 39.
6. Prose Edda, p. 40.

CHAPTER 2
1. Voluspa 19, 20.
2. Prose Edda
3. Bauschatz, Paul. The Well and the Tree (hereafter Bauschatz).
4. Bauschatz.
5. Ibid., pp. 122—124.
6. Grimnismal 26.

CHAPTER 4
1.   Rune-lore, p. 8.
2. Elliot, R. W. V. Runes, pp. 12—13.
3. Rune-lore, p. 57.

CHAPTER 5
3. Rune-lore.
4. Sigrdrifumal 17—18.
5. Havamal 138—139.
6. Sigrdrifumal 20.
7. Futhark, pp. 32—33; Rune-lore.
8. Rune-lore, p. 17.
9. Grettir's Saga, Chapter: LXXXI.
10. Gudhrunarkvida II.

CHAPTER 6
1. Futhark.

CHAPTER 7

FEHU
1.Gudhrunarkvida 126.
2.Reginsmal 1.
3.Voluspa 21—24.

URUZ
1.Grimnismal 25—26.
THURISAZ
1.Skirriismal 36—37.

RAIDHO
1.Hastrup.
2.Ibid.
3.Ibid.

KENAZ
1.Davidson, H. R. Ellis. Pagan Scandinavia (hereafter Pagan Scandina
via), p. 35.
2.Rune-lore, p. 119.

GEBO
1. Anderson, Poul (tr., ed.). Hrolf Kraki's Saga, p. 257.
2.Havamal 41—42,48.
3.Grimnismal 2—3.
4.Havamal 138.
5.Havamal 145.

WUNJO
1.Fafnismal 29.

HAGALAZ
1.Rune-lore.
2.Futhark, Rune-lore

NALITHIZ
1.Sigrdrifumal 8.

EIHWAZ
1.von List, Guido (tr. Stephen Flowers). The Secret of the Runes (here
after von List), pp. 62—64).
2.Havamal 164.
3.Vafthrudismal 55.
4.Baldrs draumar 5.
5.Rune-lore.

PERTHRO
1.Tacitus, Germania (hereafter Tacitus).

ELHAZ
1.Futhark, p. 48.
SOWILO
1.Rune-lore, p. 127.

TIWAZ
1.Futhark, p. 54.
2.Sigrdrifumal 7.

BERKANO
1.Lokasenna 29.
2.Prose Edda, p.44 3. Heaney, Seamus. North.

MANNAZ
1.Rigsthula 37—38.
2.Ibid. 46.
4.Rune-lore.
5.Voluspa.
6.Futhark, p.60.

LAGUZ
1. Sigrdrifumal 235.

DAGAZ
1.Sigrdrifumal 2.
2.Sigrdrifumal 2; the use of this holy song with this rune is suggested by
Thorsson in Futhark, p. 66.

OTHALA
1.Hastrup.

CHAPTER 8
1. Schneider, Karl. Die German ische Runennamen.
2. Crowley, Aleister. Book 4.

CHAPTER 9
1. At the Well of Wyrd.

CHAPTER 10
1. Futhark, p. 89.
2.Ibid., p. 89.

CHAPTER 11
1. Rune-lore.
2. Futhark, p. 83.
3. Storms, Dr. C. Anglo-Saxon Magic (hereafter Storms).
4. Rune-lore, p. 170.

CHAPTER 12
1. McCullough. Mythology of All Races, vol. II: Eddic Mythology (hereafter
Eddic Mythology).
2. Fafnismal, Reginsmal.
3. Hastrup.

CHAPTER 13
1. Grieve, Mrs. M. A Modern Herbal (hereafter Grieve).
2. Grieve.
3. Hollander, Lee. Notes to Gudhrunarkvida I, Poetic Edda p. 249.
4. Gudhrunarkvida 118.
5. Grimm, Jacob. Teutonic Mythology (hereafter Grimm), pp. 1202—03.
6. Nine Herbs Charm (Nigon Wyrta Galdor), Lacnunga.
7. Grieve, p. 575.
8.Grimm, p. 1208.

CHAPTER 14
1.Locasenna 95.
2.Ynglinga Saga, Chapter: VII.
3.Saga of Eirik the Red, Chapter: IV. (Keyser, Rudolph, tr. Pennock, Barclay),   p.
290.
4.Hastrnp, p. 105.

CHAPTER 15
1.Grimm.

CHAPTER 16
1.Rune-lore
2.Branston, Brian. Lost Gods of England (hereafter Lost Gods of England), p.   94.
3.Harbardzljod 44.
4.Grimm.
5.Voluspa 62.
6.Eddic Mythology.
7.Vafthrudhnismal 51.
8.Eddic Mythology, p. 183.
9.Grimmnismal 7.

CHAPTER 17
1.Rune-lore, p. 155.
2.Tacitus.
3.Davidson, H. R. Ellis. Gods and Myths of the Viking Age (hereafter Gods and Myths of the Viking Age).
4.Turville-Petre, E. o. C. Myth and Religion of the North (hereafter Turvi   le-
Petre), p. 170.
5.Gods and Myths of the Viking Age.
6.Dumezil, Georges. Gods of the Ancient Northmen (hereafter Dumezil).
7.Prose Edda.
8.Beowulf.
9.Rune-lore.
10.Prose Edda, p. 59.
11.Locasenna 20.
12.Locasenna 21.
13.Ynglinga Saga.
14.Locasenna.
15.Branston, Brian. Gods of the North (hereafter Gods of the North), p. 164.
16.Locasenna.
17.Ynglina Saga, Chapter: VIII.
18.Turville-Petre.
19.Lokasenna 51.
20. Ingvisson, Ingvar Solve writing as Ingramsson, Ragnar Solve. "Some Ideas For Sacralizing Regular Events. Northways, vol. 1, no. 1. Yule 2238.

CHAPTER 18
1.Prose Edda, p.48.
2.Ynglinga Saga, Chapter: XXIX.
3.Njals Saga.
4.Jomsvikinga Saga.
5.Storms, p. 51.
6.Harbarzljod 44.
7.Eddic Mythology, p. 264.
8.Dvergatal 12.
9.Olaf Tryggvason's Saga, Chapter: 33.
10.Njals Saga.

CHAPTER 19
1.Hastrup, p.154.
2.Hastrup, p.144.
3.Baring-Gould, Rev. Sabine. The Book of Werewolves (hereafter Bar
ing-Gould), p.48.
4. Hastrup.
5.Harbarzljod 80.
6.Holmverja Saga.
7.Egils Saga.
8.Grimm.
9.Grettix's Saga, Chapter: XVIII.
10.Grettir's Saga, Chapter: XXXV.
11.Rune-lore.
12.Skirnismal.
13.Helgakvidha Hundingsbana I.
14.Beowulf 111—12.
15.Grundy, Stephan. "Maera Mearc-Stapa: Beowulf and the Borders of Wyrd".
16.Marwick, Ernest W. Folklore of the Orkneys and Shetlands.

CHAPTER 20
1.Grimm.
2.Fafnismal.
3.Grimm, pp. 678-80.
4.Ibid., pp. 682—83.
5.Gods and Myths of the Viking Age, p. 99.
6.Grimm.
7.Grimm.
8.Helgakvidha Hundingsbana 1138.
9.Fafnismal 2.
10.Rune-lore, p.187.
11.Helgi Hundingsbana II.
12.von List, p. 56.
13.Vafthrudhnismal 37.
14.Grimm, p.633.
15.Turville-Petre, pp.256-58.
16.Grimm, p.661.
17.Grimm, p.671.
18.Gripisspa 10.
19.Bauschatz, p. 130.
20.Ibid.

BIBLIOGRAPHY

(With occasional annotations)

Anderson, George (tr.). The Saga of the Volsungs. East Brunswick, NJ: Associated University Press, 1982. A good book which includes not only translations, but comments on the historical origins and backgrounds of the various versions of the Volsung Saga.

Baring-Gould, Sabine. The Book of Werewolves. New York, NY: Causeway Books, 1973. Contains a vast amount of fascinating information presented in a well-organized and relatively unbiased fashion.

Bauschatz, Paul. The Well And The Tree. Amherst: The University of Massachusetts Press, 1982. The book to read for anyone who wants to understand the nature of Wyrd; no one attempting serious runic divination should be without it. It can still be ordered.

Baynes, H. G. Germany Possessed. London: Jonathan Cape Ltd., 1941. This book is marred from the heathen viewpoint by its rabidly Christian orientation. It was written by an Englishman during WWII, so its biases are only to be expected. Nevertheless it provides a fascinating study of the breakthrough of the dark side of the Odhinnic archetype.

Bessason, Haraldur/Glendinning, R. J. (eds.). Edda. Canada: University of Manitoba Press, 1983. A collection of short but very good essays.

Beyerl, Paul. The Master Book of Herbalism. Custer, Washington: Phoenix Publishing Co., 1984. A Wiccan or quasi-Wiccan work. His folklore and medical attributions are almost all found in Grieve. Although some of his modern magical uses are interesting and effective, a great deal of the work (particularly the attribution of various herbs to various gods) seems to be largely a product of his imagination. Warning: Beyerl does not identify poisonous or dangerous herbs as such, though he describes some of their uses. This book should not be used without external references of greater reliability and responsibility.

Bord, Janet & Cohn. The Secret Country. London: Paladin, (c) 1978, 1985. An interesting study of the folklore of the British landscape.

Branston, Brian. Gods of the North. New York: Thames & Hudson, Inc., (c) 1975, 1980. Branston ranges from brilliant to eccentric in this book, which should not be used as a single source for anything, but often provides startling insights or alternate perspectives on general problems in Germanic studies (such as the nature and identity of Heimdallr).

Lost Gods of England. London: Thames & Hudson Ltd., 1957, 1974. Generally more reliable than Gods of the North, although his comparisons of the Norse myths to Mediterranean cults in the latter parts of the book do not seem to me particularly well-founded.

Chisholm, James (tr. and commentary). Poetic Edda. (c) 1989. An excellent literal translation which is exceedingly valuable to the study of Teutonic magic. This version was created specifically to aid magical and deep religious understanding among those who are not able to use the Old Norse original and is the only one recommended for purely magical use.

Cooper, Jason D. Using the Runes. Wellingborough, Northampton-shire: the Aquarian Press, 1986. Not a terribly impressive book, although Cooper does offer some interesting thoughts on the relative developments of the cults of Tyr and Odhinn.

Crossley-Holland, Kevin. The Norse Myths. New York: Pantheon Books, 1980. A very good introduction to Norse mythology. The Eddic stories have been competently rewritten here to appeal to the modern mind without mauling the stories themselves or their meanings. Give a copy to all your friends.

Crowley, Aleister. Book 4. Dallas, TX: Sangreal Foundation, Inc., 1972. Like all of Crowley's books, this is greatly valuable to the experienced magician who understands Crowley's work and mind, and quite dangerous to the novice.

Cunningham, Scott. Encyclopedia of Magical Herbs. St. Paul, MN: Llewellyn Publications, 1985. A reference work dealing solely with folkloric and/or Wiccan magical uses of herbs and trees.

Magical Herbalism.. St. Paul, MN: Llewehlyn Publications, (c) 1982, 1983, rep. 1985, 1986. A very good manual of practical instructions for anyone who is interested in magical herbalism, blending their own recels (incenses), etc.

Davidson, H. R. Ellis. Gods and Myths of the Viking Age. New York: Bell Publishing Co., 1981. An excellent work and most highly recommended, as are all of Ms. Davidson's writings. Her books are particularly informative concerning the mysteries of the Vanic cults.

Pagan Scandinavia. London: Thames & Hudson, 1987. This book deals more with pre-viking Age customs and artifacts.

Dumezil, Georges. Gods of the Ancient Northmen. Berkeley/Los Angeles/London: University of California Press, 1973. A highly speculative work, dealing with Indo-European roots and comparisons of European myths to the Rig Veda. Scholarly Teutonic heathens tend to become either Dumezihians who go about talking about the tripartite functions of society (king/judge/priest, warrior, and provider) or anti-Dumezihians who froth at the mouth when this stuff is mentioned, claiming that these divisions could not be supported in any Teutonic society. I do not think much of Dumezil myself, but his work has been very influential. The serious student of Teutonic subjects should read it for him/ herself and draw her/his own conclusions.

Eliade, Mircea; W. R. Trask (tr.). Shamanism: Archaic Techniques of Ecstasy. Bohlingen Series 46. Princeton, NJ: Princeton University Press, 1972. The book on shamanic initiation.

Elliott, R. W. V. Runes. Manchester: Manchester University Press, (c) 1959, rep. 1971. A good book on scholarly runology.

Glob, P. V.; Rupert Bruce-Mitford (tr.). The Bog People. Ithaca, NY:

Cornell University Press, 1969. A nice book on, as it says, the bog people (early sacrifices, possibly to Nerthus, preserved by the acids of the peat bogs in which they were buried). Valuable for information on and contemplation of the early Vanic cults.

Glob, P. V. (Bulman, Joan tr.). The Mound People. London: Faber and Faber Limited, 1970.

Grieve, Mrs. M. A Modern Herbal (2 vols.). New York: Dover Publications, Inc., 1971; Harcourt, Brace, & Co., 1931. The best collection of herbal folklore and medical uses available.

Grimm, Jacob; James Steven Stallybrass (tr.). Teutonic Mythology (4 vols.).

Gloucester, Mass: Peter Smith, 1976. A major collection of Teutonic religion, folklore, and etymologies, which I have found indispensable.

Guerber, H. A, Myths of Northern Lands. New York/Cincinnati/Chicago: American Book Company, 1895.

Gundarsson, Kveldulf. "The Northern Dragon" in Northways, vol.1, no. 1. (Yule 2238)/ Arlington, TX: North Texas Kindred, 1988. A brilliant article I think, but then I also wrote it.

Gumdas. Gemm Elixirs and Vibrational Healing. Boulder, CO: Cassandra Press, 1985. Good information on the properties of stones and different ways to use them. As well as the channeled information, there is a great deal of legitimate folklore concerning gems in this book.

Hastrup, Kirsten. Culture and History in Medieval Iceland. Oxford: Clarendon Press, 1985. An excellent work which thoroughly details several major elements of Teutonic thought, particularly concerning innangardhs and utangardhs.

Heaney, Seamus. North. London: Faber & Faber Ltd., 1975. Beautiful poetry, including a number of poems about the bog people.

Hollander, Lee (tr.). The Poetic Edda. Austin: University of Texas Press, (c) 1962, rep. in paperback 1986. A beautiful poetic translation which is good for Teutonic liturgical use, especially when working with those who are less deeply initiated into the frequently obscure mysteries of Northern poetic usages. Unfortunately, Hollander was often forced to sacrifice accuracy for the sake of meter and alliteration~ do not try to use this version for detailed magical study, especially when working with kennings and other aspects of the language used in these holy poems. What Hollander does offer is a stunning example of the use of Germanic English (as opposed to latinized) as it should be used in Teutonic rituals.

Saga of the Joms vikings. Austin, TX: University of Texas Press, 1955. A good translation of an interesting saga.

Ingramsson, Ragnar Solve. "Some Ideas for Sacralizing Regular Events" in Northways, vol. 1, no. 1 (Yule 2238). Arlington, TX: North Texas Kindred, 1988. Jones, Gwyn (tr.). Vatnsdaela Saga.. Princeton, NJ: Princeton University Press, 1944.

Keyser, Rudolph (Pennock, Barclay tr.). Religion of the Northmen. New York: Charles B. Norton, 1854. An excellent book, dealing with the actual practice of the religion and music in Viking times.

Lehmann, Ruth P. M. (tr.). Beowulf. Austin: University of Texas Press, 1988. A really beautiful poetic translation.

List, Guido von; Stephen Flowers (tr.). The Secret of the Runes. Rochester: Destiny Books, 1988. A fascinating book by the father of modern runology and creator (discoverer?) of the Armanen futhark. Although sometimes von List ranges into the romantic, airy, or downright bizarre, his intense depth of understanding and brilliance of approach make this an important book to any student of runic magic.

MacCullough, John. Mythology of All Races, vol. 2: Eddic. New York, NY: Cooper Square Publishers, Inc., (c) 1930, 1958, 1964. One of the best books available on Teutonic religion as viewed from an Eddic standpoint, although MacCullough also works quite a bit with folklore. Highly recommended.

Magnusson, Eirikr/Morris, William (trs.). Grettir the Strong. Totowa, NJ: Cooper Square Publishers, 1980 (facsimile reprint of the first edition 1869).

Magnusson, Magnus/Palsson, Hermann (trs.). The Vinland Sagas. New York: New York University Press, 1966.

Marwick, Ernest W. The Folklore of Orkney and Shetland. Totowa, NJ:

Rowman and Littlefield, 1975. A good guide to the survivals of Teutonic metaphysical views in a relatively isolated area.

Munch, Peter Andreas. Scandinavian Classics, vol. XXVII: Norse Mythology. New York: The American Scandinavian foundation, 1942.

Osburn, Marijane/Longland, Stella. Rune Games. London/New York: Routledge & Kegan, Paul Ltd., 1982, 1986, 1987. This book deals solely with the Anglo—Saxon futhark; a number of their interpretations of the Rune Poem are very good. The attempts to set the runes on the Qabalistic Tree of Life are wholly ludicrous, but their generally experimental attitude seems a very good thing, and they do offer some valuable alternate perspectives.

Page, R. I. An Introduction to English Runes. London: Methuen & Co., Ltd., 1973. A wholly mundane work of scholarship which should be read by magical runologists to keep their historical fantasies in perspective. Page is quite skeptical of magical interpretations in general.

Pennick, Nigel. The Ancient Science of Geomancy. London: Thames & Hudson, Ltd, 1979. Sebastopol: CRC Publications, Ltd. 1987.

Raphaell, Katrina. Crystal Enlightenment. New York, NY: Aurora Press, 1985, 1986. The basic New Age crystal text.

Schutz, Herbert. The Prehistory of Germanic Europe. New Haven and London: Yale University Press, 1983.

Storms, Dr. G. Anglo-Saxon Magic. The Hague: Martinus Nijhoff, 1948. The only book that I have yet seen analyzing the charm spells; a text that is both fascinating and infinitely informative. It contains a great deal of material which can be found nowhere else.

Sturlusson, Snorri (Hollander, Lee tr.). Heimskringla.. Austin: University Press, 1964.
Sturlusson, Snorri (Young, Jean I. tr.) Prose Edda.. Cambridge: Bowes & Bowes Publishers Ltd., 1954.

Tacitus; W. Hamilton Pyfe (tr.) Dialogus Agricola and Germania. Oxford: Clarendon Press., 1908. A major source of information on the lives and practices of the continental Germanic people, although its reliability may be questioned because of the didactic purpose and natural biases of the author.

Rune-lore. York Beach, ME: Samuel Weiser, Inc., 1987. The theory of which Fut hark is the practice,

Turville-Petre, E. o. G. Myth and Religion of the North. London: Weidenfeld and Nicolson, 1964. An excellent reference work.

Tyson, Donald. Rune Magic. St. Paul, MN: Llewellyn Publications, 1988. Tyson is primarily a ceremonial magician, best known as the author of The New Magus. Rune Magic shows a great deal of research and thought. It also is written from the perspective of someone who is at best a little dubious about heathen deities and at worst sees them as unpredictable and dangerous beings which must be controlled by a transcendental "All-Father." Many of his practices, such as the use of the pentagram in ritual, are taken directly from ceremonial magic and have little place in Teutonic workings. However, Tyson is a very good practical magician; some of his suggestions in that department and some of his insights into the runes make this book worth the trouble, though it is recommended to check his interpretations against those of other writers.

BIOGRAPHY

From his humble beginnings, Gundarsson would make his mark on the world by writing on the most rare and obscure myths breathing new life into them, for a new generation of readers. His fictional works written under Stephan Grundy focused on mythology and history and were met with international success. Along with his fictional works, Gundarsson made a name for himself writing books on Germanic Paganism (also known as heathenry) and Germanic Culture. He is an Elder in the organization The Troth where he has dedicated a majority of his life influencing major changes in the organization, including the development of anti-racist and anti-sexist ideals. He has fought for equality in trans-gendered communities, as well as fighting for the acceptance of Loki. Gundarsson has shaped heathenry through his numerous academic and fictional works as well as his extensive articles, thesis papers and his creation and sustainment of the lore program within The Troth. His hobbies included wood-working, jewelry making and gardening as well as historical re-enactment. He is currently attending medical school in Ireland supported by his loving wife Melodi where they maintain a local hof called The Tribe of Thor.

The Three Little Sisters

The Three Little Sisters is an indie publisher that puts authors first. We specialize in the strange and unusual. From titles about pagan and heathen spirituality to traditional fiction we bring books to life.

https://shop.the3littlesisters.com

www.ingramcontent.com/pod-product-compliance
Lightning Source LLC
Chambersburg PA
CBHW080954120626
46546CB00010B/2892